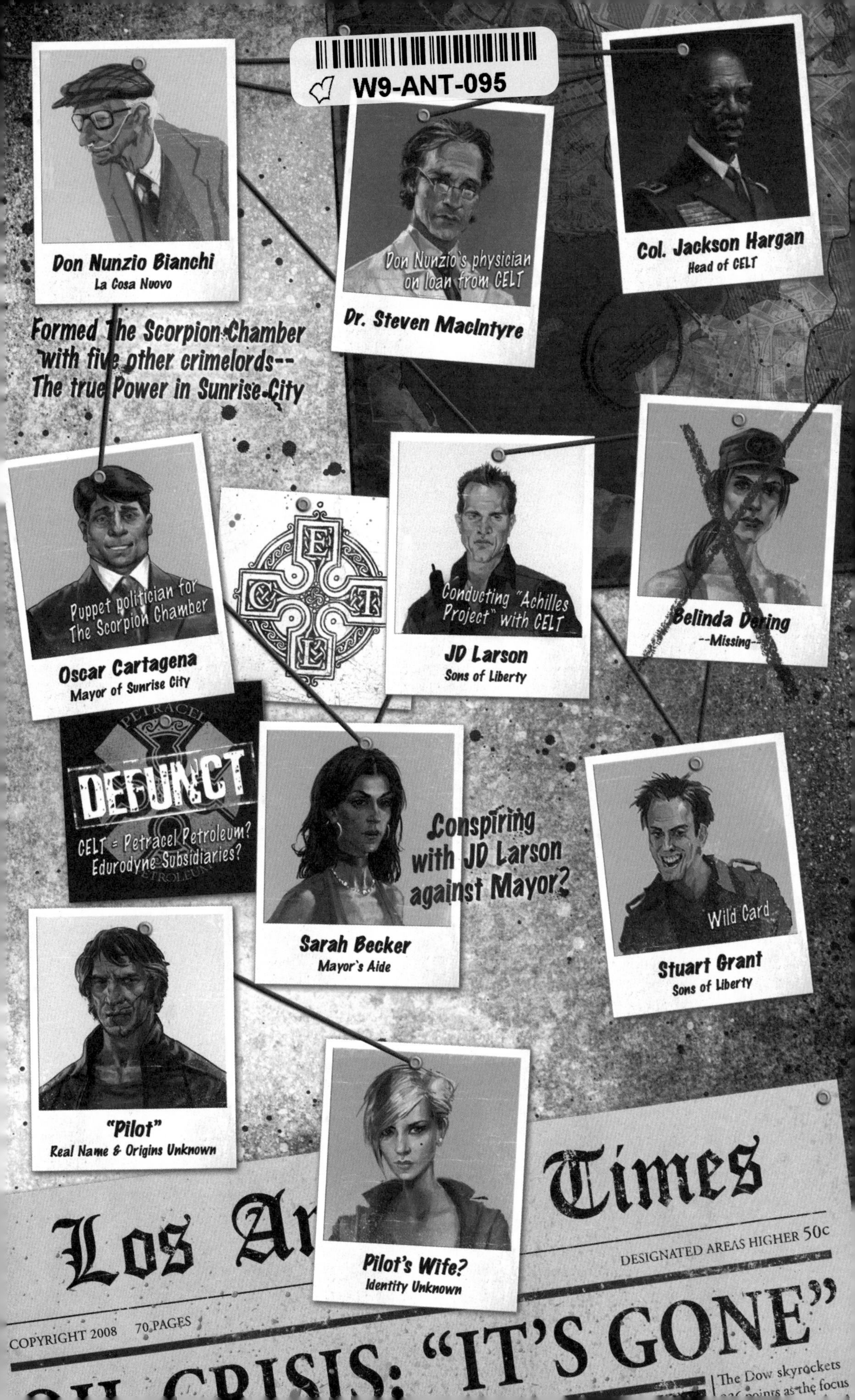

Don Nunzio Bianchi
La Cosa Nuovo
Don Nunzio's physician on loan from CELT
Dr. Steven MacIntyre
Col. Jackson Hargan
Head of CELT
Formed The Scorpion Chamber with five other crimelords--
The true Power in Sunrise City
Puppet politician for The Scorpion Chamber
Oscar Cartagena
Mayor of Sunrise City
E C T L
Conducting "Achilles Project" with CELT
JD Larson
Sons of Liberty
Belinda Dering
--Missing--
PETRACEL
DEFUNCT
CELT = Petracel Petroleum?
Edurodyne Subsidiaries?
PETROLEUM
Sarah Becker
Mayor's Aide
Conspiring with JD Larson against Mayor?
Wild Card
Stuart Grant
Sons of Liberty
"Pilot"
Real Name & Origins Unknown
Pilot's Wife?
Identity Unknown
Los An Times
DESIGNATED AREAS HIGHER 50c
COPYRIGHT 2008 70 PAGES
OIL CRISIS: "IT'S GONE"
The Dow skyrockets
points as the focus

An **Archaia Black Label** and **Vogster Entertainment** Production

BLEEDOUT™

ARCHAIA ENTERTAINMENT LLC
WWW.ARCHAIA.COM

VOGSTER™ ENTERTAINMENT
WWW.VOGSTER.COM

An **Archaia Black Label** and **Vogster Entertainment** Production

BLEEDOUT ™

Written by **Mike Kennedy**	Illustrated by **Nathan Fox**
Colors by **Andrey Shcherbak** **Oscar Pinto** **Jesus Aburto** **Alexey Sklarov**	**Zach Howard** **Sanford Greene** **David Williams**
Interstitial Illustrations by **Andrey Shcherbak**	**Ben Templesmith** **Gary Erskine**
Cover by **Tim Bradstreet**	**Howard Chaykin** **Glenn Fabry**
Logo Design by **Vladimir Kuzmin** Lettered by **Troy Peteri**	**Vince Proce**
Executive Producer for Vogster Entertainment **Michael Mendheim**	**Trevor Hairsine**

Published by **Archaia**

Archaia Entertainment LLC
1680 Vine Street, Suite 912
Los Angeles, California, 90028, USA
www.archaia.com

BLEEDOUT Hardcover. May 2011. FIRST PRINTING.

10 9 8 7 6 5 4 3 2 1

ISBN: 1-936393-18-2

ISBN 13: 978-1-936393-18-3

ARCHAIA
BLACK LABEL ™

ENTERTAINMENT

WWW.CRIMECRAFT.COM

Forest Lawn
Memorial Park

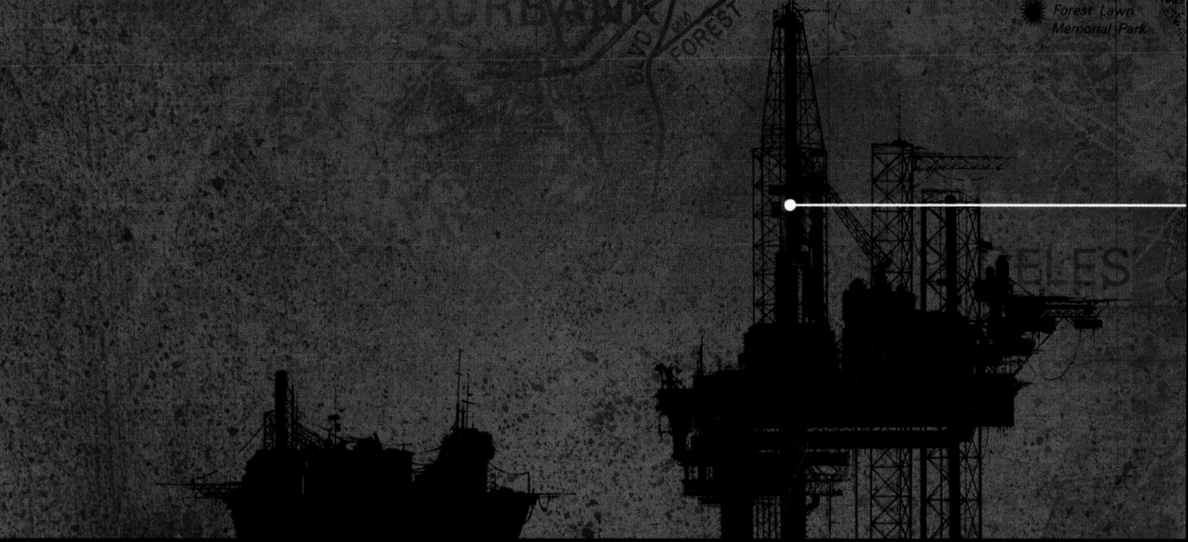

TABLE OF CONTENTS

April 20, 2010: An explosion on the *Deepwater Horizon* drilling rig causes a massive oil leak that releases an estimated 5 million barrels of crude into the Gulf of Mexico, the worst oil spill on record at that time by a factor of 15.

February 8, 2012: A massive chunk of the Norwegian continental shelf triggers a series of "Svartann Tsunamis" which sever multiple offshore drilling rigs in the North Sea, displacing nearly 28 million barrels of crude, dwarfing even the *Deepwater Horizon* disaster.

June 9, 2012: A group of eco-terrorists known as "*The Dry Earth Committee*" are murdered while sabotaging an oil field outside Hafar Al-Batin, Saudi Arabia.

August 12, 2012: Stress and frustration over steadily rising gas prices motivate a tragic shooting spree at a filling station in Washington D.C.'s poverty stricken Ward 8, taking the lives of 21 motorists and law enforcers.

December 21, 2012: Gas prices peak at an unprecedented $7.50 per gallon, reflecting an economic recession spiraling further out of control. Business closures and unemployment reach an all-time high.

INTRODUCTION

Welcome to the Bleedout

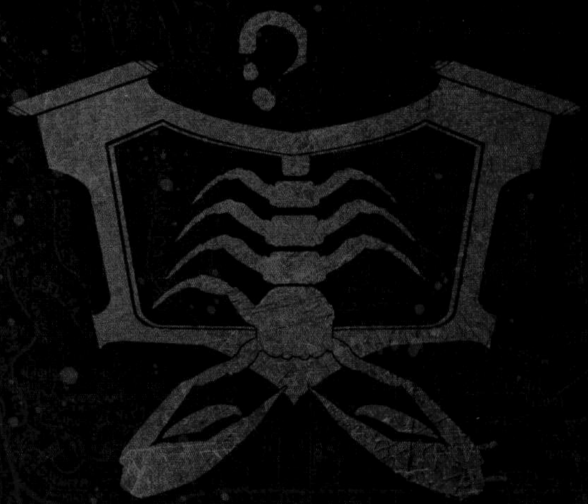

According to the United Nations Office on Drugs and Crime, there are nearly 250 million habitual drug users on the planet. That's roughly 4% of the entire global population. Compare that to the estimated 1.2 billion smokers in the world, or the 2 billion people who consume alcohol, or the estimated 5 billion people who regularly consume caffeinated beverages – that's roughly 72% of the world consciously or unconsciously hooked on one thing or another. But if all of those substances were to suddenly evaporate, civilization would survive, albeit with some potential period of withdrawal.

Now imagine a substance so subtly addictive that the entire global economy has become dependent on it. A substance that permeates every single industry, every commodity, every nation and government on the planet. A substance that almost single-handedly enables every simple thing we take for granted every day. An addiction so insidious, it could destroy the world as we know it.

Oil.

Every single industry on the planet is anchored in some way to the use of petrochemicals. Whether it's in the creation of raw materials *(plastics, detergents, dyes, pesticides, additives, fertilizers)*, the manufacturing of composite goods *(diesel factory engines, assembly and packaging plants)*, or the distribution of those final goods *(via air, sea, and ground freight)*, no piece of our daily life goes by without owing

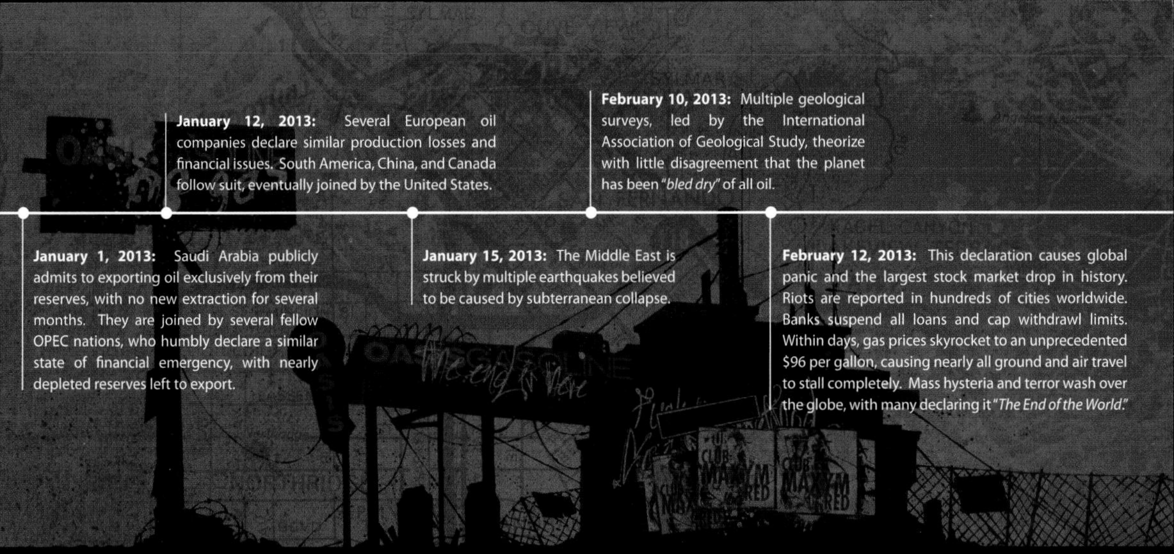

January 1, 2013: Saudi Arabia publicly admits to exporting oil exclusively from their reserves, with no new extraction for several months. They are joined by several fellow OPEC nations, who humbly declare a similar state of financial emergency, with nearly depleted reserves left to export.

January 12, 2013: Several European oil companies declare similar production losses and financial issues. South America, China, and Canada follow suit, eventually joined by the United States.

January 15, 2013: The Middle East is struck by multiple earthquakes believed to be caused by subterranean collapse.

February 10, 2013: Multiple geological surveys, led by the International Association of Geological Study, theorize with little disagreement that the planet has been *"bled dry"* of all oil.

February 12, 2013: This declaration causes global panic and the largest stock market drop in history. Riots are reported in hundreds of cities worldwide. Banks suspend all loans and cap withdrawl limits. Within days, gas prices skyrocket to an unprecedented $96 per gallon, causing nearly all ground and air travel to stall completely. Mass hysteria and terror wash over the globe, with many declaring it *"The End of the World."*

some credit to oil. Without it, our simplest assumptions would never see the light of day.

Geologists worldwide agree that there is an undeniable end to oil, and that at the rate at which we blindly consume petroleum on a daily basis, that end is already in sight. On a global level, we are producing less and consuming more. In 2008, we were consuming nearly 85 million barrels of oil per day, but only producing roughly 9 million barrels per day. That means that, in 2008, we were tapping into 76 million barrels of reserve each day. It is simple mathematics -- crunch those numbers and we will deplete the estimated 1.3 trillion barrels in the global reserve in roughly 45 years. Sure, 2056 may sound like The Distant Future, full of robot butlers and jetpacks, but so did 2011 a few years ago. And considering that average daily production is decreasing while global consumption is increasing, that end-date is probably quite generous. We are burning through our global savings with no viable back-up plans, and very little encouragement to figure one out quickly.

Electric cars, bio-diesel engines, hydrogen cells, even solar advancements all sound exciting, but at the current rate of study, none of those options are practicable enough to carry even a fraction of our current global demand. And as long as there are still billions to be made by keeping things the way they are, that research will continue to be shortchanged until it is too late. The cost to retrofit the entire global infrastructure would be monumental, perhaps prohibitively so. Imagine what it would cost to replace every automobile, airplane, freight tanker, train car, farming device, and diesel generator on the planet. Who in their right mind would want to pick up that bill?

Bleedout explores a world in which that bill has come suddenly and unexpectedly due. The 45-year scenario described above is compressed into an all-too-sudden 9-month disaster that forces the world to respond to its lack of preparation. Desperation gives foothold to criminal empires, and survival becomes the driving agenda, by any means necessary. And while the artificial cause of this extraordinary disaster may seem rooted in science fiction, the fallout is not. Think about how your own life would change completely if all oil were to disappear overnight -- our consumer-centric economy would go belly-up and individual financial priorities would quickly shift towards survival and necessity. How would your job survive a complete social/commercial meltdown? How would you get by without the variety of creature comforts you rarely think twice about? And how would you maintain such basic necessities as food and shelter?

Now think about how your life will change as this scenario happens slowly over the next 45 years. And then get ready.

The **Bleedout** is coming.

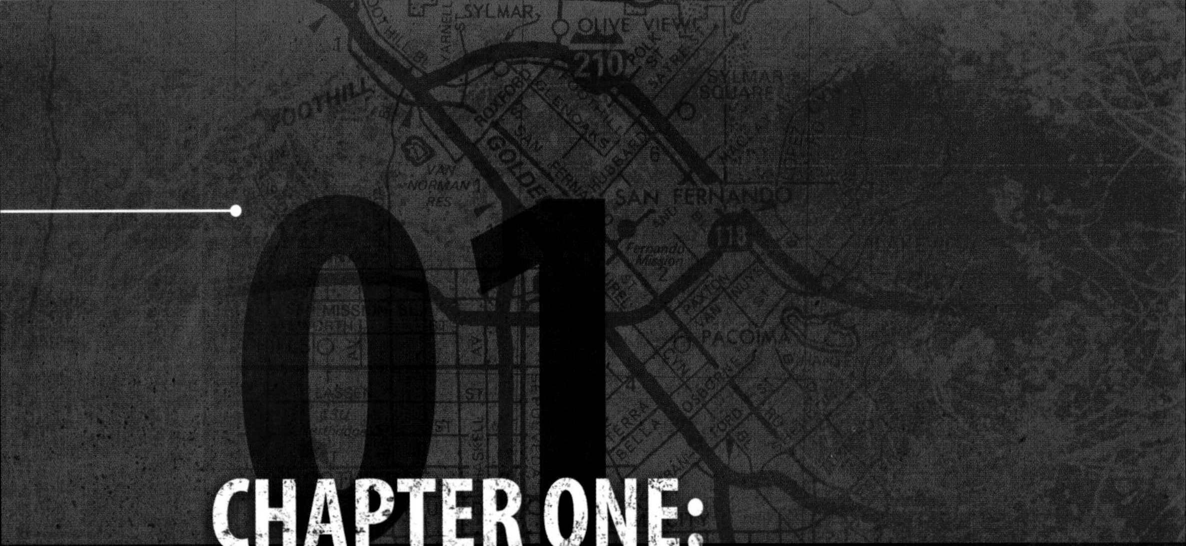
SYLMAR
OLIVE VIEW
210
SYLMAR SQUARE
FOOTHILL
VAN NORMAN RES
SAN FERNANDO
118
PACOIMA

01

CHAPTER ONE:
History Repeating

Illustrated by
Nathan Fox

Colors by
Oscar Pinto

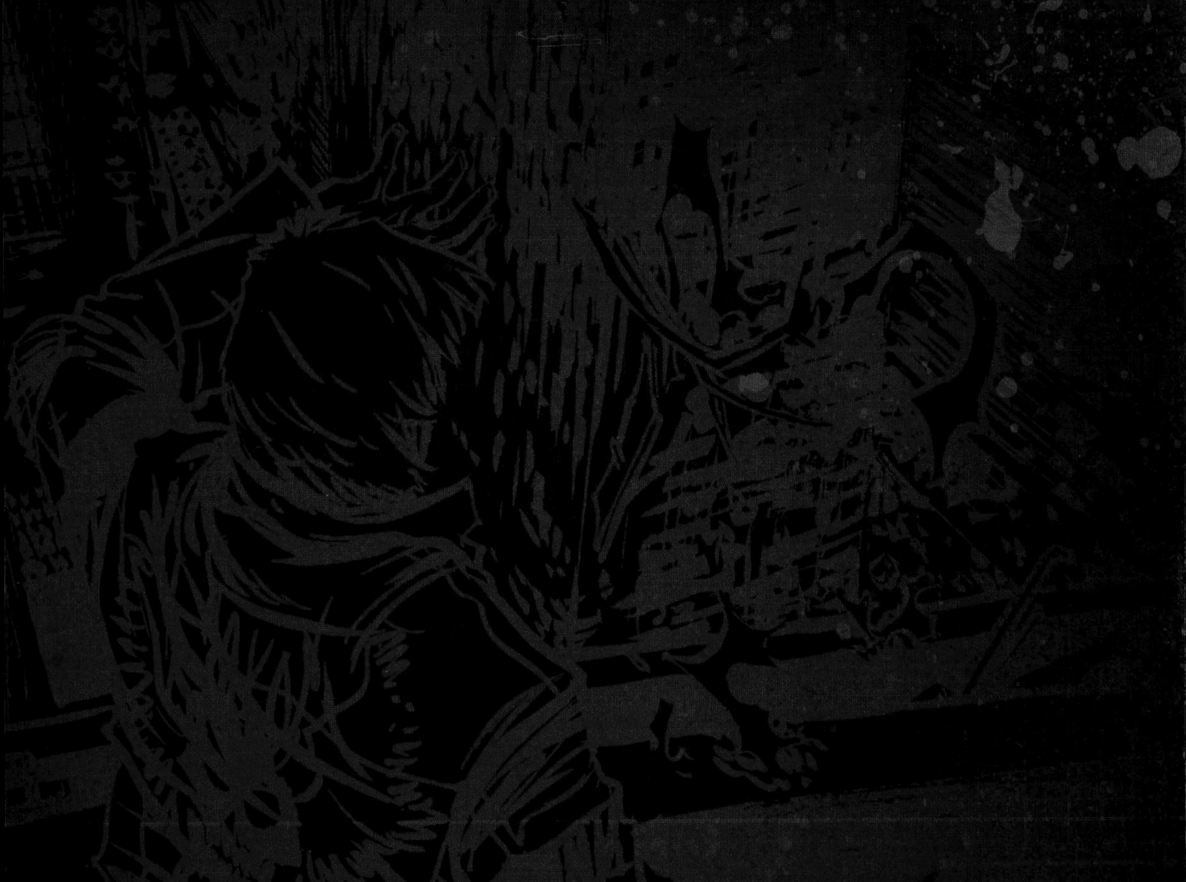

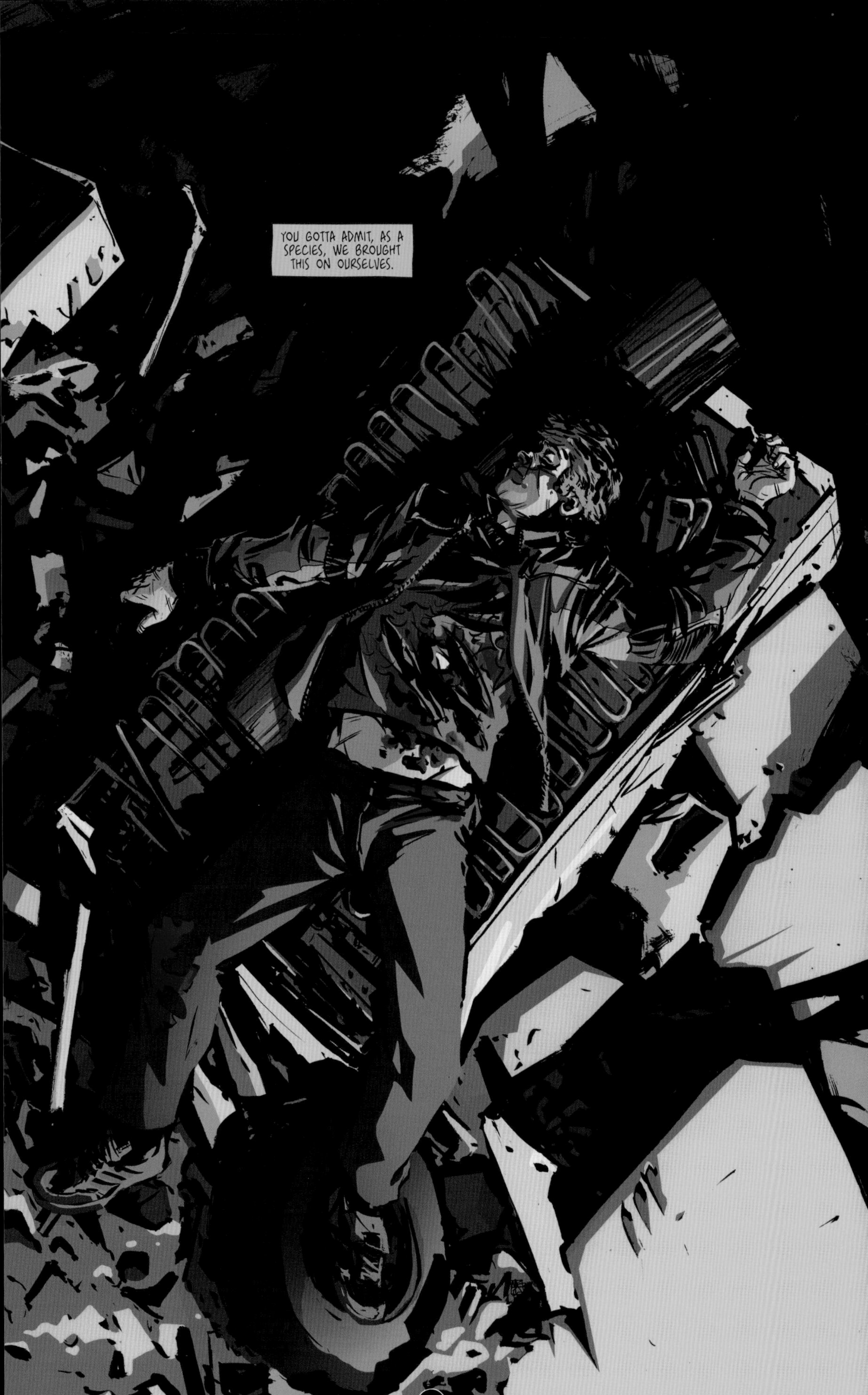
YOU GOTTA ADMIT, AS A SPECIES, WE BROUGHT THIS ON OURSELVES.

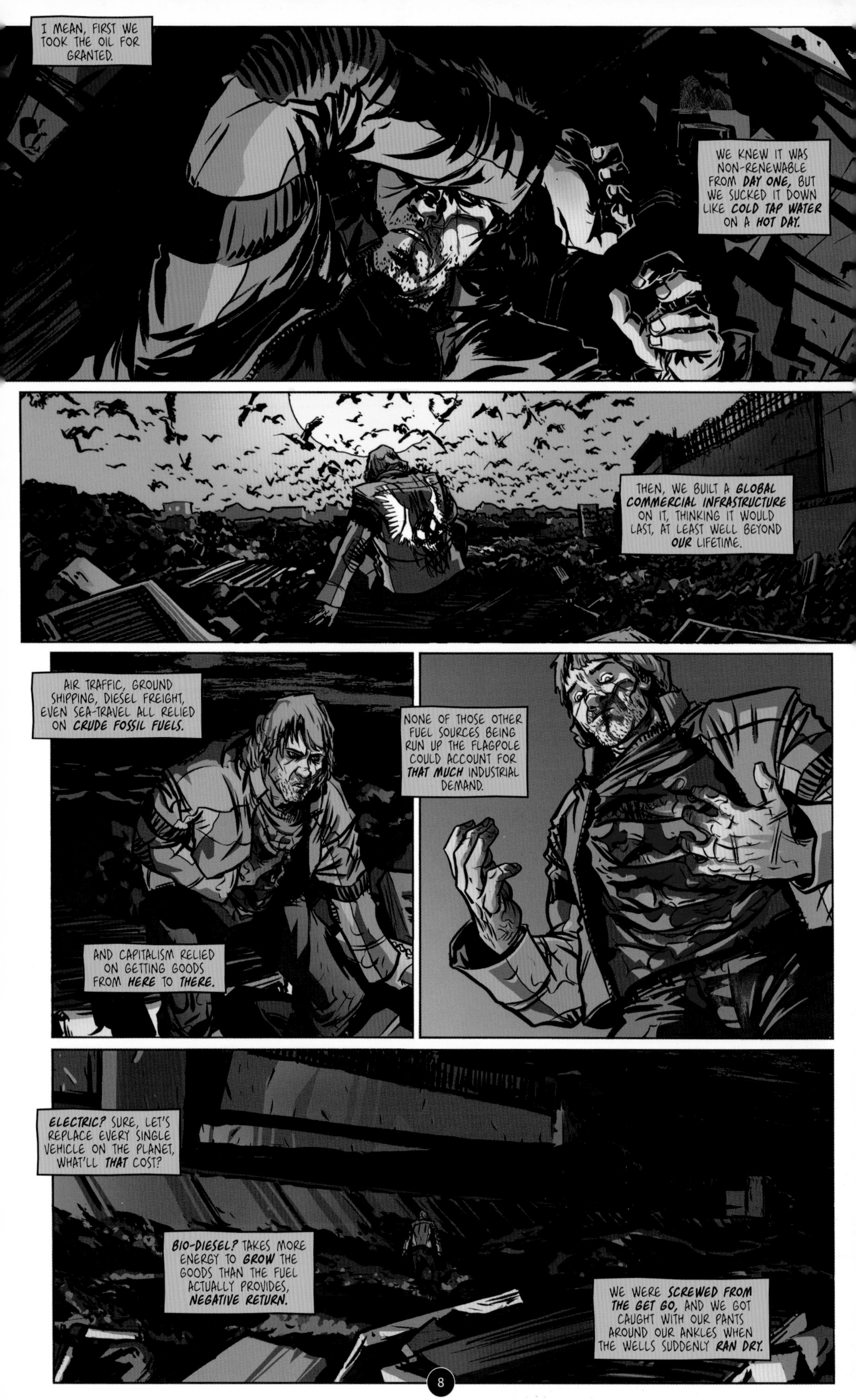
I MEAN, FIRST WE TOOK THE OIL FOR GRANTED.
WE KNEW IT WAS NON-RENEWABLE FROM DAY ONE, BUT WE SUCKED IT DOWN LIKE COLD TAP WATER ON A HOT DAY.
THEN, WE BUILT A GLOBAL COMMERCIAL INFRASTRUCTURE ON IT, THINKING IT WOULD LAST, AT LEAST WELL BEYOND OUR LIFETIME.
AIR TRAFFIC, GROUND SHIPPING, DIESEL FREIGHT, EVEN SEA-TRAVEL ALL RELIED ON CRUDE FOSSIL FUELS.
AND CAPITALISM RELIED ON GETTING GOODS FROM HERE TO THERE.
NONE OF THOSE OTHER FUEL SOURCES BEING RUN UP THE FLAGPOLE COULD ACCOUNT FOR THAT MUCH INDUSTRIAL DEMAND.
ELECTRIC? SURE, LET'S REPLACE EVERY SINGLE VEHICLE ON THE PLANET, WHAT'LL THAT COST?
BIO-DIESEL? TAKES MORE ENERGY TO GROW THE GOODS THAN THE FUEL ACTUALLY PROVIDES, NEGATIVE RETURN.
WE WERE SCREWED FROM THE GET GO, AND WE GOT CAUGHT WITH OUR PANTS AROUND OUR ANKLES WHEN THE WELLS SUDDENLY RAN DRY.

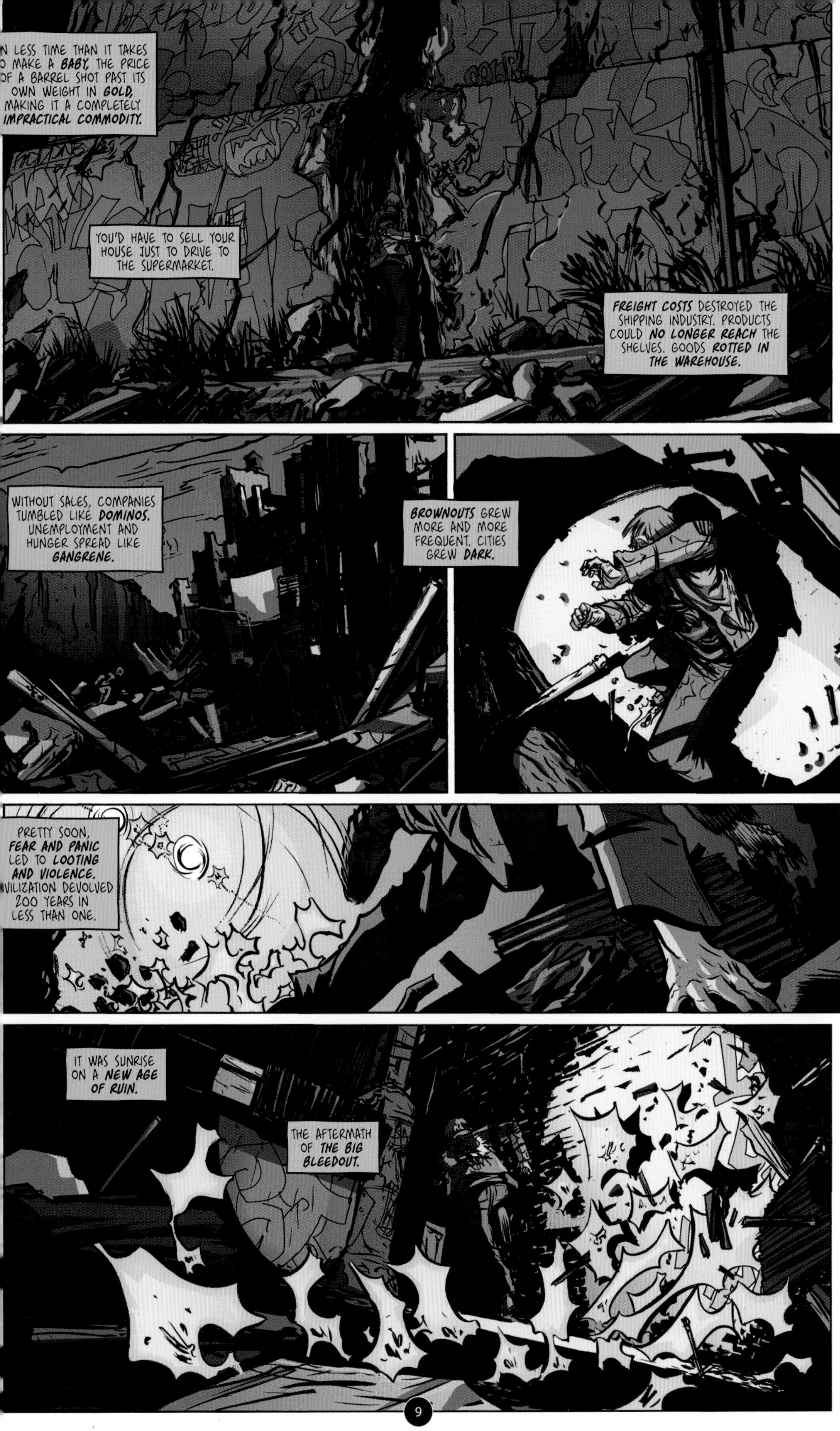
N LESS TIME THAN IT TAKES O MAKE A BABY, THE PRICE OF A BARREL SHOT PAST ITS OWN WEIGHT IN GOLD, MAKING IT A COMPLETELY IMPRACTICAL COMMODITY.
YOU'D HAVE TO SELL YOUR HOUSE JUST TO DRIVE TO THE SUPERMARKET.
FREIGHT COSTS DESTROYED THE SHIPPING INDUSTRY. PRODUCTS COULD NO LONGER REACH THE SHELVES. GOODS ROTTED IN THE WAREHOUSE.
WITHOUT SALES, COMPANIES TUMBLED LIKE DOMINOS. UNEMPLOYMENT AND HUNGER SPREAD LIKE GANGRENE.
BROWNOUTS GREW MORE AND MORE FREQUENT. CITIES GREW DARK.
PRETTY SOON, FEAR AND PANIC LED TO LOOTING AND VIOLENCE. VILIZATION DEVOLVED 200 YEARS IN LESS THAN ONE.
IT WAS SUNRISE ON A NEW AGE OF RUIN.
THE AFTERMATH OF THE BIG BLEEDOUT.

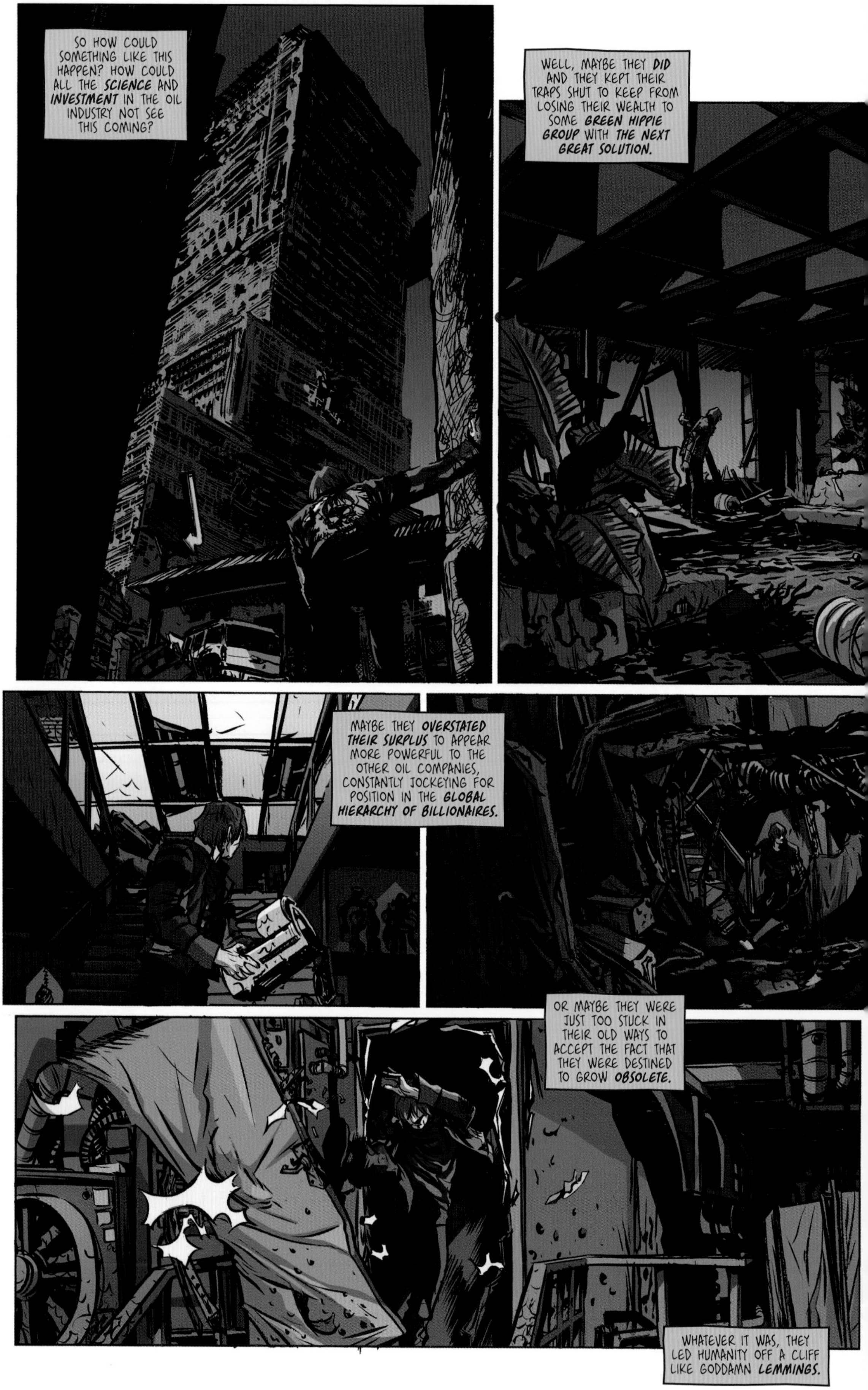
SO HOW COULD SOMETHING LIKE THIS HAPPEN? HOW COULD ALL THE **SCIENCE** AND **INVESTMENT** IN THE OIL INDUSTRY NOT SEE THIS COMING?
WELL, MAYBE THEY **DID** AND THEY KEPT THEIR TRAPS SHUT TO KEEP FROM LOSING THEIR WEALTH TO SOME **GREEN HIPPIE GROUP** WITH **THE NEXT GREAT SOLUTION.**
MAYBE THEY **OVERSTATED THEIR SURPLUS** TO APPEAR MORE POWERFUL TO THE OTHER OIL COMPANIES, CONSTANTLY JOCKEYING FOR POSITION IN THE **GLOBAL HIERARCHY OF BILLIONAIRES.**
OR MAYBE THEY WERE JUST TOO STUCK IN THEIR OLD WAYS TO ACCEPT THE FACT THAT THEY WERE DESTINED TO GROW **OBSOLETE.**
WHATEVER IT WAS, THEY LED HUMANITY OFF A CLIFF LIKE GODDAMN **LEMMINGS.**

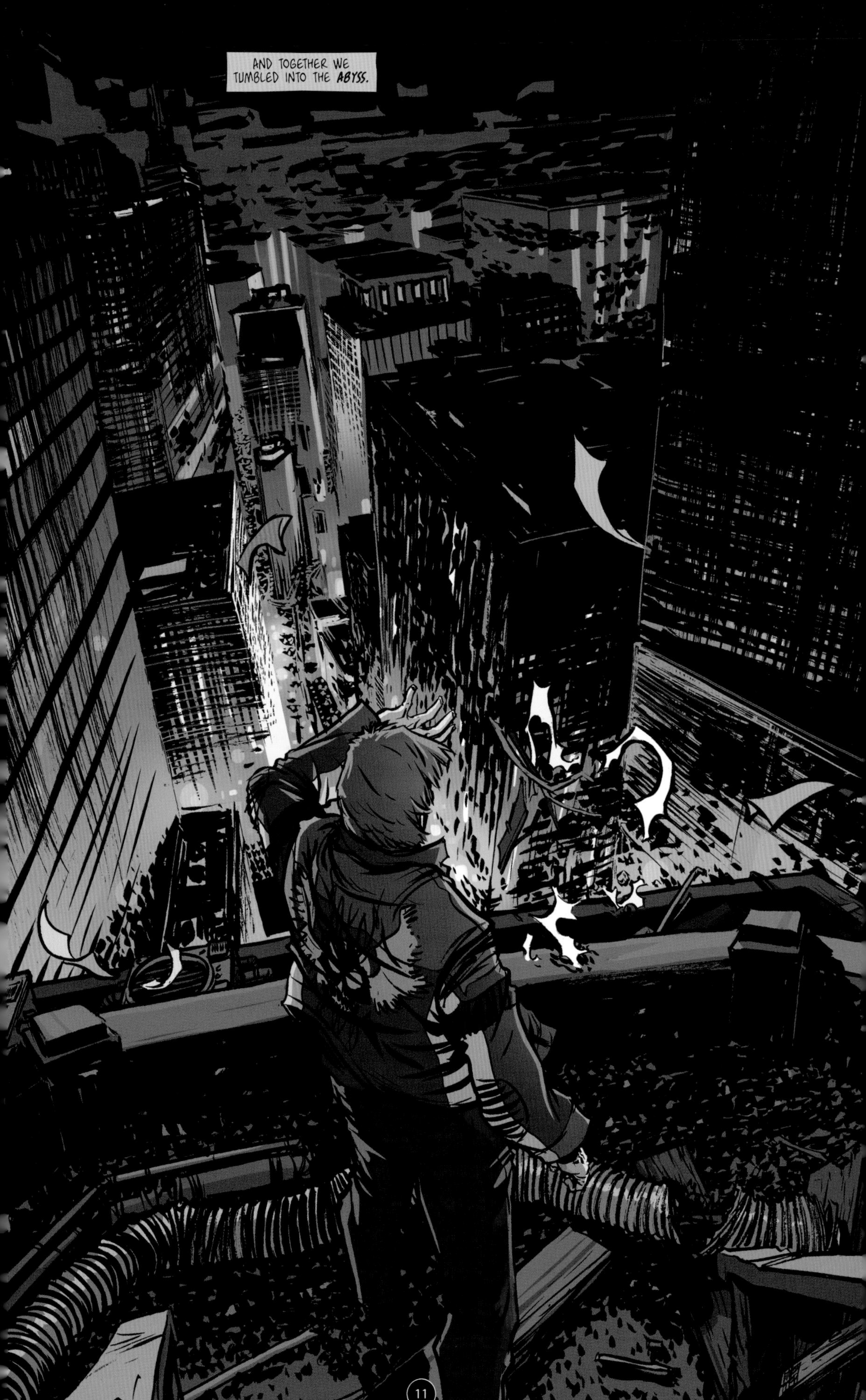
AND TOGETHER WE TUMBLED INTO THE ABYSS.

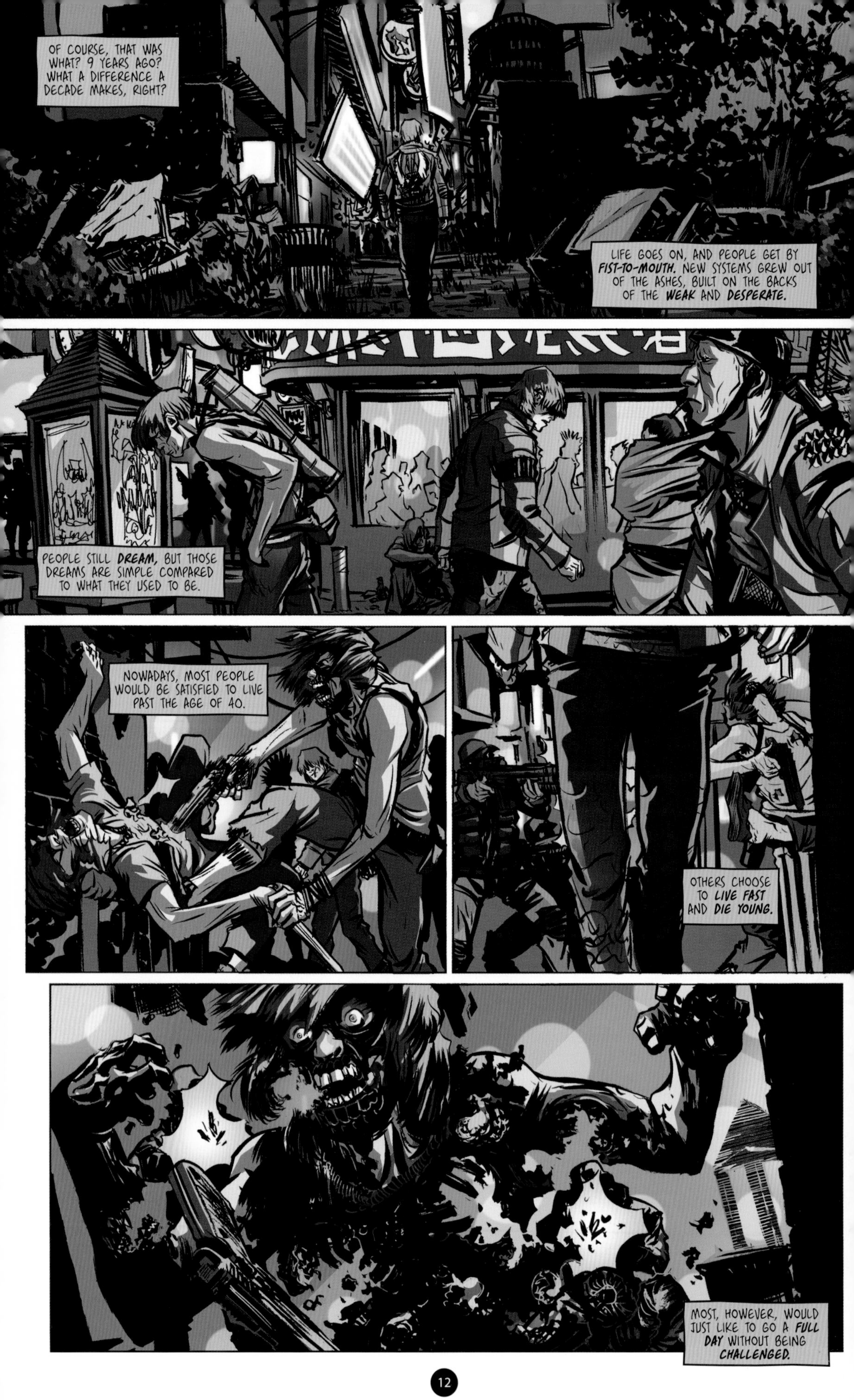
OF COURSE, THAT WAS WHAT? 9 YEARS AGO? WHAT A DIFFERENCE A DECADE MAKES, RIGHT?
LIFE GOES ON, AND PEOPLE GET BY FIST-TO-MOUTH. NEW SYSTEMS GREW OUT OF THE ASHES, BUILT ON THE BACKS OF THE WEAK AND DESPERATE.
PEOPLE STILL DREAM, BUT THOSE DREAMS ARE SIMPLE COMPARED TO WHAT THEY USED TO BE.
NOWADAYS, MOST PEOPLE WOULD BE SATISFIED TO LIVE PAST THE AGE OF 40.
OTHERS CHOOSE TO LIVE FAST AND DIE YOUNG.
MOST, HOWEVER, WOULD JUST LIKE TO GO A FULL DAY WITHOUT BEING CHALLENGED.

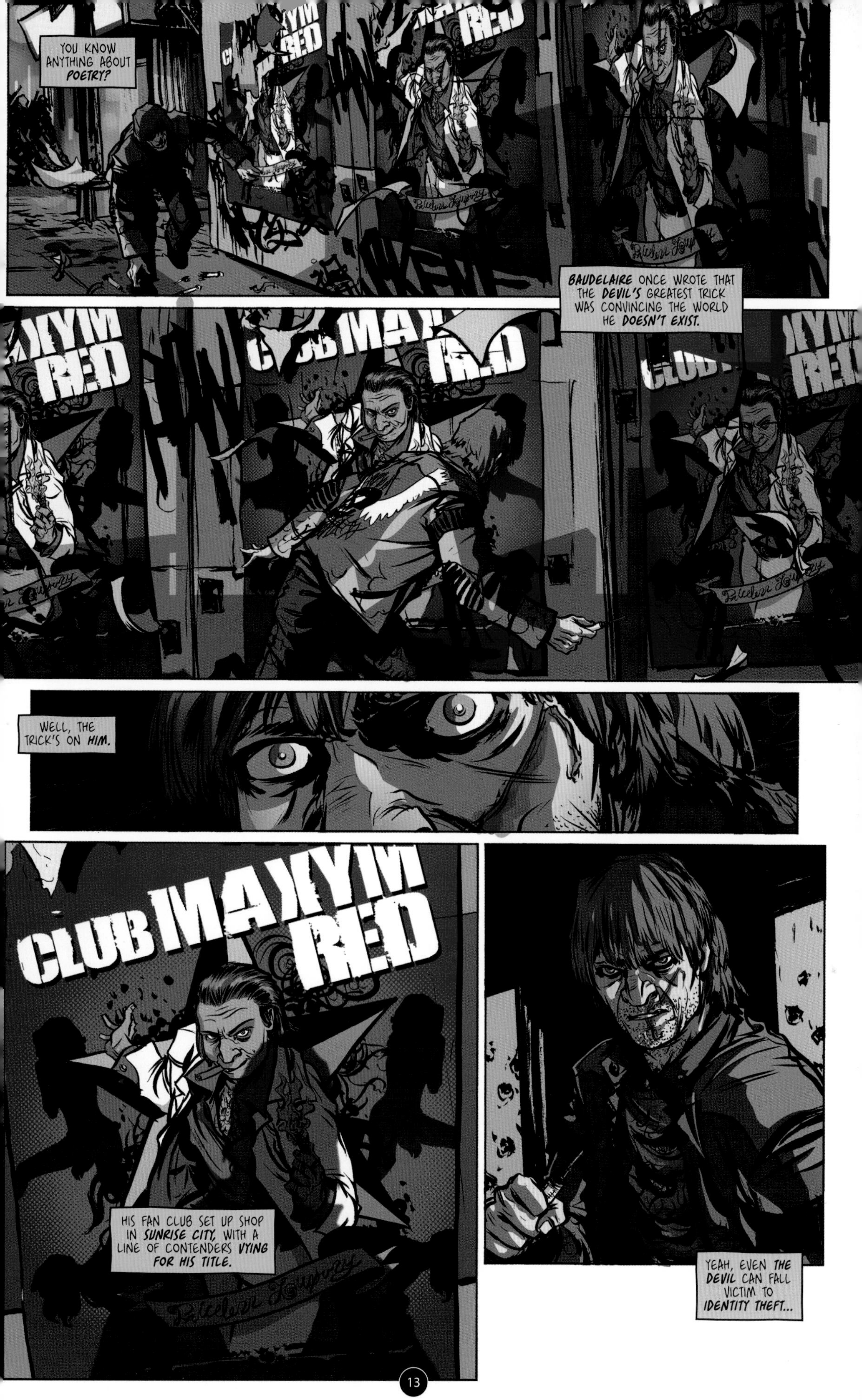
YOU KNOW ANYTHING ABOUT POETRY?
BAUDELAIRE ONCE WROTE THAT THE DEVIL'S GREATEST TRICK WAS CONVINCING THE WORLD HE DOESN'T EXIST.
WELL, THE TRICK'S ON HIM.
CLUB MAXYM RED
HIS FAN CLUB SET UP SHOP IN SUNRISE CITY, WITH A LINE OF CONTENDERS VYING FOR HIS TITLE.
YEAH, EVEN THE DEVIL CAN FALL VICTIM TO IDENTITY THEFT...

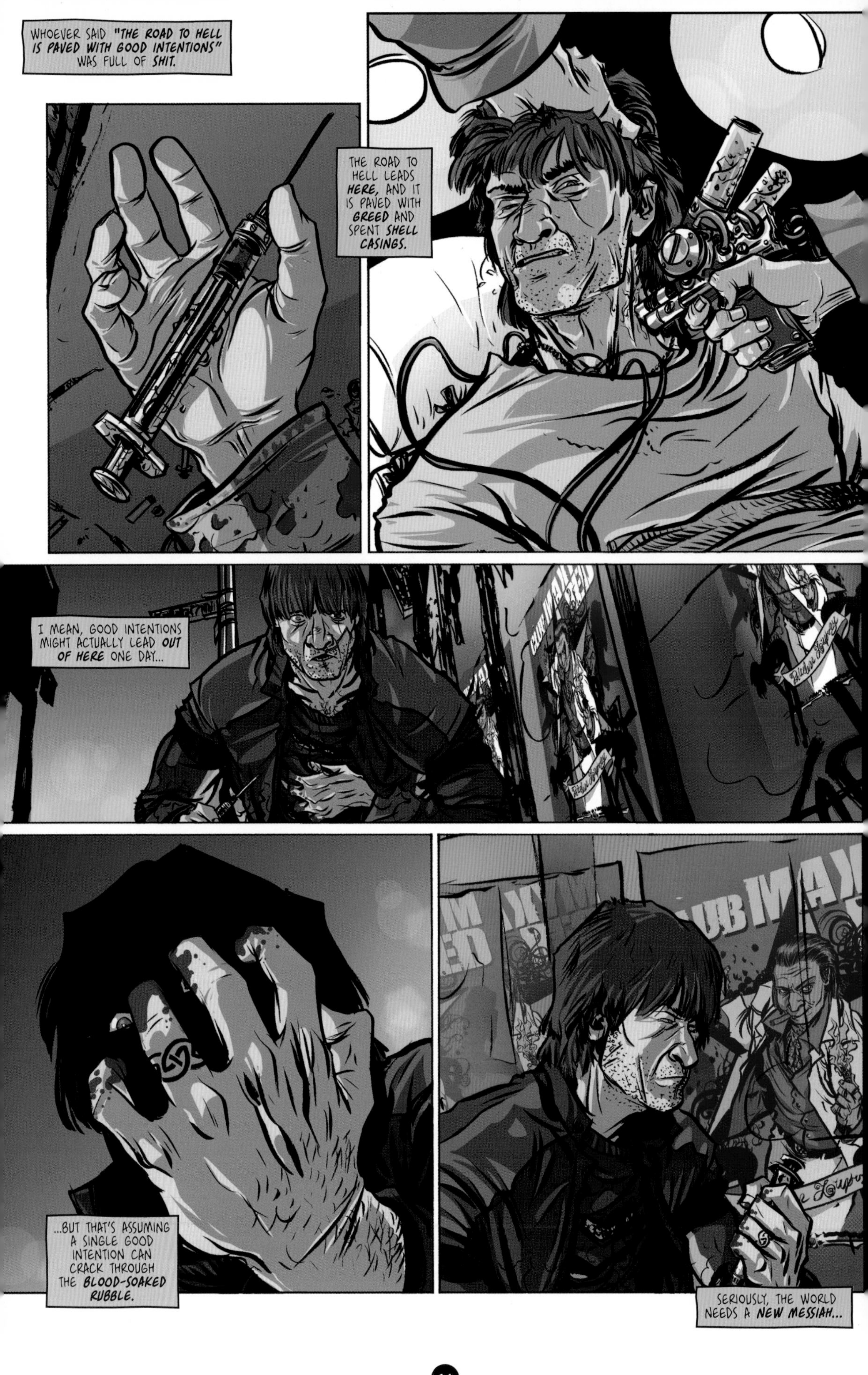
WHOEVER SAID "THE ROAD TO HELL IS PAVED WITH GOOD INTENTIONS" WAS FULL OF SHIT.
THE ROAD TO HELL LEADS HERE, AND IT IS PAVED WITH GREED AND SPENT SHELL CASINGS.
I MEAN, GOOD INTENTIONS MIGHT ACTUALLY LEAD OUT OF HERE ONE DAY...
...BUT THAT'S ASSUMING A SINGLE GOOD INTENTION CAN CRACK THROUGH THE BLOOD-SOAKED RUBBLE.
SERIOUSLY, THE WORLD NEEDS A NEW MESSIAH...

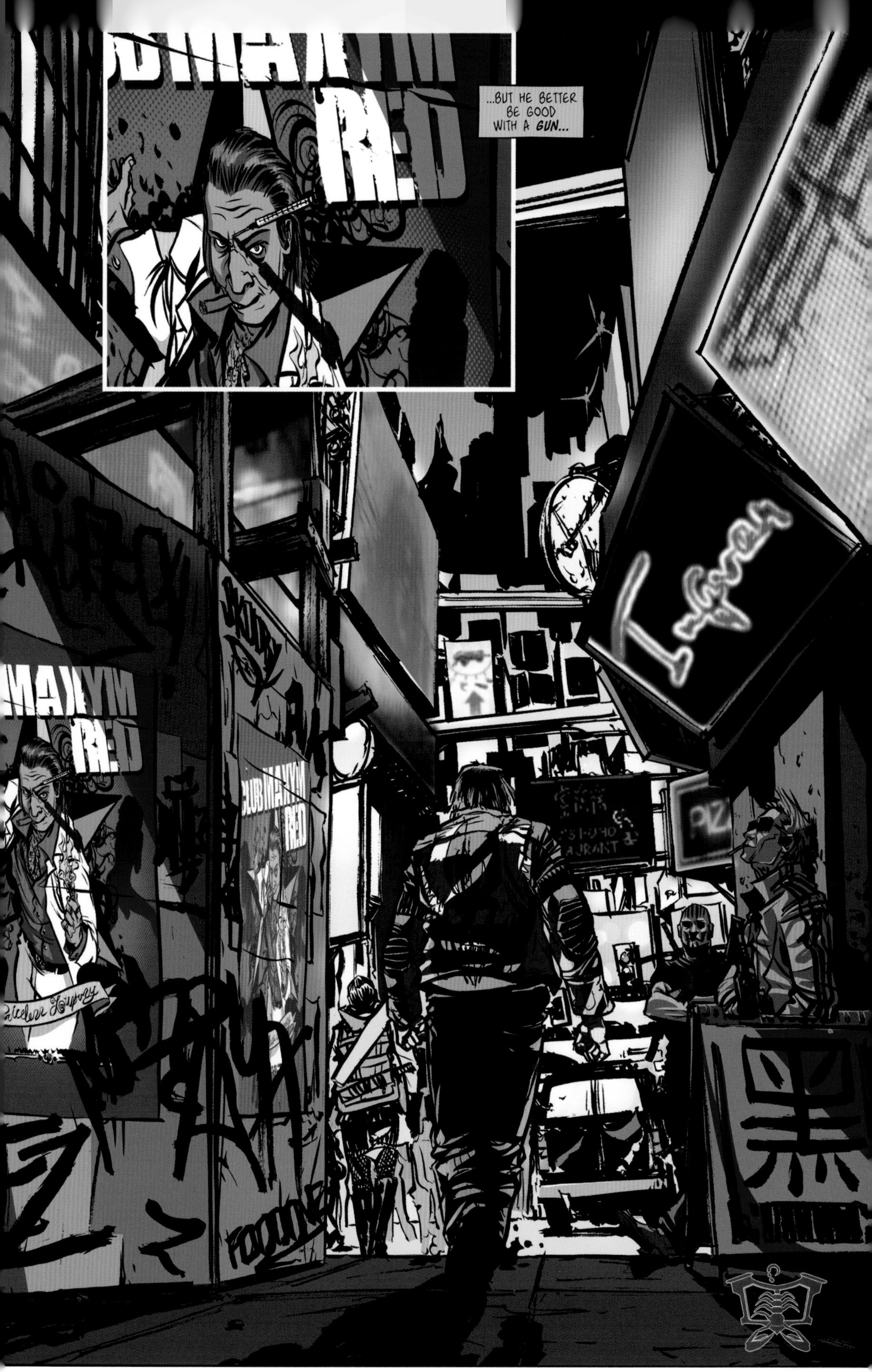
...BUT HE BETTER BE GOOD WITH A GUN...
MAXYM RED
CLUB MAXYM RED

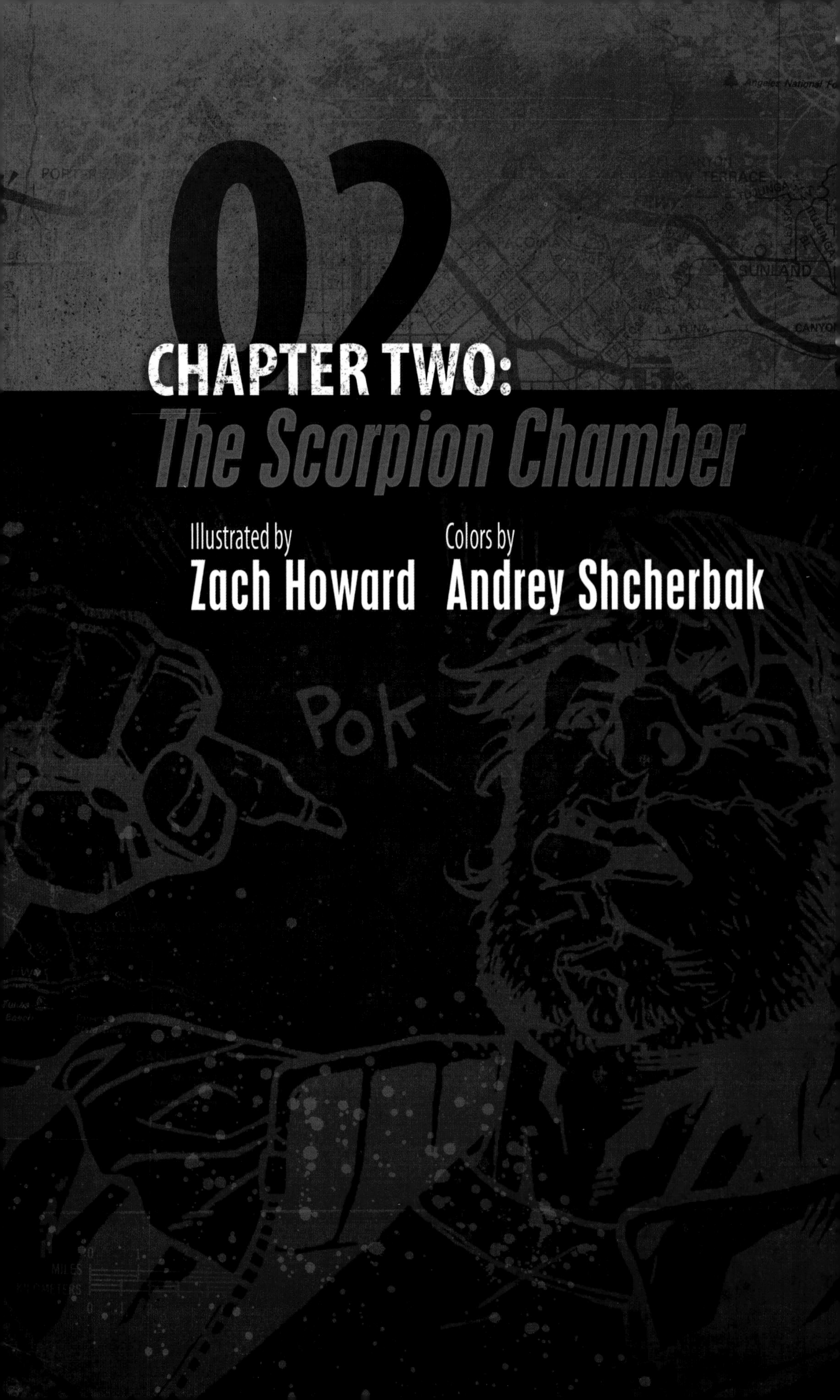
Pok
SUNLAND
TERRACE

02

CHAPTER TWO: *The Scorpion Chamber*

Illustrated by
Zach Howard

Colors by
Andrey Shcherbak

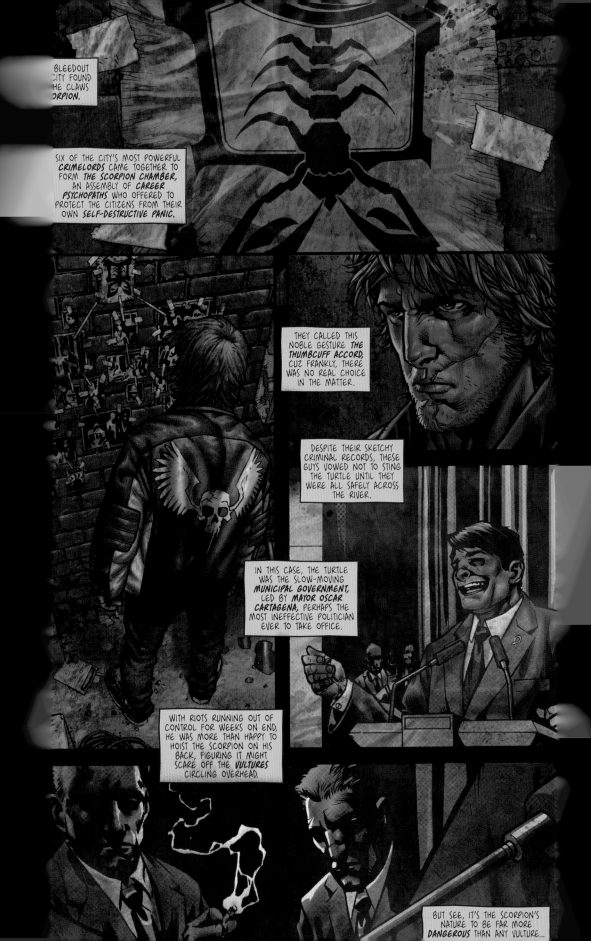

BLEEDOUT
CITY FOUND
THE CLAWS
[SC]ORPION.

SIX OF THE CITY'S MOST POWERFUL *CRIMELORDS* CAME TOGETHER TO FORM *THE SCORPION CHAMBER*, AN ASSEMBLY OF *CAREER PSYCHOPATHS* WHO OFFERED TO PROTECT THE CITIZENS FROM THEIR OWN *SELF-DESTRUCTIVE PANIC*.

THEY CALLED THIS NOBLE GESTURE *THE THUMBCUFF ACCORD*, CUZ FRANKLY, THERE WAS NO REAL CHOICE IN THE MATTER.

DESPITE THEIR SKETCHY CRIMINAL RECORDS, THESE GUYS VOWED NOT TO STING THE TURTLE UNTIL THEY WERE ALL SAFELY ACROSS THE RIVER.

IN THIS CASE, THE TURTLE WAS THE SLOW-MOVING *MUNICIPAL GOVERNMENT*, LED BY *MAYOR OSCAR CARTAGENA*, PERHAPS THE MOST INEFFECTIVE POLITICIAN EVER TO TAKE OFFICE.

WITH RIOTS RUNNING OUT OF CONTROL FOR WEEKS ON END, HE WAS MORE THAN HAPPY TO HOIST THE SCORPION ON HIS BACK, FIGURING IT MIGHT SCARE OFF THE *VULTURES* CIRCLING OVERHEAD.

BUT SEE, IT'S THE SCORPION'S NATURE TO BE FAR MORE *DANGEROUS* THAN ANY VULTURE...

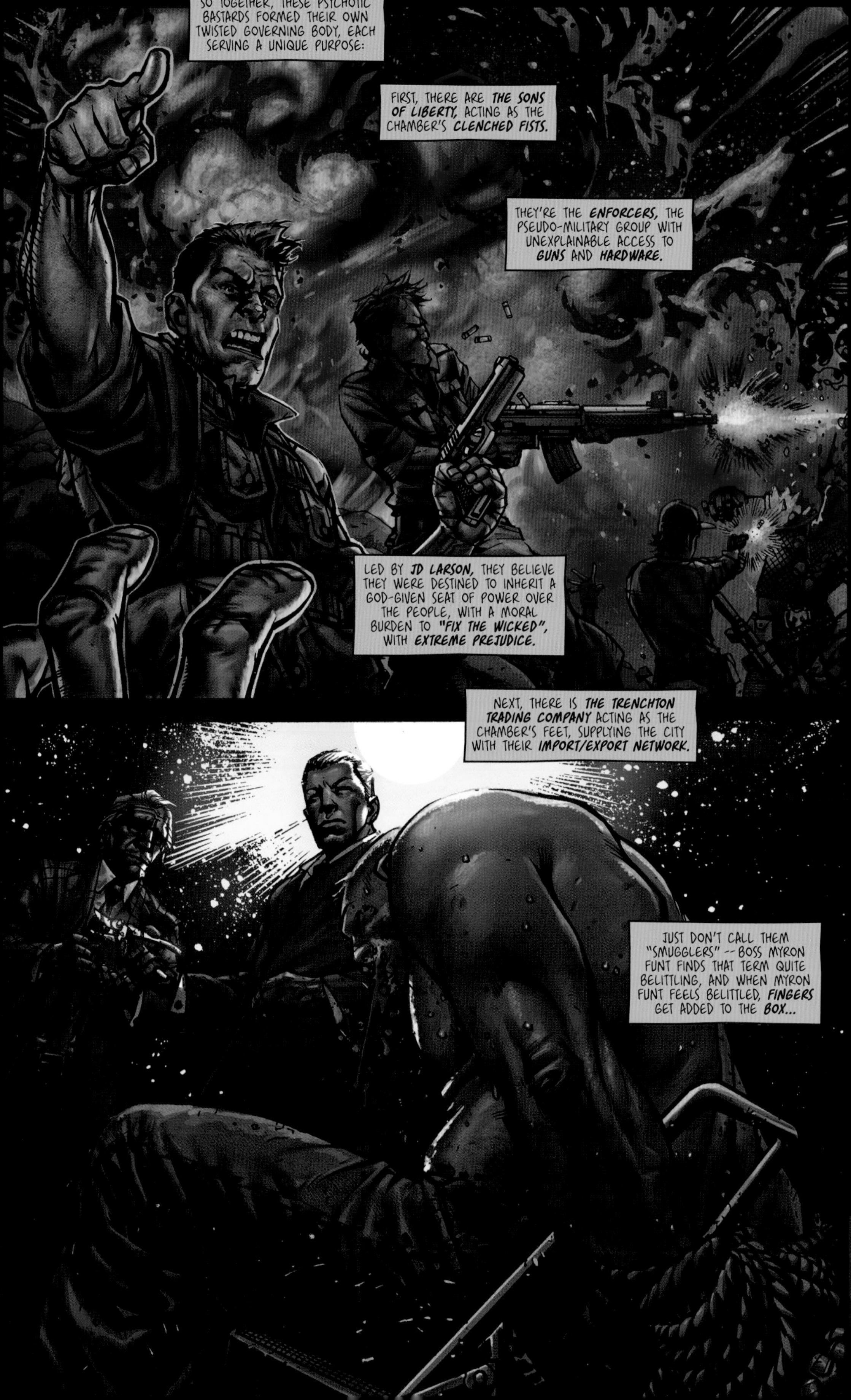
SO TOGETHER, THESE PSYCHOTIC BASTARDS FORMED THEIR OWN TWISTED GOVERNING BODY, EACH SERVING A UNIQUE PURPOSE:
FIRST, THERE ARE THE SONS OF LIBERTY, ACTING AS THE CHAMBER'S CLENCHED FISTS.
THEY'RE THE ENFORCERS, THE PSEUDO-MILITARY GROUP WITH UNEXPLAINABLE ACCESS TO GUNS AND HARDWARE.
LED BY JD LARSON, THEY BELIEVE THEY WERE DESTINED TO INHERIT A GOD-GIVEN SEAT OF POWER OVER THE PEOPLE, WITH A MORAL BURDEN TO "FIX THE WICKED", WITH EXTREME PREJUDICE.
NEXT, THERE IS THE TRENCHTON TRADING COMPANY ACTING AS THE CHAMBER'S FEET, SUPPLYING THE CITY WITH THEIR IMPORT/EXPORT NETWORK.
JUST DON'T CALL THEM "SMUGGLERS" -- BOSS MYRON FUNT FINDS THAT TERM QUITE BELITTLING, AND WHEN MYRON FUNT FEELS BELITTLED, FINGERS GET ADDED TO THE BOX...

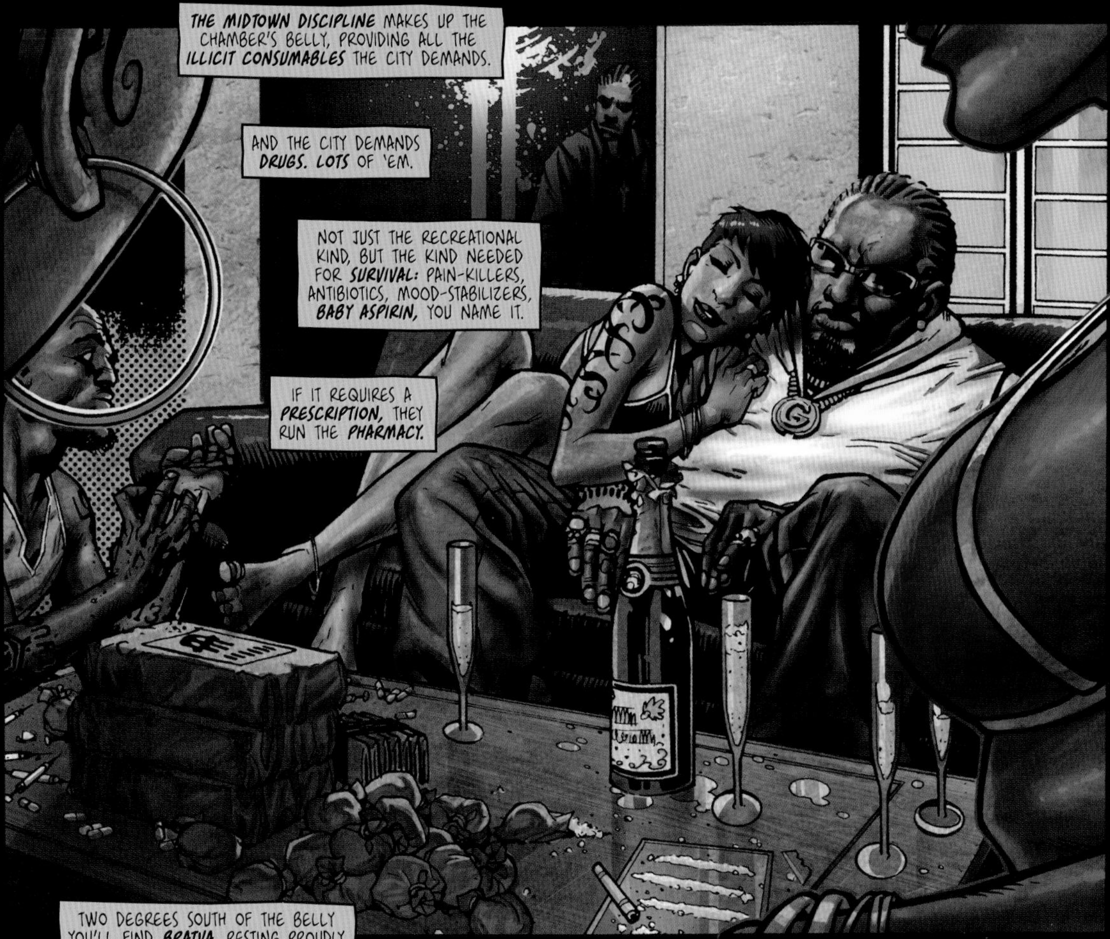
THE MIDTOWN DISCIPLINE MAKES UP THE CHAMBER'S BELLY, PROVIDING ALL THE ILLICIT CONSUMABLES THE CITY DEMANDS.
AND THE CITY DEMANDS DRUGS. LOTS OF 'EM.
NOT JUST THE RECREATIONAL KIND, BUT THE KIND NEEDED FOR SURVIVAL: PAIN-KILLERS, ANTIBIOTICS, MOOD-STABILIZERS, BABY ASPIRIN, YOU NAME IT.
IF IT REQUIRES A PRESCRIPTION, THEY RUN THE PHARMACY.

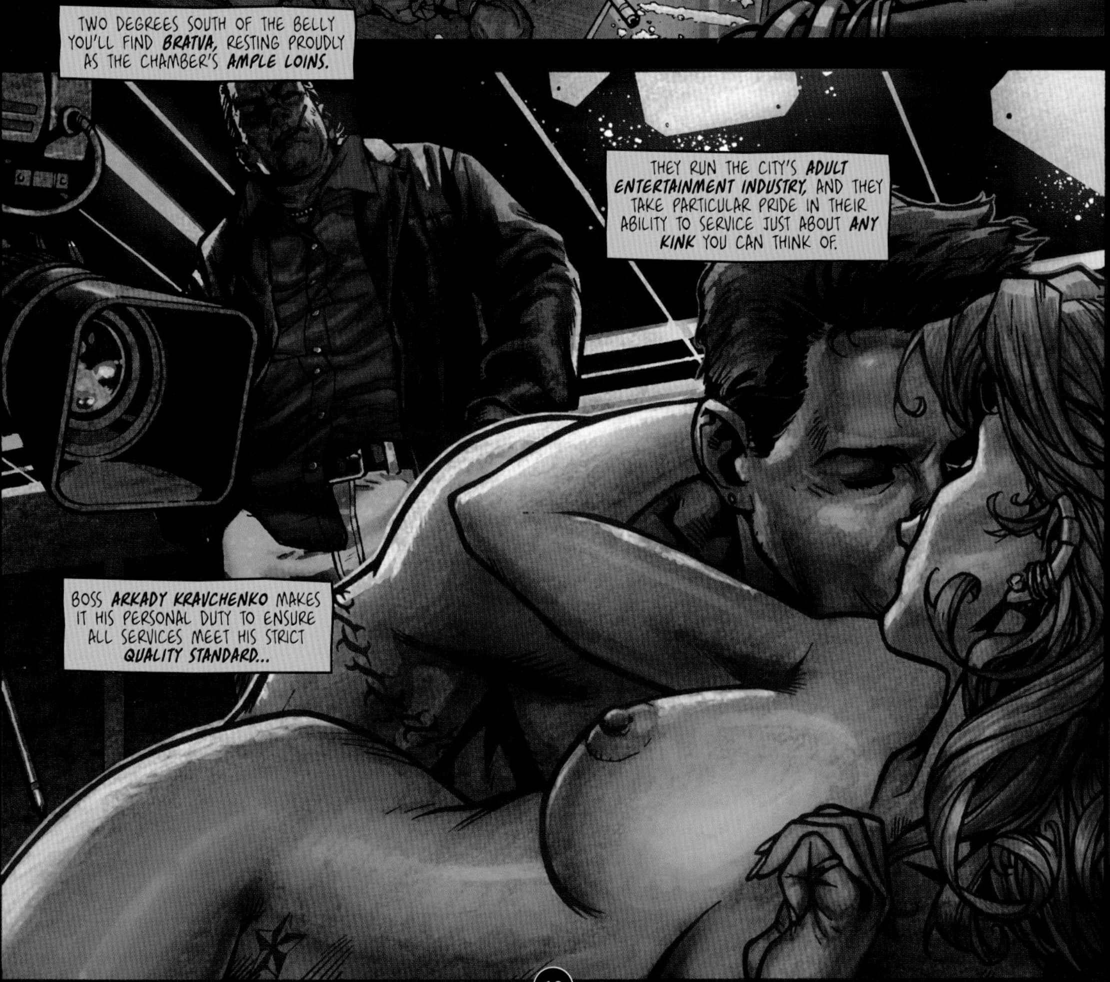
TWO DEGREES SOUTH OF THE BELLY YOU'LL FIND BRATVA, RESTING PROUDLY AS THE CHAMBER'S AMPLE LOINS.
THEY RUN THE CITY'S ADULT ENTERTAINMENT INDUSTRY, AND THEY TAKE PARTICULAR PRIDE IN THEIR ABILITY TO SERVICE JUST ABOUT ANY KINK YOU CAN THINK OF.
BOSS ARKADY KRAVCHENKO MAKES IT HIS PERSONAL DUTY TO ENSURE ALL SERVICES MEET HIS STRICT QUALITY STANDARD...

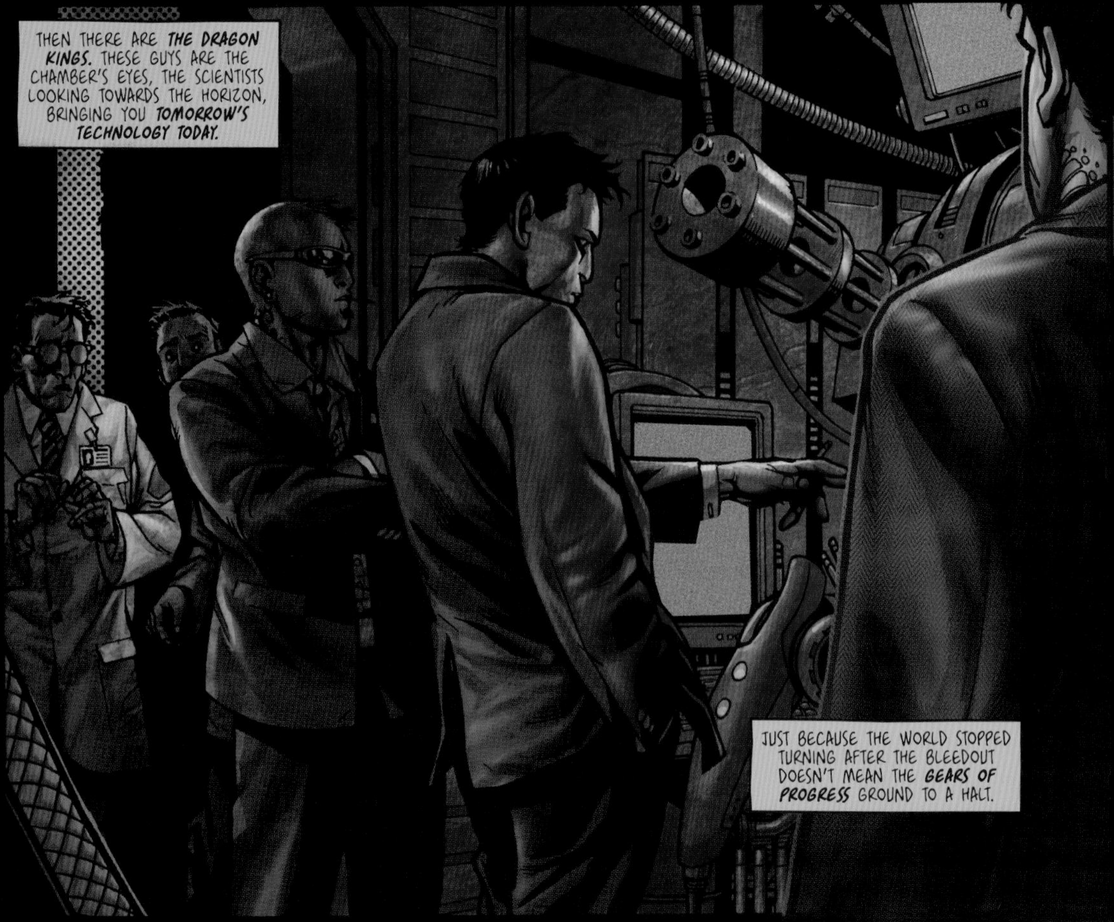
THEN THERE ARE THE DRAGON KINGS. THESE GUYS ARE THE CHAMBER'S EYES, THE SCIENTISTS LOOKING TOWARDS THE HORIZON, BRINGING YOU TOMORROW'S TECHNOLOGY TODAY.
JUST BECAUSE THE WORLD STOPPED TURNING AFTER THE BLEEDOUT DOESN'T MEAN THE GEARS OF PROGRESS GROUND TO A HALT.

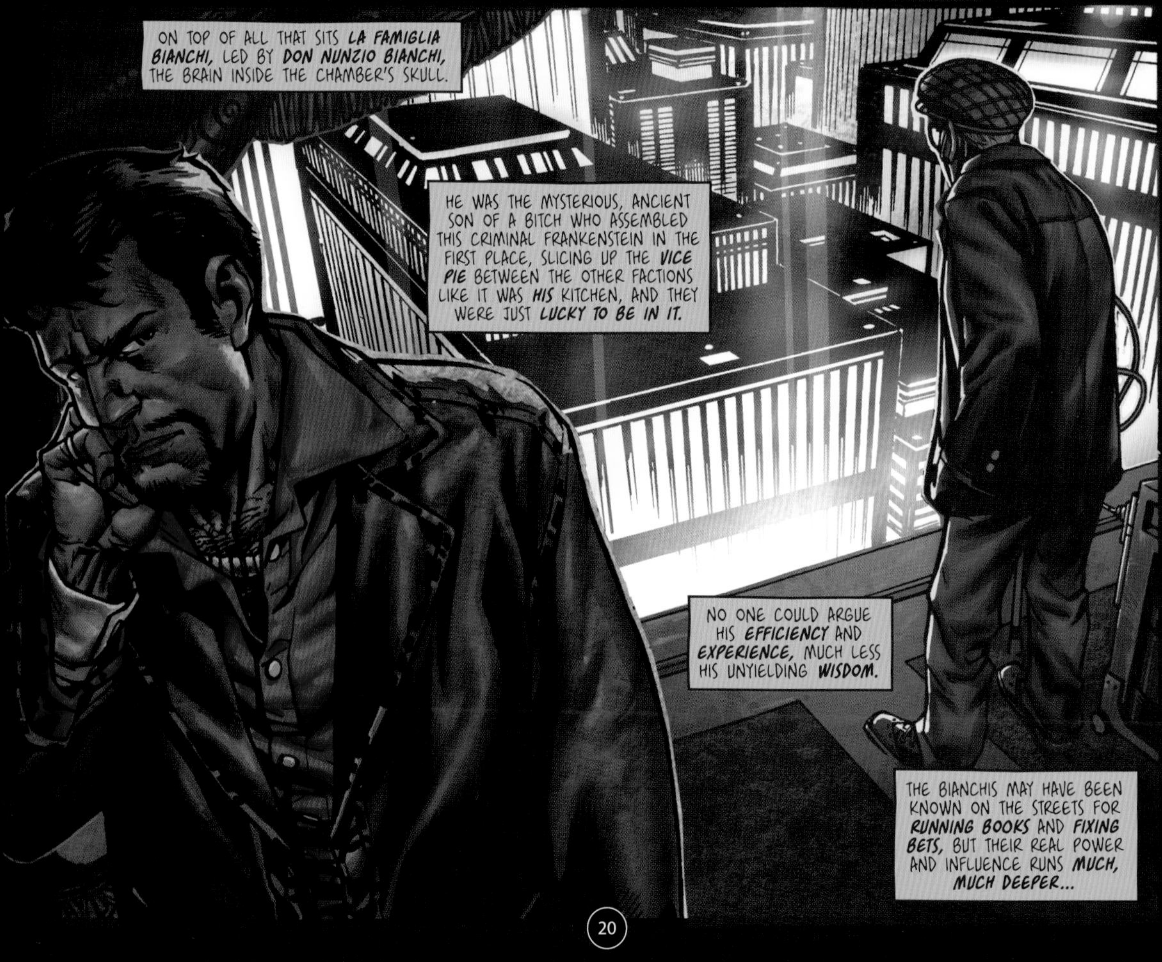
ON TOP OF ALL THAT SITS LA FAMIGLIA BIANCHI, LED BY DON NUNZIO BIANCHI, THE BRAIN INSIDE THE CHAMBER'S SKULL.
HE WAS THE MYSTERIOUS, ANCIENT SON OF A BITCH WHO ASSEMBLED THIS CRIMINAL FRANKENSTEIN IN THE FIRST PLACE, SLICING UP THE VICE PIE BETWEEN THE OTHER FACTIONS LIKE IT WAS HIS KITCHEN, AND THEY WERE JUST LUCKY TO BE IN IT.
NO ONE COULD ARGUE HIS EFFICIENCY AND EXPERIENCE, MUCH LESS HIS UNYIELDING WISDOM.
THE BIANCHIS MAY HAVE BEEN KNOWN ON THE STREETS FOR RUNNING BOOKS AND FIXING BETS, BUT THEIR REAL POWER AND INFLUENCE RUNS MUCH, MUCH DEEPER...

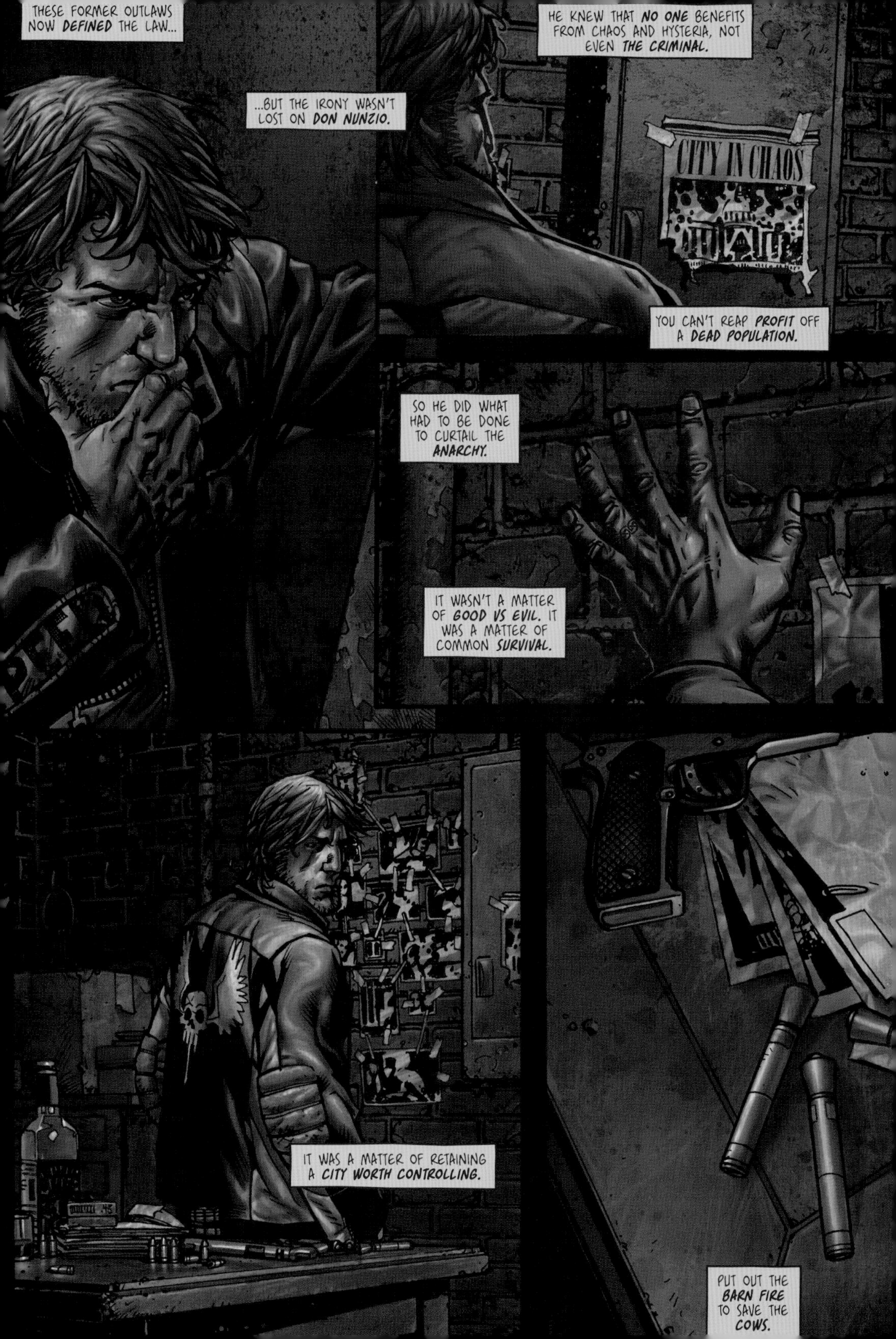
THESE FORMER OUTLAWS NOW DEFINED THE LAW...
...BUT THE IRONY WASN'T LOST ON DON NUNZIO.
HE KNEW THAT NO ONE BENEFITS FROM CHAOS AND HYSTERIA, NOT EVEN THE CRIMINAL.
CITY IN CHAOS
YOU CAN'T REAP PROFIT OFF A DEAD POPULATION.
SO HE DID WHAT HAD TO BE DONE TO CURTAIL THE ANARCHY.
IT WASN'T A MATTER OF GOOD VS EVIL. IT WAS A MATTER OF COMMON SURVIVAL.
IT WAS A MATTER OF RETAINING A CITY WORTH CONTROLLING.
PUT OUT THE BARN FIRE TO SAVE THE COWS.

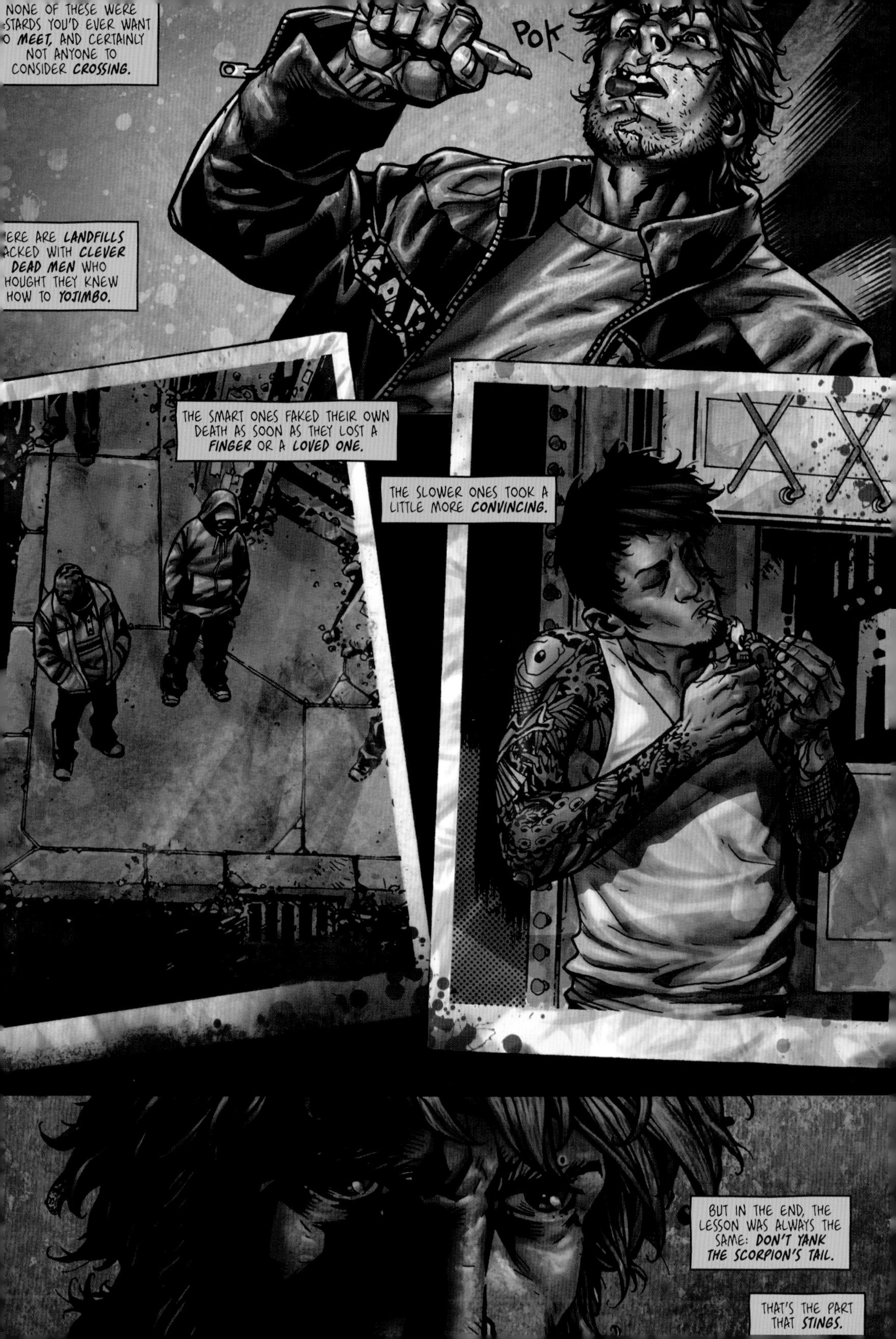
NONE OF THESE WERE
STARDS YOU'D EVER WANT
O MEET, AND CERTAINLY
NOT ANYONE TO
CONSIDER CROSSING.
POK
ERE ARE LANDFILLS
ACKED WITH CLEVER
DEAD MEN WHO
HOUGHT THEY KNEW
HOW TO YOJIMBO.
THE SMART ONES FAKED THEIR OWN DEATH AS SOON AS THEY LOST A FINGER OR A LOVED ONE.
THE SLOWER ONES TOOK A LITTLE MORE CONVINCING.
BUT IN THE END, THE LESSON WAS ALWAYS THE SAME: DON'T YANK THE SCORPION'S TAIL.
THAT'S THE PART THAT STINGS.

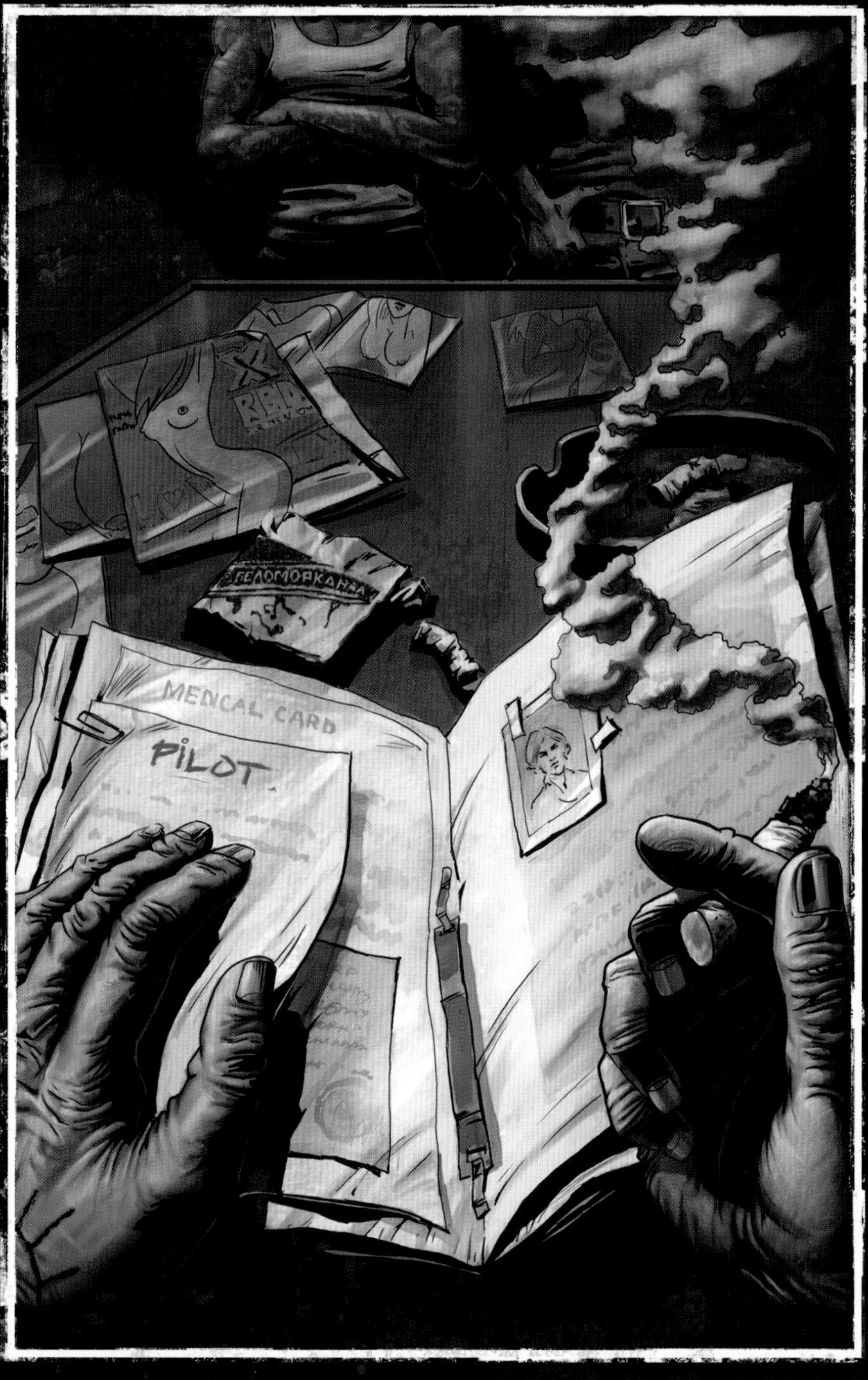
MEDICAL CARD
PILOT
БЕЛОМОРКАНАЛ

Pilot is judged by the council.

03

CHAPTER THREE: *Rat-Filled Walls*

Illustrated by

Sanford Greene

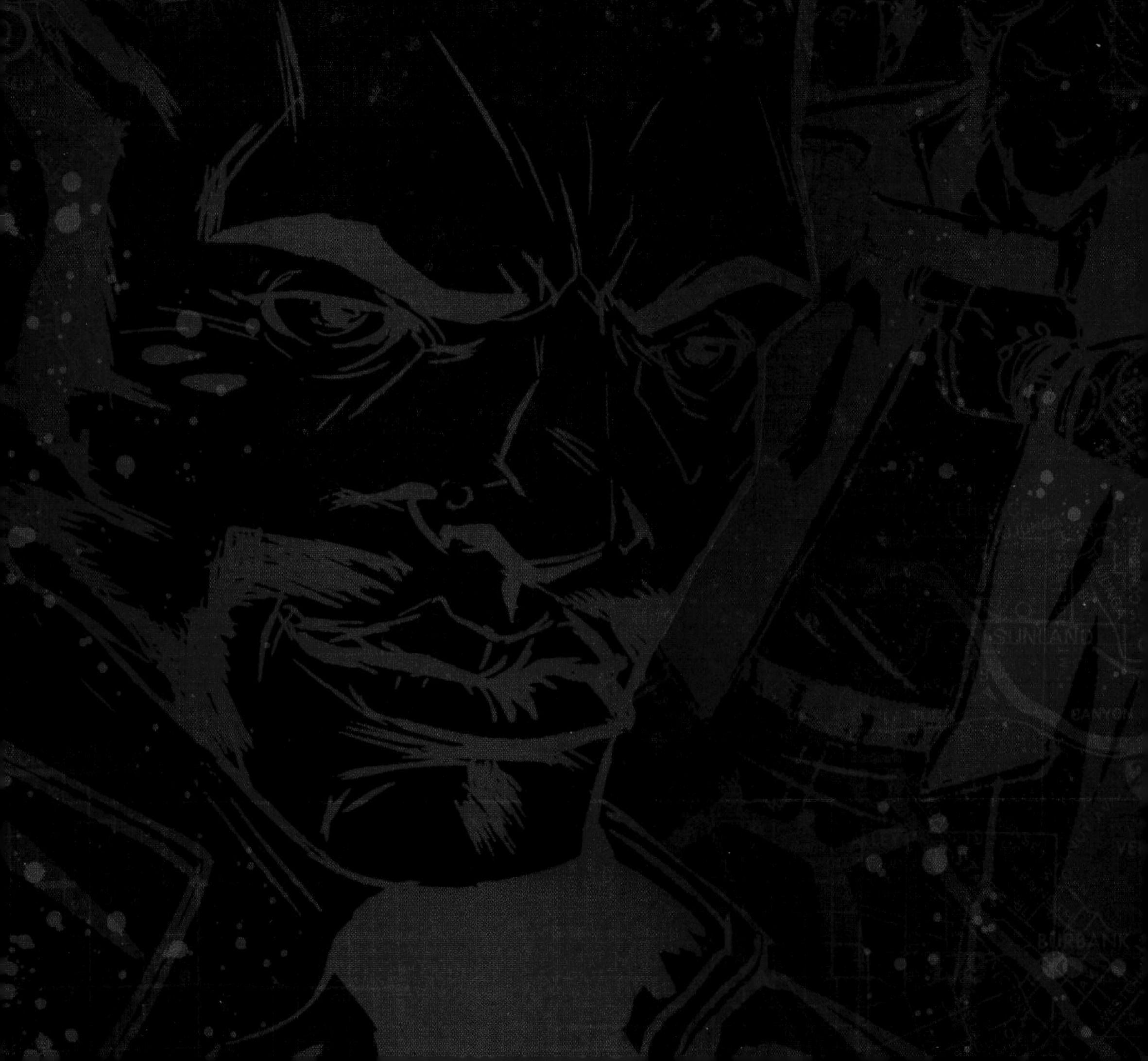

IN THE 40 YEARS AGO, A BUNCH OF PISSED OFF SOUTHSIDE **GANG BANGERS** GOT TOGETHER AND FORMED WHAT BECAME KNOWN AS THE "**BLACK AMERICAN DISCIPLINE**", A STREET GANG WITH CHAPTERS IN EVERY MAJOR METROPOLIS.

MEMBERS OF THE **'B-A-D'** CARRIED A LOT OF **PRIDE**, AND THE STRENGTH OF THEIR BOND FOLLOWED THEM WHEREVER THEY WENT, BE IT LEGITIMATE **BUSINESS**, **POLITICS**, OR EVEN **MILITARY SERVICE**.

AN OVERWHELMING NUMBER OF **BAD BROTHERS** ENDED UP FOR GOVERNMENT-SPONSORED TRAINING, NONE OF WHICH WENT WASTED ONCE THEIR STINT WAS OVER.

IN FACT, IT PROBABLY GOT A HELL OF A LOT **MORE PRACTICAL USE** ON THE STREETS **BACK HOME.**

THAT WAS BEFORE **THE BLEEDOUT.**

NOW THAT TRAINING IS PAYING OFF BETTER THAN ANY **GI COLLEGE FUND**...

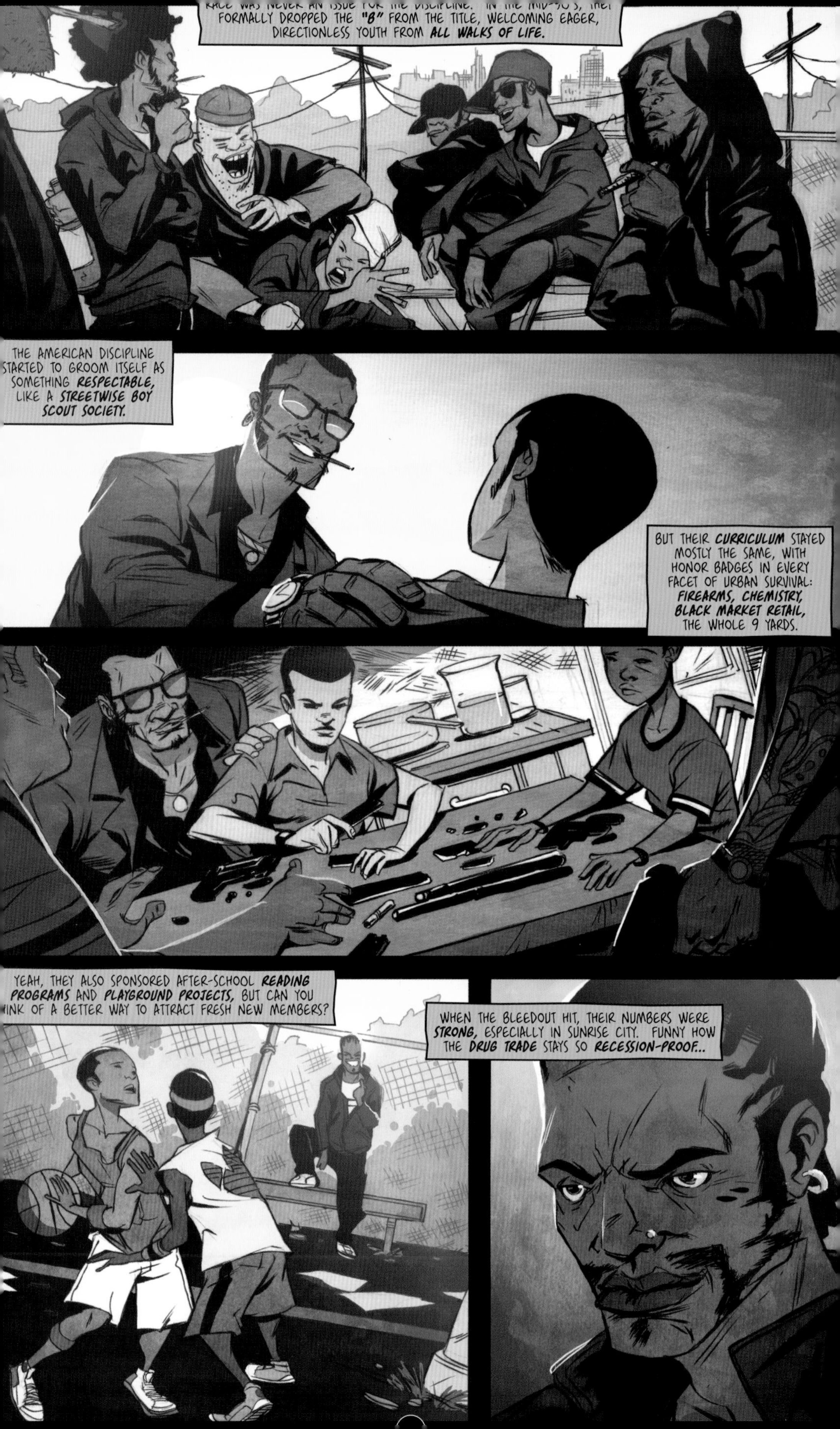
FORMALLY DROPPED THE "B" FROM THE TITLE, WELCOMING EAGER, DIRECTIONLESS YOUTH FROM ALL WALKS OF LIFE.
THE AMERICAN DISCIPLINE STARTED TO GROOM ITSELF AS SOMETHING RESPECTABLE, LIKE A STREETWISE BOY SCOUT SOCIETY.
BUT THEIR CURRICULUM STAYED MOSTLY THE SAME, WITH HONOR BADGES IN EVERY FACET OF URBAN SURVIVAL: FIREARMS, CHEMISTRY, BLACK MARKET RETAIL, THE WHOLE 9 YARDS.
YEAH, THEY ALSO SPONSORED AFTER-SCHOOL READING PROGRAMS AND PLAYGROUND PROJECTS, BUT CAN YOU
INK OF A BETTER WAY TO ATTRACT FRESH NEW MEMBERS?
WHEN THE BLEEDOUT HIT, THEIR NUMBERS WERE STRONG, ESPECIALLY IN SUNRISE CITY. FUNNY HOW THE DRUG TRADE STAYS SO RECESSION-PROOF...

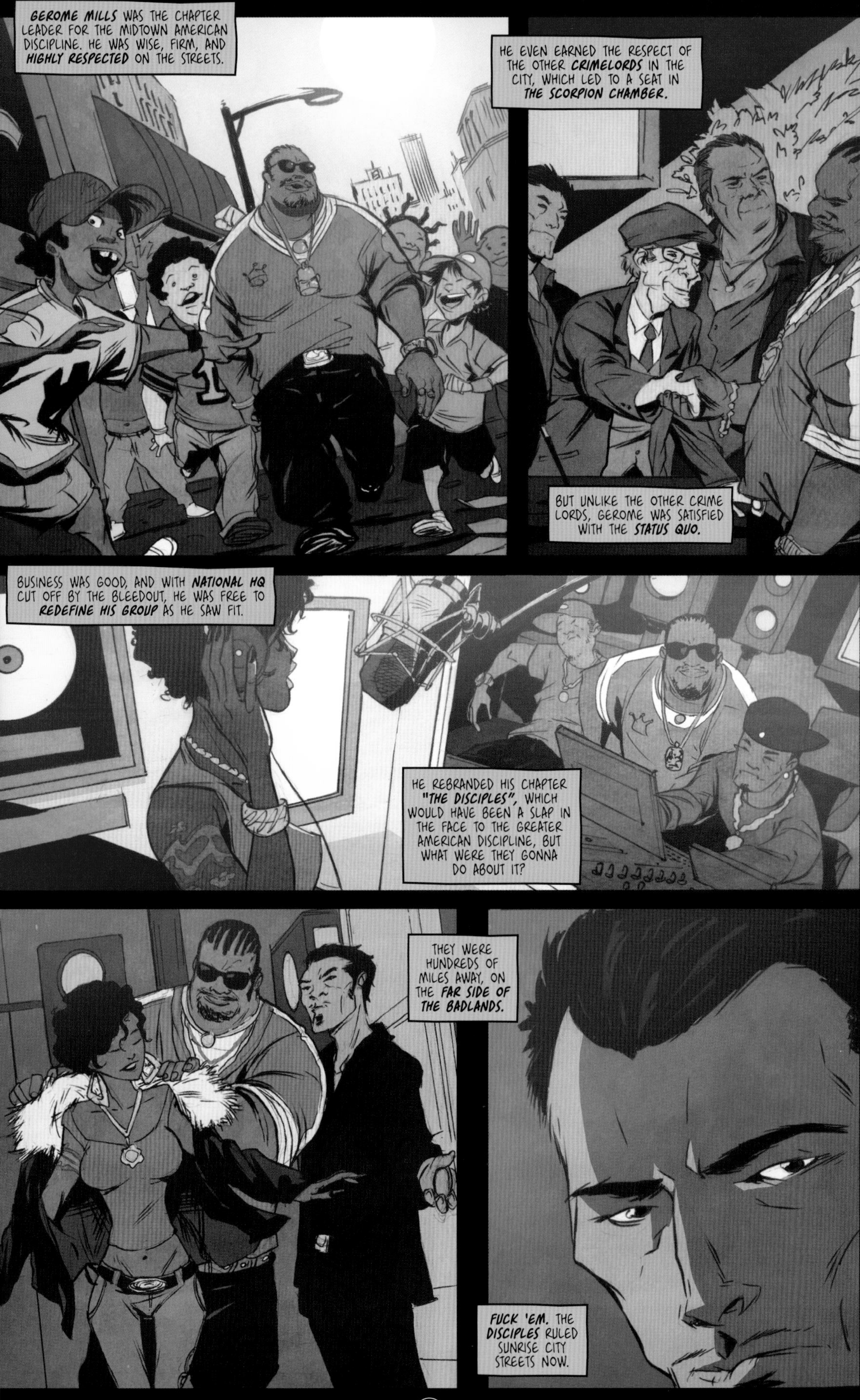
GEROME MILLS WAS THE CHAPTER LEADER FOR THE MIDTOWN AMERICAN DISCIPLINE. HE WAS WISE, FIRM, AND HIGHLY RESPECTED ON THE STREETS.
HE EVEN EARNED THE RESPECT OF THE OTHER CRIMELORDS IN THE CITY, WHICH LED TO A SEAT IN THE SCORPION CHAMBER.
BUT UNLIKE THE OTHER CRIME LORDS, GEROME WAS SATISFIED WITH THE STATUS QUO.
BUSINESS WAS GOOD, AND WITH NATIONAL HQ CUT OFF BY THE BLEEDOUT, HE WAS FREE TO REDEFINE HIS GROUP AS HE SAW FIT.
HE REBRANDED HIS CHAPTER "THE DISCIPLES", WHICH WOULD HAVE BEEN A SLAP IN THE FACE TO THE GREATER AMERICAN DISCIPLINE, BUT WHAT WERE THEY GONNA DO ABOUT IT?
THEY WERE HUNDREDS OF MILES AWAY, ON THE FAR SIDE OF THE BADLANDS.
FUCK 'EM. THE DISCIPLES RULED SUNRISE CITY STREETS NOW.

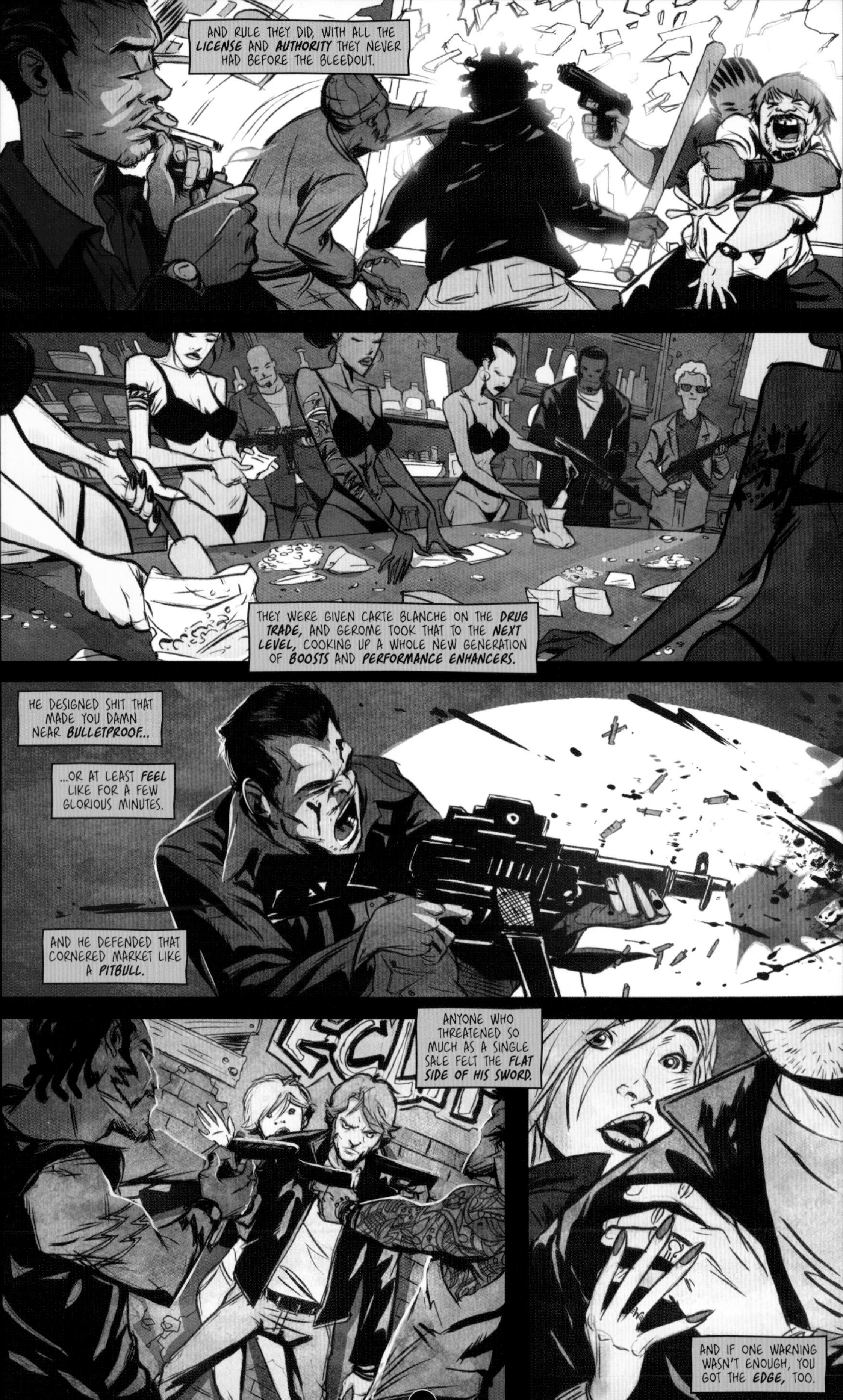
AND RULE THEY DID, WITH ALL THE LICENSE AND AUTHORITY THEY NEVER HAD BEFORE THE BLEEDOUT.
THEY WERE GIVEN CARTE BLANCHE ON THE DRUG TRADE, AND GEROME TOOK THAT TO THE NEXT LEVEL, COOKING UP A WHOLE NEW GENERATION OF BOOSTS AND PERFORMANCE ENHANCERS.
HE DESIGNED SHIT THAT MADE YOU DAMN NEAR BULLETPROOF...
...OR AT LEAST FEEL LIKE FOR A FEW GLORIOUS MINUTES.
AND HE DEFENDED THAT CORNERED MARKET LIKE A PITBULL.
ANYONE WHO THREATENED SO MUCH AS A SINGLE SALE FELT THE FLAT SIDE OF HIS SWORD.
AND IF ONE WARNING WASN'T ENOUGH, YOU GOT THE EDGE, TOO.

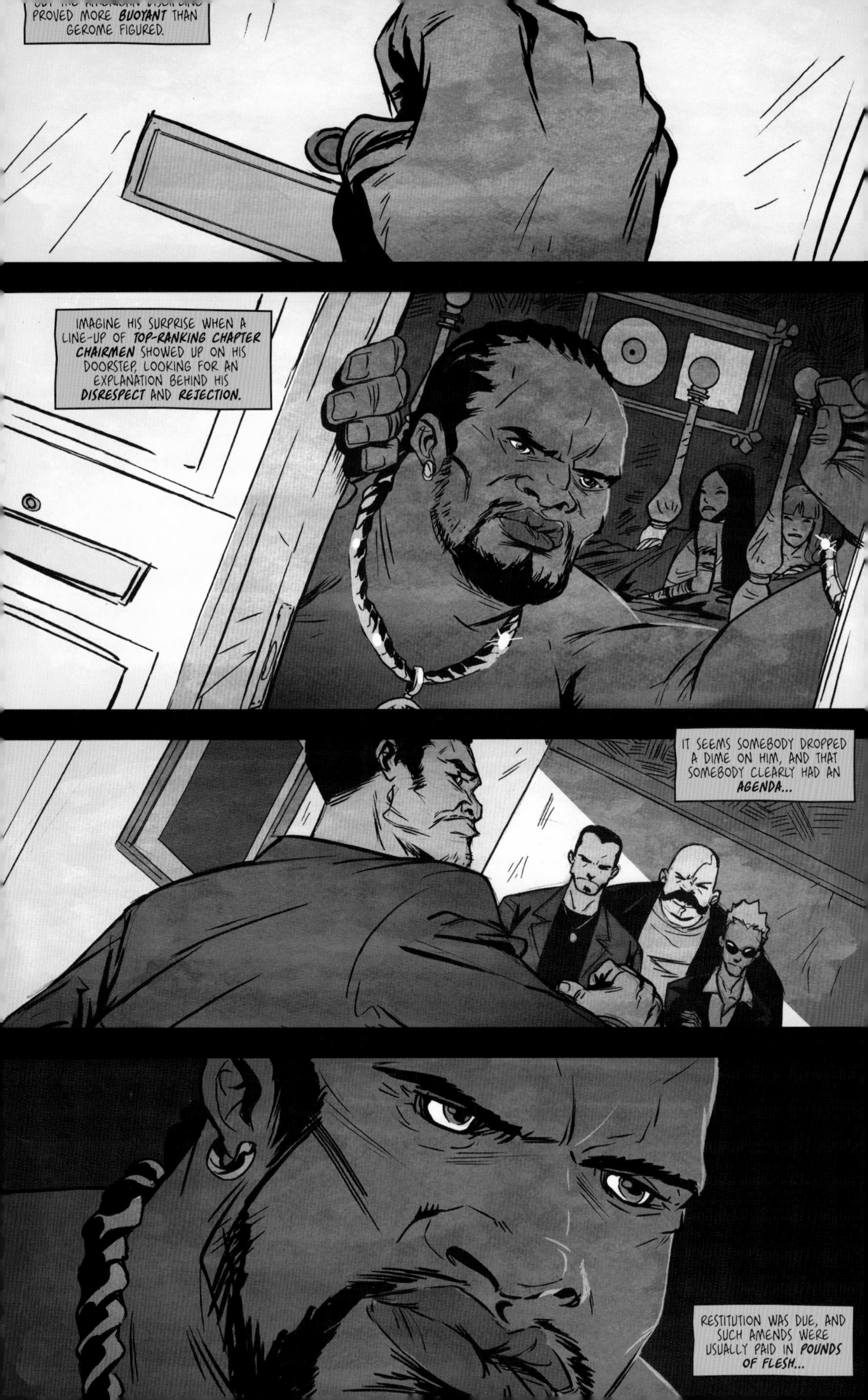
PROVED MORE BUOYANT THAN GEROME FIGURED.
IMAGINE HIS SURPRISE WHEN A LINE-UP OF TOP-RANKING CHAPTER CHAIRMEN SHOWED UP ON HIS DOORSTEP, LOOKING FOR AN EXPLANATION BEHIND HIS DISRESPECT AND REJECTION.
IT SEEMS SOMEBODY DROPPED A DIME ON HIM, AND THAT SOMEBODY CLEARLY HAD AN AGENDA...
RESTITUTION WAS DUE, AND SUCH AMENDS WERE USUALLY PAID IN POUNDS OF FLESH...

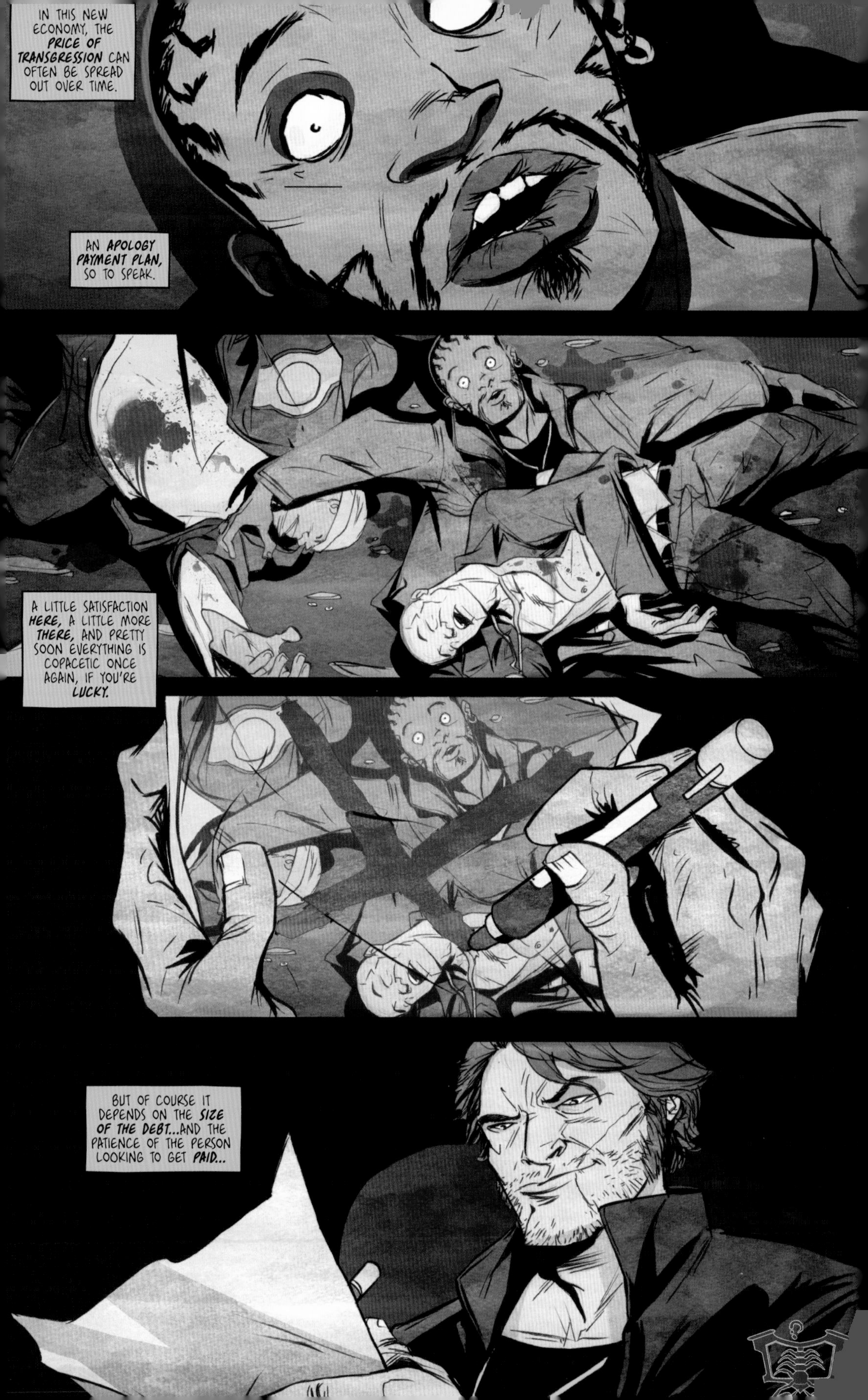
IN THIS NEW ECONOMY, THE PRICE OF TRANSGRESSION CAN OFTEN BE SPREAD OUT OVER TIME.
AN APOLOGY PAYMENT PLAN, SO TO SPEAK.
A LITTLE SATISFACTION HERE, A LITTLE MORE THERE, AND PRETTY SOON EVERYTHING IS COPACETIC ONCE AGAIN, IF YOU'RE LUCKY.
BUT OF COURSE IT DEPENDS ON THE SIZE OF THE DEBT...AND THE PATIENCE OF THE PERSON LOOKING TO GET PAID...

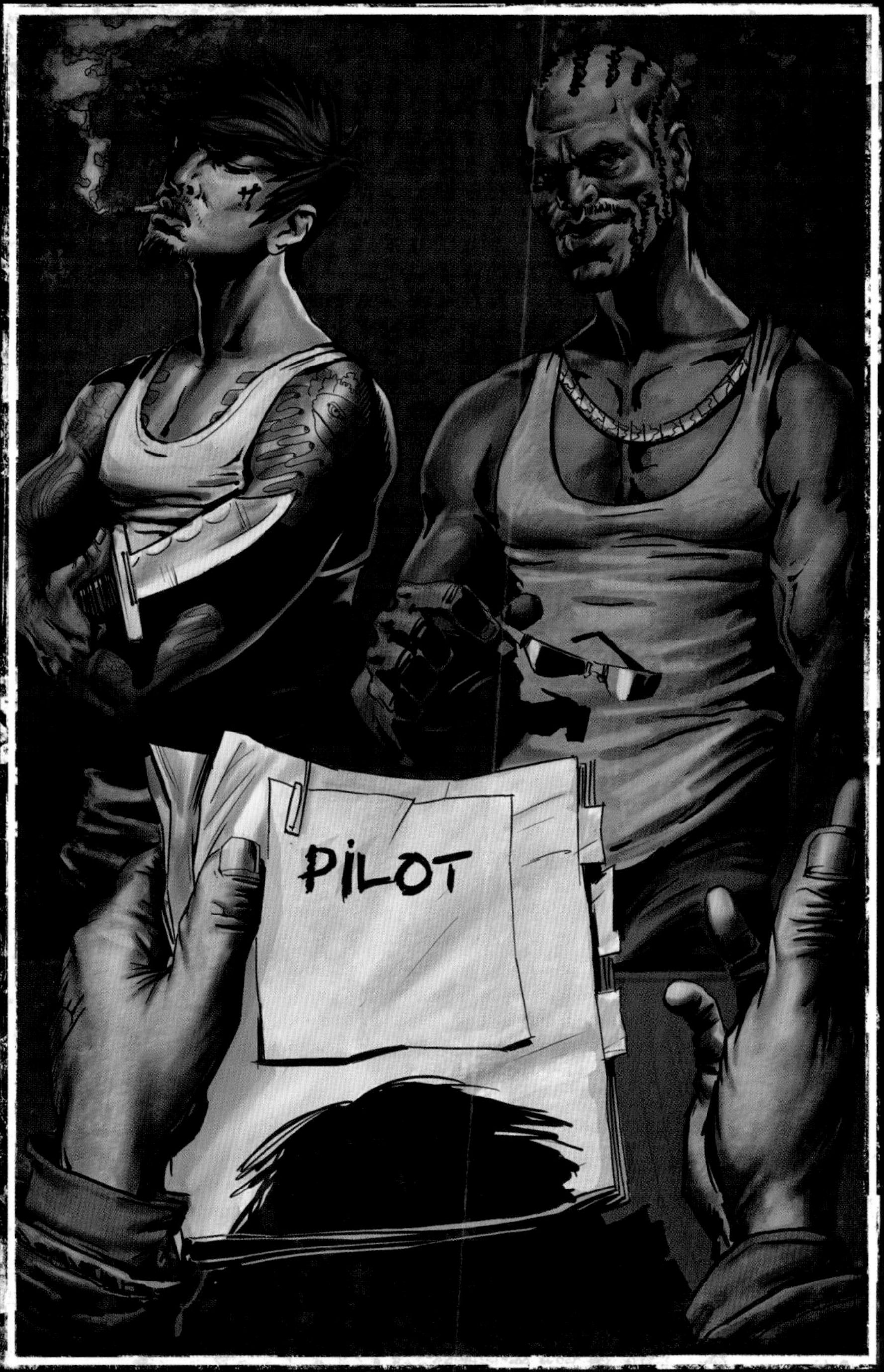
PILOT

Pilot is condemned.

04

CHAPTER FOUR:
Grim Stains

Illustrated by
David Williams

Colors by
Andrey Shcherbak

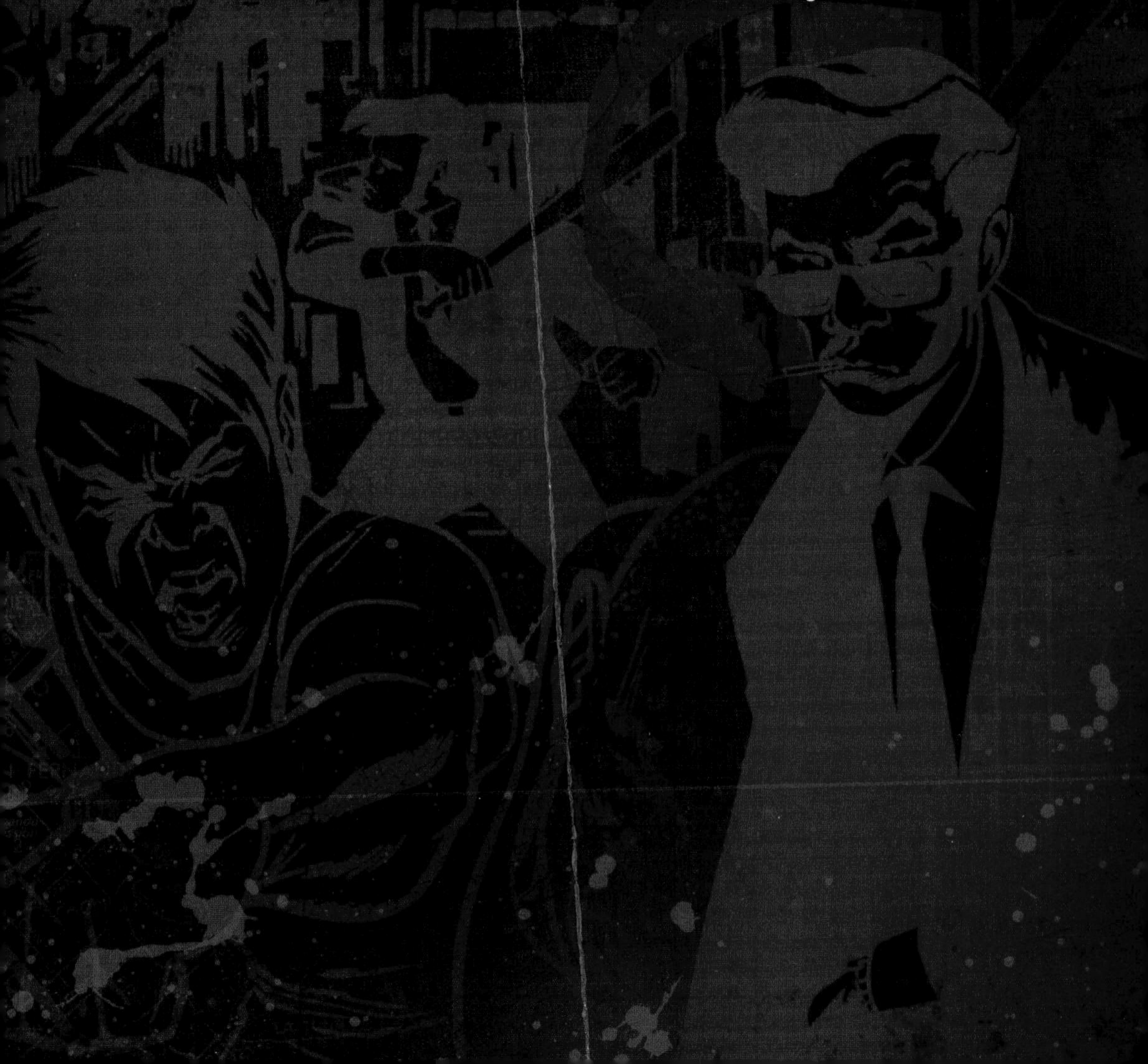

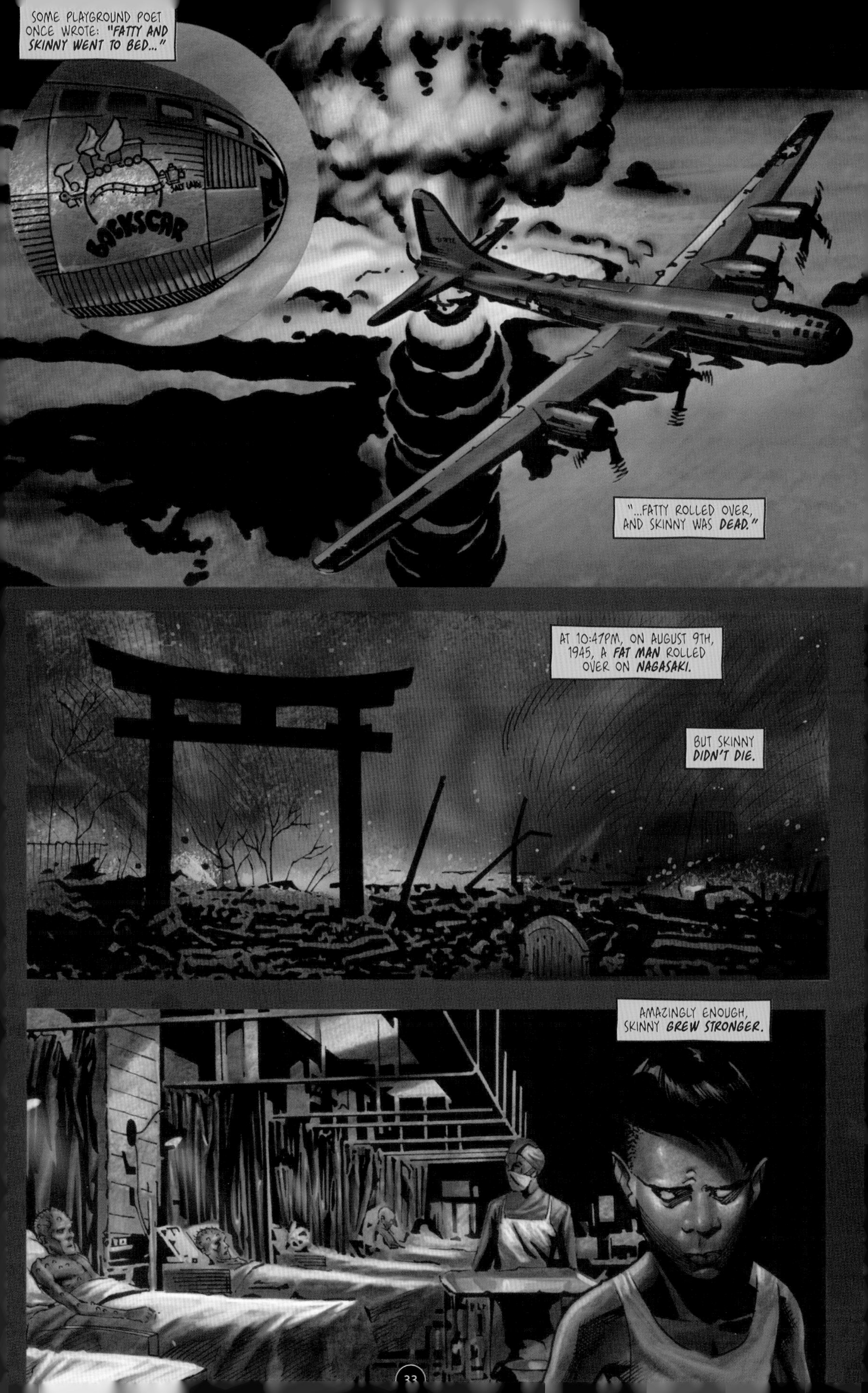

SOME PLAYGROUND POET ONCE WROTE: "FATTY AND SKINNY WENT TO BED..."
"...FATTY ROLLED OVER, AND SKINNY WAS DEAD."
AT 10:47PM, ON AUGUST 9TH, 1945, A FAT MAN ROLLED OVER ON NAGASAKI.
BUT SKINNY DIDN'T DIE.
AMAZINGLY ENOUGH, SKINNY GREW STRONGER.

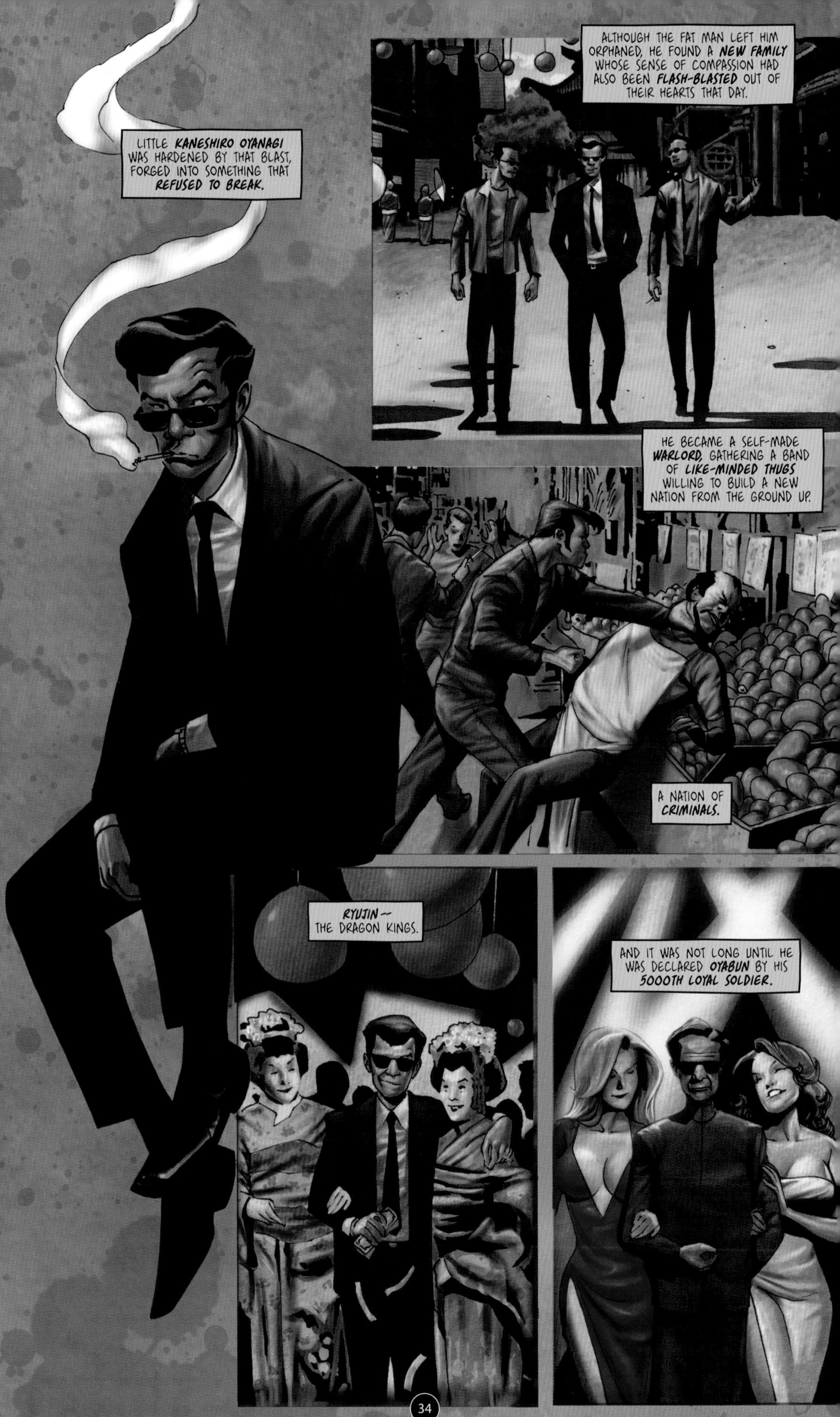
LITTLE KANESHIRO OYANAGI WAS HARDENED BY THAT BLAST, FORGED INTO SOMETHING THAT REFUSED TO BREAK.
ALTHOUGH THE FAT MAN LEFT HIM ORPHANED, HE FOUND A NEW FAMILY WHOSE SENSE OF COMPASSION HAD ALSO BEEN FLASH-BLASTED OUT OF THEIR HEARTS THAT DAY.
HE BECAME A SELF-MADE WARLORD, GATHERING A BAND OF LIKE-MINDED THUGS WILLING TO BUILD A NEW NATION FROM THE GROUND UP.
A NATION OF CRIMINALS.
RYUJIN-- THE DRAGON KINGS.
AND IT WAS NOT LONG UNTIL HE WAS DECLARED OYABUN BY HIS 5000TH LOYAL SOLDIER.

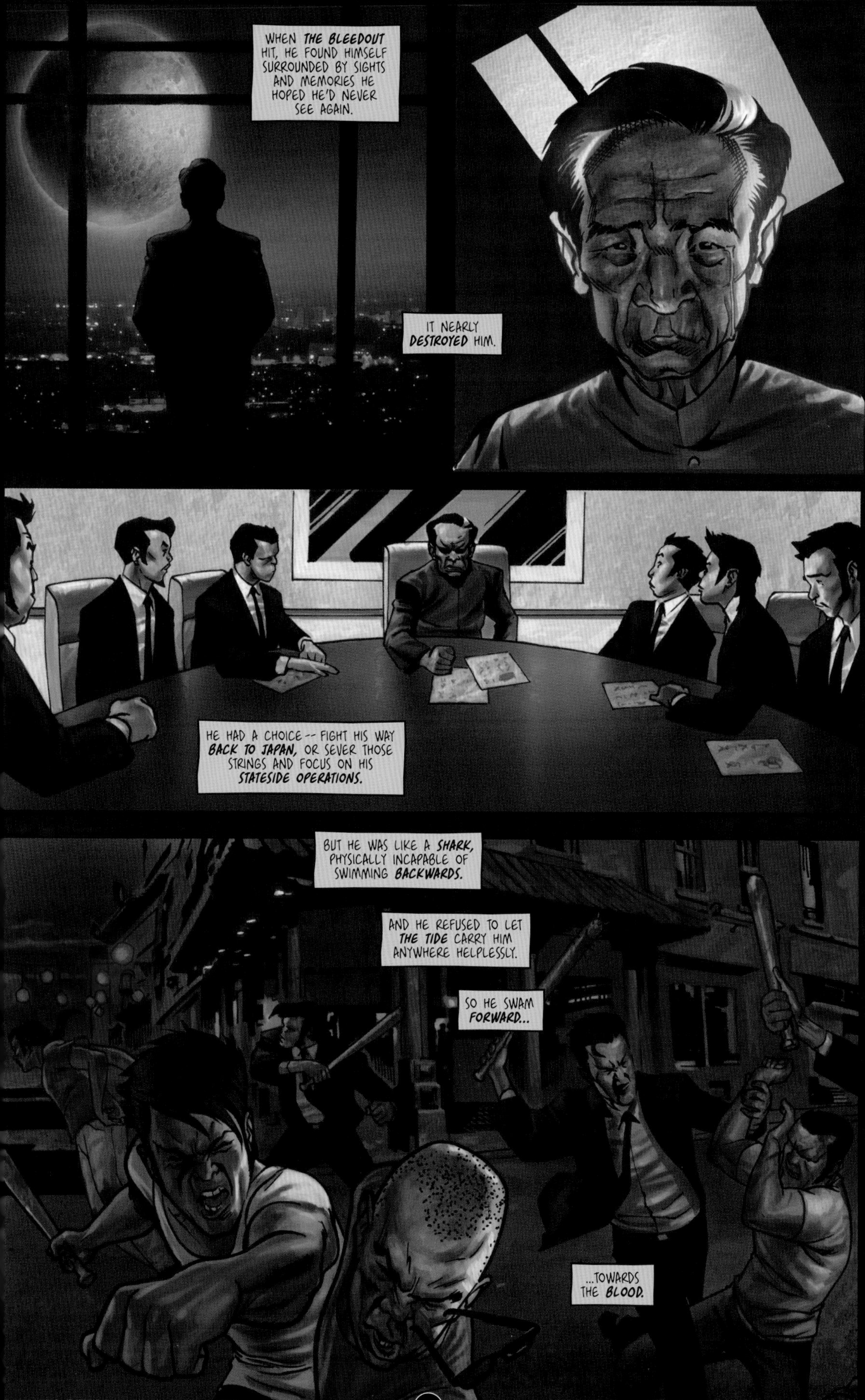
WHEN THE BLEEDOUT HIT, HE FOUND HIMSELF SURROUNDED BY SIGHTS AND MEMORIES HE HOPED HE'D NEVER SEE AGAIN.
IT NEARLY DESTROYED HIM.
HE HAD A CHOICE-- FIGHT HIS WAY BACK TO JAPAN, OR SEVER THOSE STRINGS AND FOCUS ON HIS STATESIDE OPERATIONS.
BUT HE WAS LIKE A SHARK, PHYSICALLY INCAPABLE OF SWIMMING BACKWARDS.
AND HE REFUSED TO LET THE TIDE CARRY HIM ANYWHERE HELPLESSLY.
SO HE SWAM FORWARD...
...TOWARDS THE BLOOD.

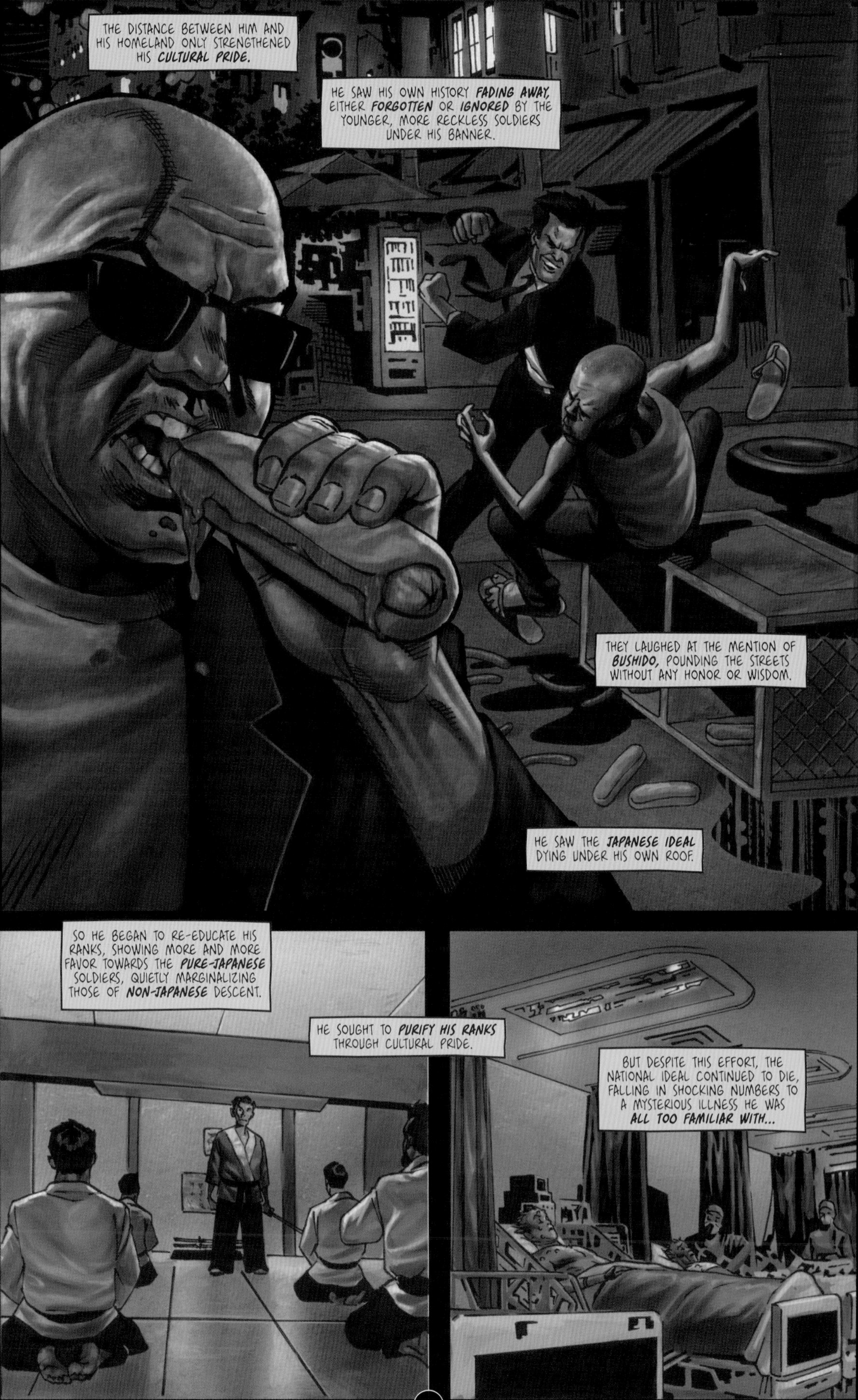
THE DISTANCE BETWEEN HIM AND HIS HOMELAND ONLY STRENGTHENED HIS CULTURAL PRIDE.
HE SAW HIS OWN HISTORY FADING AWAY, EITHER FORGOTTEN OR IGNORED BY THE YOUNGER, MORE RECKLESS SOLDIERS UNDER HIS BANNER.
THEY LAUGHED AT THE MENTION OF BUSHIDO, POUNDING THE STREETS WITHOUT ANY HONOR OR WISDOM.
HE SAW THE JAPANESE IDEAL DYING UNDER HIS OWN ROOF.
SO HE BEGAN TO RE-EDUCATE HIS RANKS, SHOWING MORE AND MORE FAVOR TOWARDS THE PURE-JAPANESE SOLDIERS, QUIETLY MARGINALIZING THOSE OF NON-JAPANESE DESCENT.
HE SOUGHT TO PURIFY HIS RANKS THROUGH CULTURAL PRIDE.
BUT DESPITE THIS EFFORT, THE NATIONAL IDEAL CONTINUED TO DIE, FALLING IN SHOCKING NUMBERS TO A MYSTERIOUS ILLNESS HE WAS ALL TOO FAMILIAR WITH...

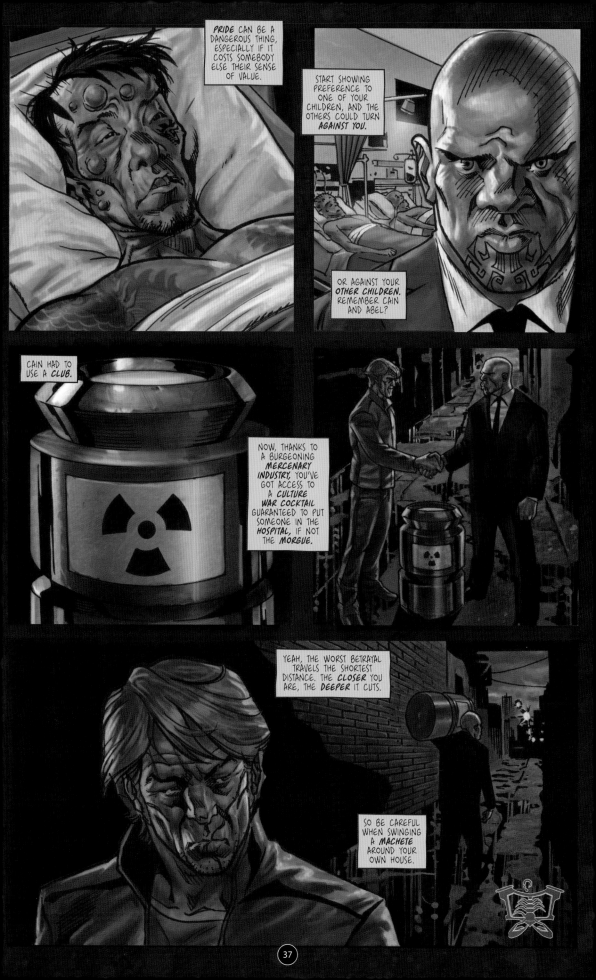

PRIDE CAN BE A DANGEROUS THING, ESPECIALLY IF IT COSTS SOMEBODY ELSE THEIR SENSE OF VALUE.

START SHOWING PREFERENCE TO ONE OF YOUR CHILDREN, AND THE OTHERS COULD TURN *AGAINST YOU.*

OR AGAINST YOUR *OTHER CHILDREN.* REMEMBER CAIN AND ABEL?

CAIN HAD TO USE A *CLUB.*

NOW, THANKS TO A BURGEONING *MERCENARY INDUSTRY,* YOU'VE GOT ACCESS TO A *CULTURE WAR COCKTAIL* GUARANTEED TO PUT SOMEONE IN THE *HOSPITAL,* IF NOT THE *MORGUE.*

YEAH, THE WORST BETRAYAL TRAVELS THE SHORTEST DISTANCE. THE *CLOSER* YOU ARE, THE *DEEPER* IT CUTS.

SO BE CAREFUL WHEN SWINGING A *MACHETE* AROUND YOUR OWN HOUSE.

05

CHAPTER FIVE:
Youth Bulge

Illustrated by
Ben Templesmith

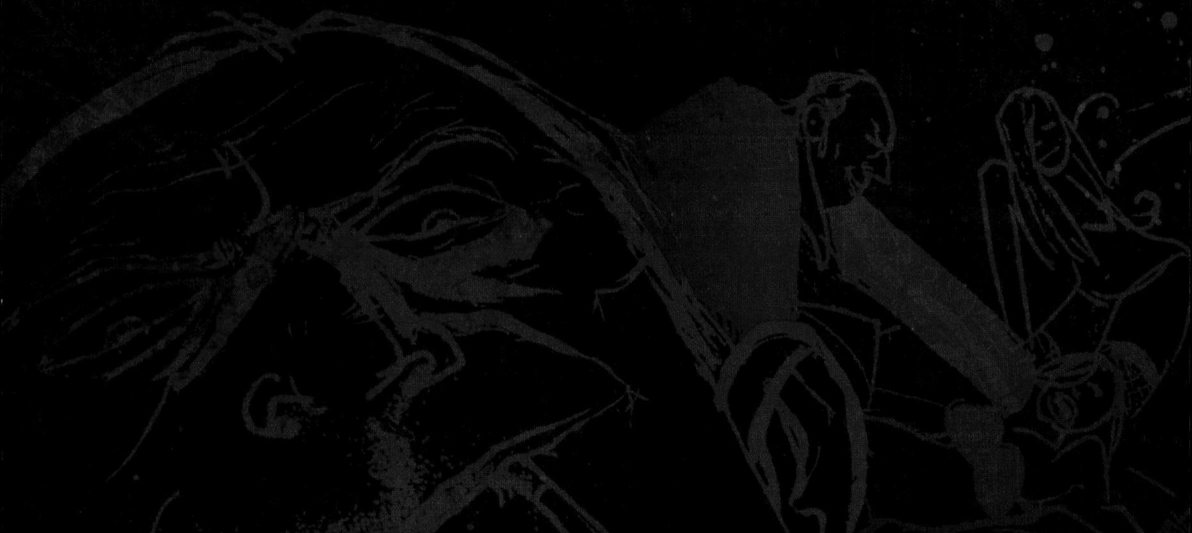

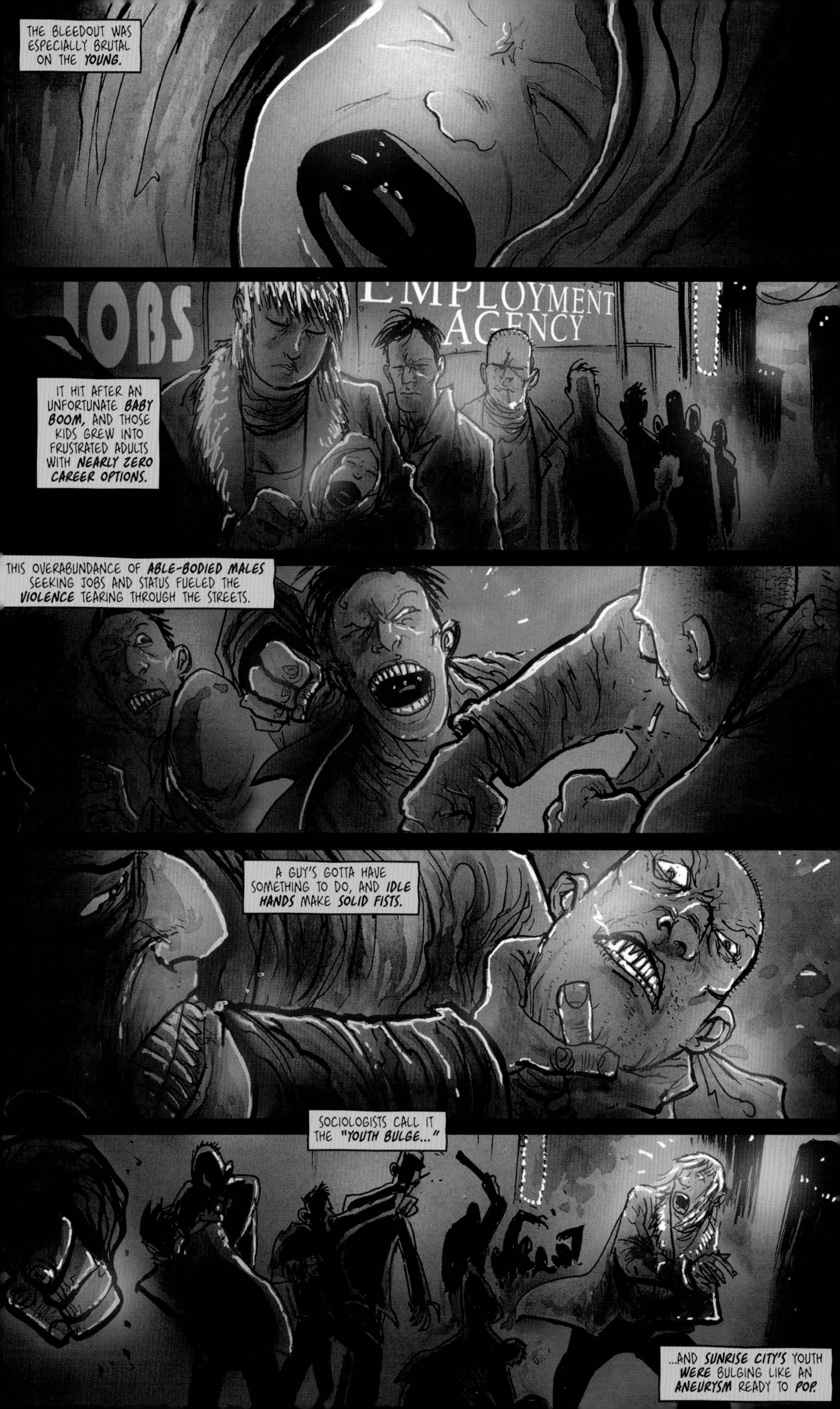
THE BLEEDOUT WAS ESPECIALLY BRUTAL ON THE YOUNG.
EMPLOYMENT AGENCY
JOBS
IT HIT AFTER AN UNFORTUNATE BABY BOOM, AND THOSE KIDS GREW INTO FRUSTRATED ADULTS WITH NEARLY ZERO CAREER OPTIONS.
THIS OVERABUNDANCE OF ABLE-BODIED MALES SEEKING JOBS AND STATUS FUELED THE VIOLENCE TEARING THROUGH THE STREETS.
A GUY'S GOTTA HAVE SOMETHING TO DO, AND IDLE HANDS MAKE SOLID FISTS.
SOCIOLOGISTS CALL IT THE "YOUTH BULGE..."
...AND SUNRISE CITY'S YOUTH WERE BULGING LIKE AN ANEURYSM READY TO POP.

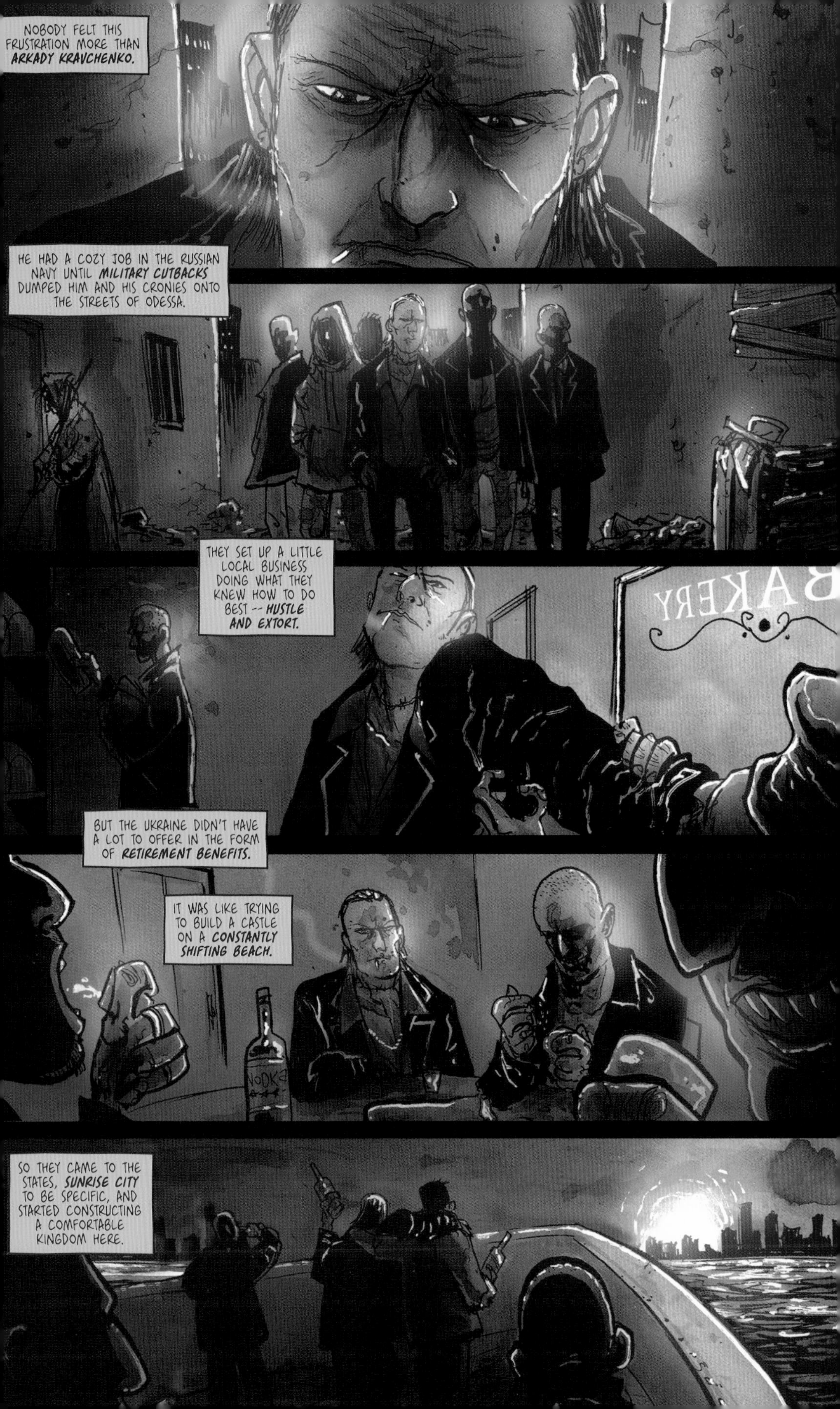
NOBODY FELT THIS FRUSTRATION MORE THAN ARKADY KRAVCHENKO.
HE HAD A COZY JOB IN THE RUSSIAN NAVY UNTIL MILITARY CUTBACKS DUMPED HIM AND HIS CRONIES ONTO THE STREETS OF ODESSA.
THEY SET UP A LITTLE LOCAL BUSINESS DOING WHAT THEY KNEW HOW TO DO BEST -- HUSTLE AND EXTORT.
BAKERY
BUT THE UKRAINE DIDN'T HAVE A LOT TO OFFER IN THE FORM OF RETIREMENT BENEFITS.
IT WAS LIKE TRYING TO BUILD A CASTLE ON A CONSTANTLY SHIFTING BEACH.
VODKA
SO THEY CAME TO THE STATES, SUNRISE CITY TO BE SPECIFIC, AND STARTED CONSTRUCTING A COMFORTABLE KINGDOM HERE.

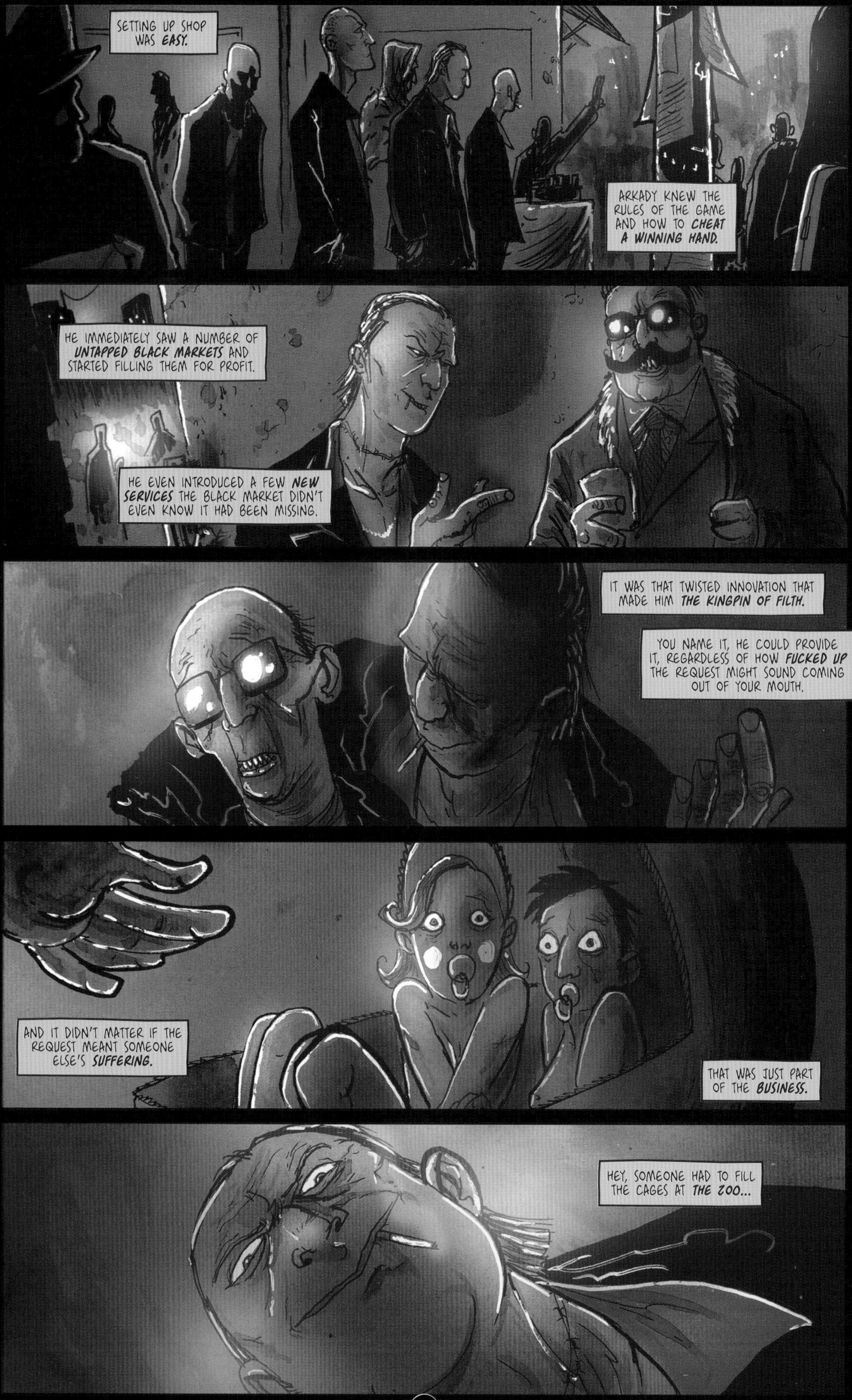
SETTING UP SHOP WAS EASY.
ARKADY KNEW THE RULES OF THE GAME AND HOW TO CHEAT A WINNING HAND.
HE IMMEDIATELY SAW A NUMBER OF UNTAPPED BLACK MARKETS AND STARTED FILLING THEM FOR PROFIT.
HE EVEN INTRODUCED A FEW NEW SERVICES THE BLACK MARKET DIDN'T EVEN KNOW IT HAD BEEN MISSING.
IT WAS THAT TWISTED INNOVATION THAT MADE HIM THE KINGPIN OF FILTH.
YOU NAME IT, HE COULD PROVIDE IT, REGARDLESS OF HOW FUCKED UP THE REQUEST MIGHT SOUND COMING OUT OF YOUR MOUTH.
AND IT DIDN'T MATTER IF THE REQUEST MEANT SOMEONE ELSE'S SUFFERING.
THAT WAS JUST PART OF THE BUSINESS.
HEY, SOMEONE HAD TO FILL THE CAGES AT THE ZOO...

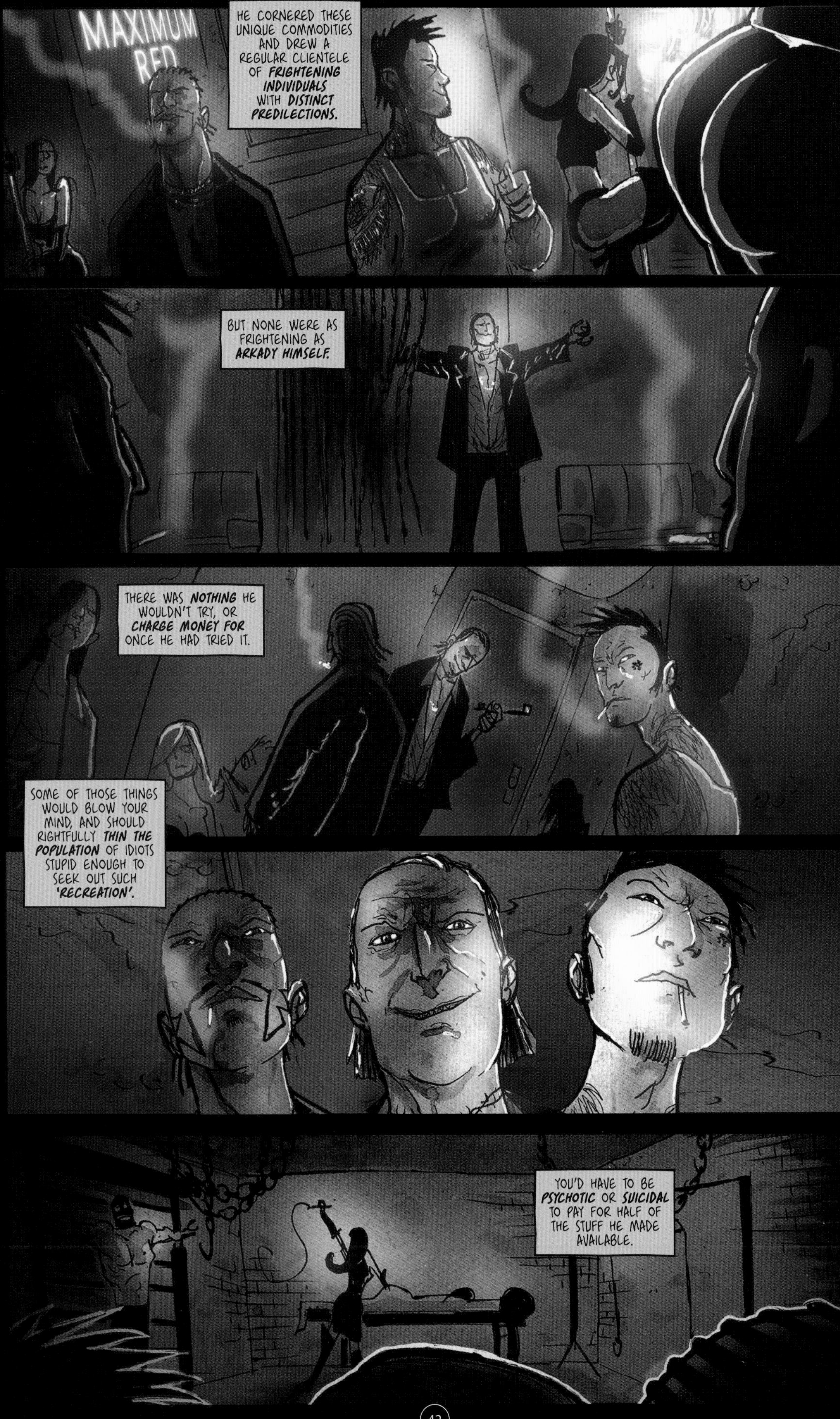
MAXIMUM RED
HE CORNERED THESE UNIQUE COMMODITIES AND DREW A REGULAR CLIENTELE OF **FRIGHTENING INDIVIDUALS** WITH **DISTINCT PREDILECTIONS.**
BUT NONE WERE AS FRIGHTENING AS **ARKADY HIMSELF.**
THERE WAS **NOTHING** HE WOULDN'T TRY, OR **CHARGE MONEY FOR** ONCE HE HAD TRIED IT.
SOME OF THOSE THINGS WOULD BLOW YOUR MIND, AND SHOULD RIGHTFULLY **THIN THE POPULATION** OF IDIOTS STUPID ENOUGH TO SEEK OUT SUCH **'RECREATION'.**
YOU'D HAVE TO BE **PSYCHOTIC** OR **SUICIDAL** TO PAY FOR HALF OF THE STUFF HE MADE AVAILABLE.

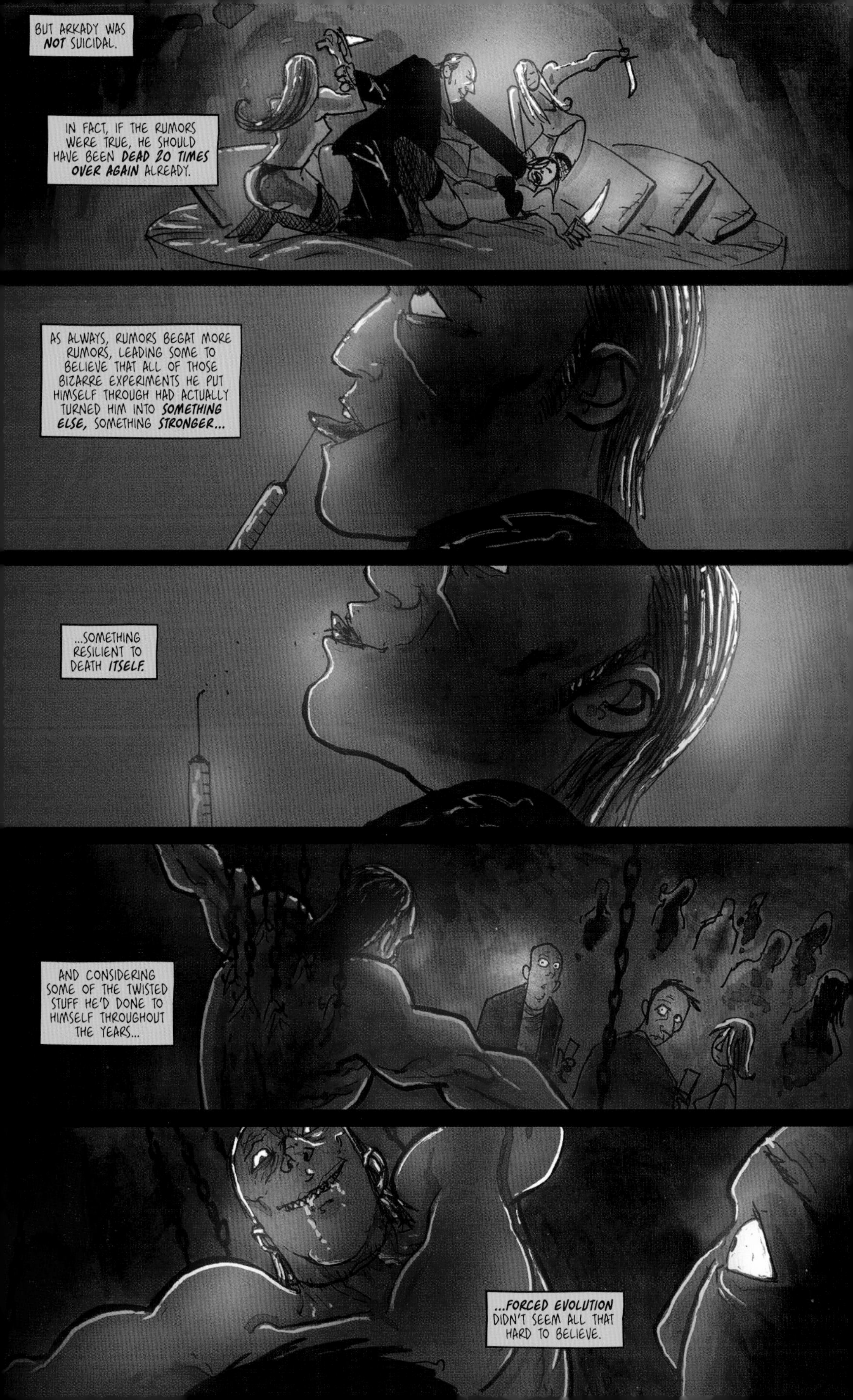

BUT ARKADY WAS **NOT** SUICIDAL.
IN FACT, IF THE RUMORS WERE TRUE, HE SHOULD HAVE BEEN **DEAD 20 TIMES OVER AGAIN** ALREADY.
AS ALWAYS, RUMORS BEGAT MORE RUMORS, LEADING SOME TO BELIEVE THAT ALL OF THOSE BIZARRE EXPERIMENTS HE PUT HIMSELF THROUGH HAD ACTUALLY TURNED HIM INTO **SOMETHING ELSE,** SOMETHING **STRONGER...**
...SOMETHING RESILIENT TO DEATH **ITSELF.**
AND CONSIDERING SOME OF THE TWISTED STUFF HE'D DONE TO HIMSELF THROUGHOUT THE YEARS...
...FORCED EVOLUTION DIDN'T SEEM ALL THAT HARD TO BELIEVE.

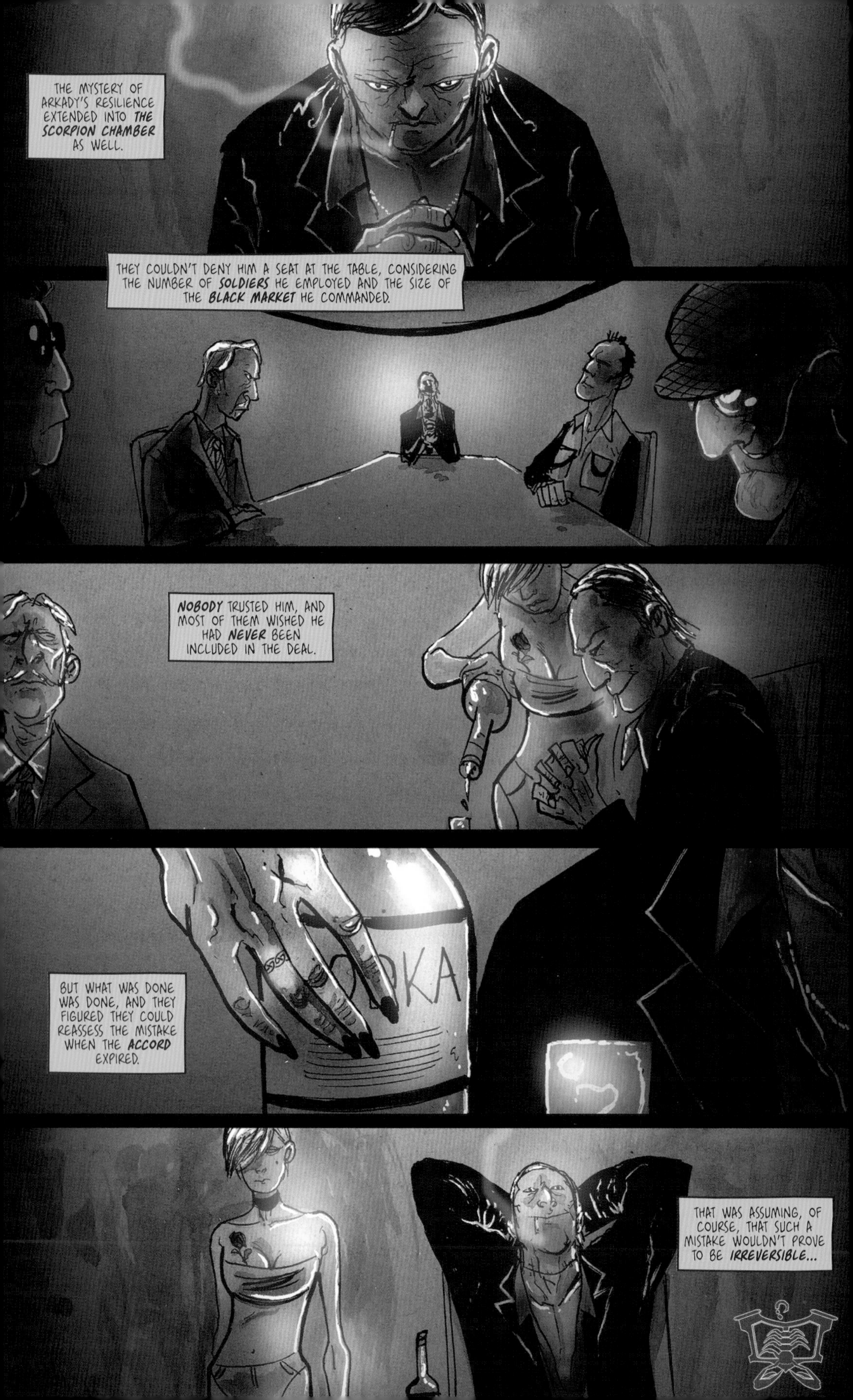
THE MYSTERY OF ARKADY'S RESILIENCE EXTENDED INTO THE SCORPION CHAMBER AS WELL.
THEY COULDN'T DENY HIM A SEAT AT THE TABLE, CONSIDERING THE NUMBER OF SOLDIERS HE EMPLOYED AND THE SIZE OF THE BLACK MARKET HE COMMANDED.
NOBODY TRUSTED HIM, AND MOST OF THEM WISHED HE HAD NEVER BEEN INCLUDED IN THE DEAL.
BUT WHAT WAS DONE WAS DONE, AND THEY FIGURED THEY COULD REASSESS THE MISTAKE WHEN THE ACCORD EXPIRED.
THAT WAS ASSUMING, OF COURSE, THAT SUCH A MISTAKE WOULDN'T PROVE TO BE IRREVERSIBLE...

Pilot is betrayed.

06

CHAPTER SIX:
The Achilles Helix

Illustrated by
Gary Erskine

Colors by
Andrey Shcherbak

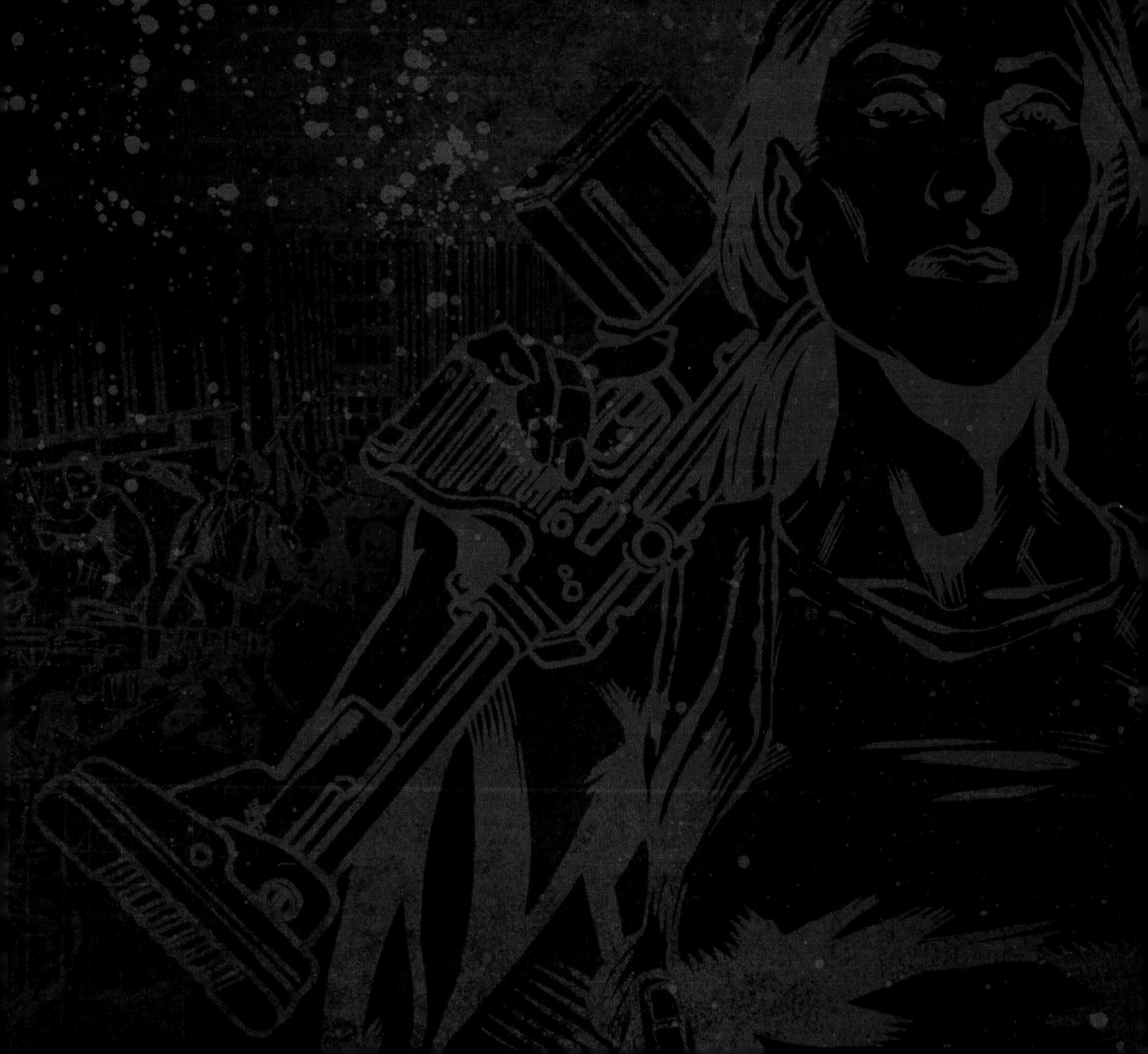

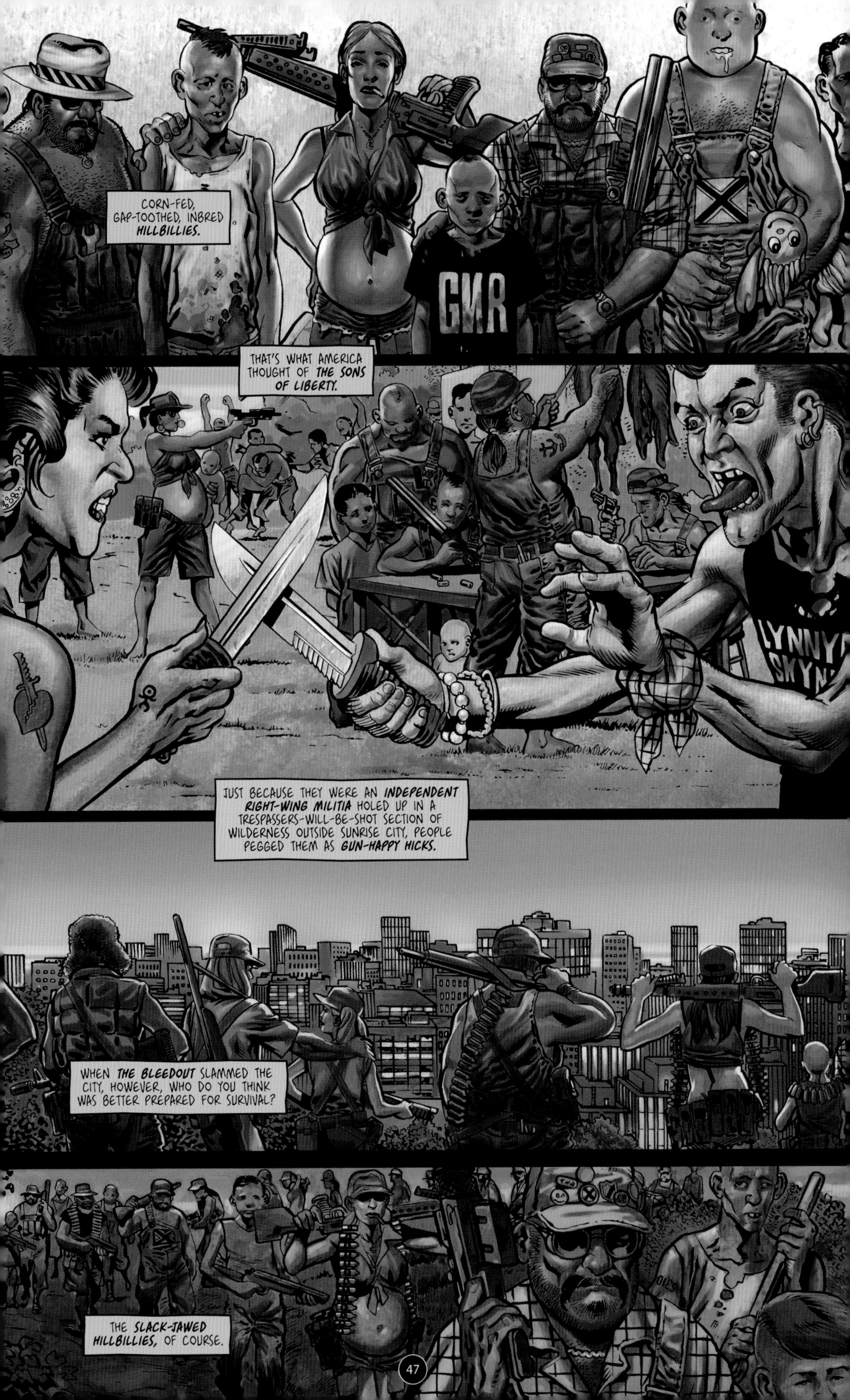

CORN-FED, GAP-TOOTHED, INBRED HILLBILLIES.
GMR
THAT'S WHAT AMERICA THOUGHT OF THE SONS OF LIBERTY.
JUST BECAUSE THEY WERE AN INDEPENDENT RIGHT-WING MILITIA HOLED UP IN A TRESPASSERS-WILL-BE-SHOT SECTION OF WILDERNESS OUTSIDE SUNRISE CITY, PEOPLE PEGGED THEM AS GUN-HAPPY HICKS.
WHEN THE BLEEDOUT SLAMMED THE CITY, HOWEVER, WHO DO YOU THINK WAS BETTER PREPARED FOR SURVIVAL?
THE SLACK-JAWED HILLBILLIES, OF COURSE.

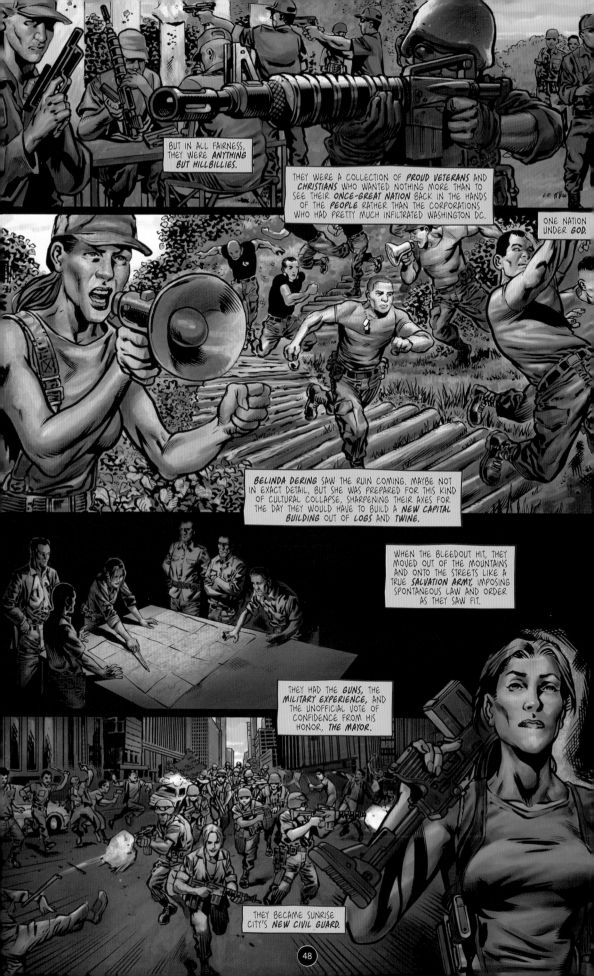

BUT IN ALL FAIRNESS, THEY WERE *ANYTHING BUT HILLBILLIES.*

THEY WERE A COLLECTION OF *PROUD VETERANS* AND *CHRISTIANS* WHO WANTED NOTHING MORE THAN TO SEE THEIR *ONCE-GREAT NATION* BACK IN THE HANDS OF THE *PEOPLE* RATHER THAN THE CORPORATIONS WHO HAD PRETTY MUCH INFILTRATED WASHINGTON DC.

ONE NATION UNDER *GOD.*

BELINDA DERING SAW THE RUIN COMING. MAYBE NOT IN EXACT DETAIL, BUT SHE WAS PREPARED FOR THIS KIND OF CULTURAL COLLAPSE, SHARPENING THEIR AXES FOR THE DAY THEY WOULD HAVE TO BUILD A *NEW CAPITAL BUILDING* OUT OF *LOGS* AND *TWINE.*

WHEN THE BLEEDOUT HIT, THEY MOVED OUT OF THE MOUNTAINS AND ONTO THE STREETS LIKE A TRUE *SALVATION ARMY,* IMPOSING SPONTANEOUS LAW AND ORDER AS THEY SAW FIT.

THEY HAD THE *GUNS,* THE *MILITARY EXPERIENCE,* AND THE UNOFFICIAL VOTE OF CONFIDENCE FROM HIS HONOR, *THE MAYOR.*

THEY BECAME SUNRISE CITY'S *NEW CIVIL GUARD.*

48

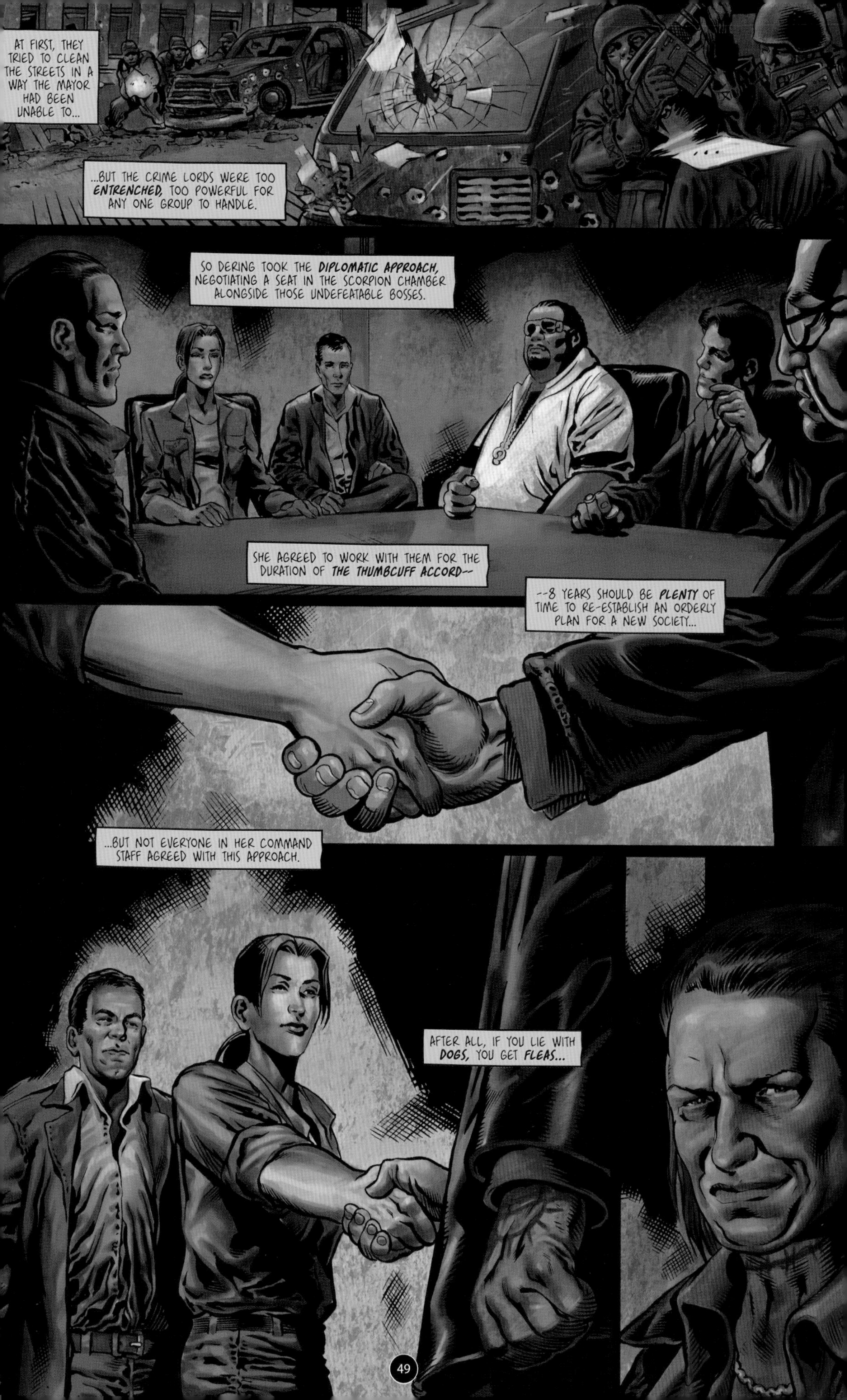
AT FIRST, THEY TRIED TO CLEAN THE STREETS IN A WAY THE MAYOR HAD BEEN UNABLE TO...
...BUT THE CRIME LORDS WERE TOO ENTRENCHED, TOO POWERFUL FOR ANY ONE GROUP TO HANDLE.
SO DERING TOOK THE DIPLOMATIC APPROACH, NEGOTIATING A SEAT IN THE SCORPION CHAMBER ALONGSIDE THOSE UNDEFEATABLE BOSSES.
SHE AGREED TO WORK WITH THEM FOR THE DURATION OF THE THUMBCUFF ACCORD--
--8 YEARS SHOULD BE PLENTY OF TIME TO RE-ESTABLISH AN ORDERLY PLAN FOR A NEW SOCIETY...
...BUT NOT EVERYONE IN HER COMMAND STAFF AGREED WITH THIS APPROACH.
AFTER ALL, IF YOU LIE WITH DOGS, YOU GET FLEAS...

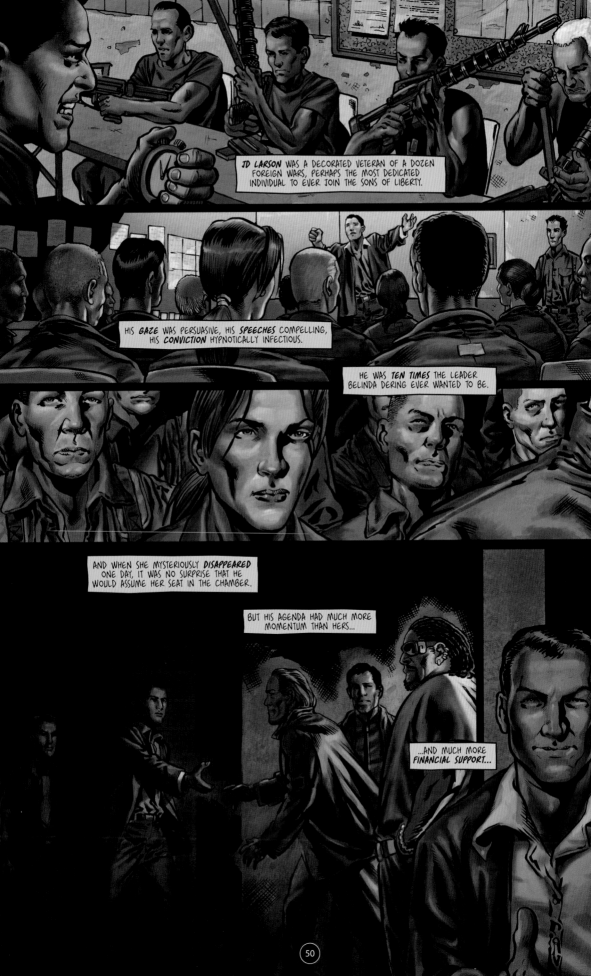

JD LARSON WAS A DECORATED VETERAN OF A DOZEN FOREIGN WARS, PERHAPS THE MOST DEDICATED INDIVIDUAL TO EVER JOIN THE SONS OF LIBERTY.

HIS *GAZE* WAS PERSUASIVE, HIS *SPEECHES* COMPELLING, HIS *CONVICTION* HYPNOTICALLY INFECTIOUS.

HE WAS *TEN TIMES* THE LEADER BELINDA DERING EVER WANTED TO BE.

AND WHEN SHE MYSTERIOUSLY *DISAPPEARED* ONE DAY, IT WAS NO SURPRISE THAT HE WOULD ASSUME HER SEAT IN THE CHAMBER.

BUT HIS AGENDA HAD MUCH MORE MOMENTUM THAN HERS...

...AND MUCH MORE *FINANCIAL SUPPORT...*

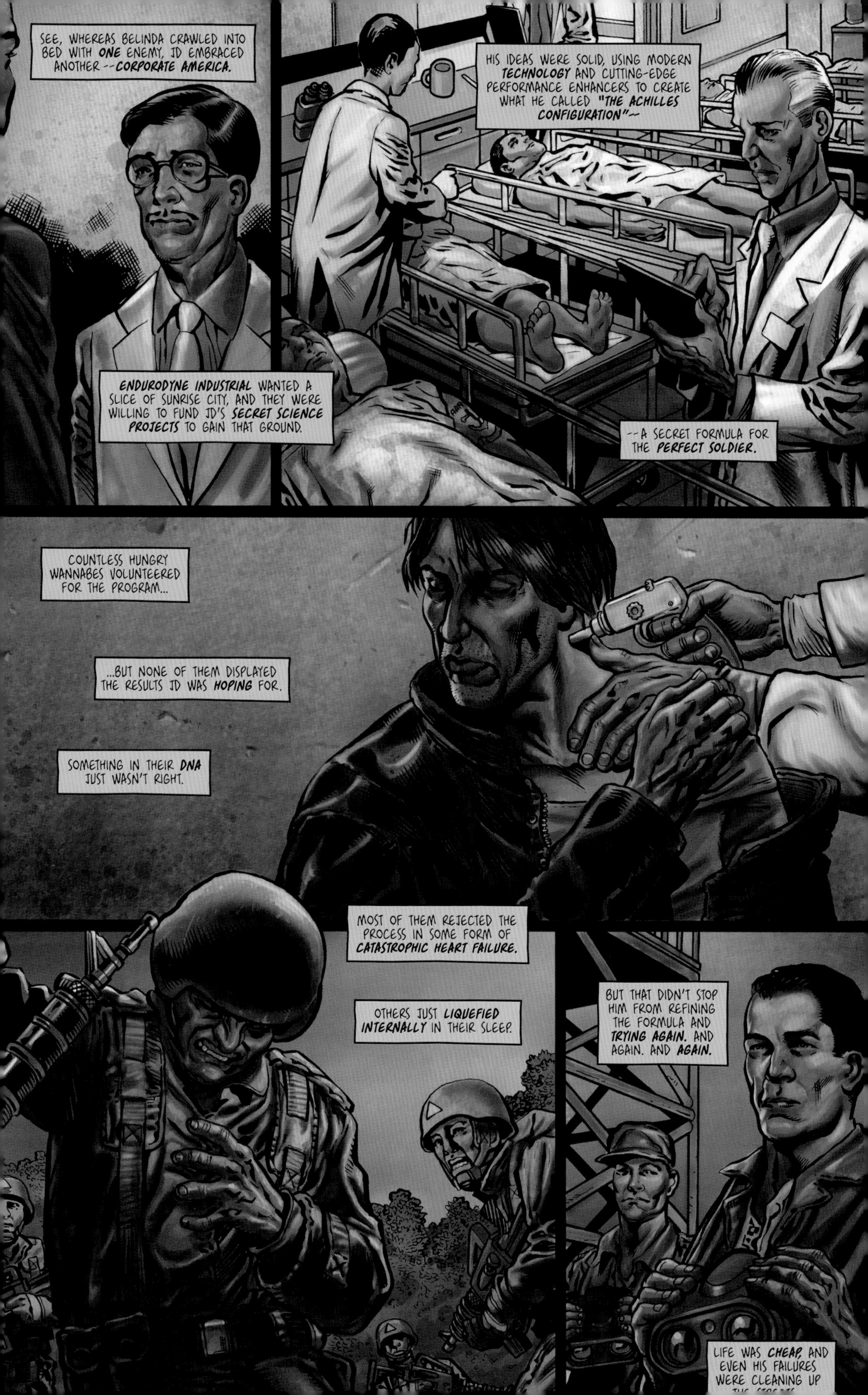
SEE, WHEREAS BELINDA CRAWLED INTO BED WITH ONE ENEMY, JD EMBRACED ANOTHER--CORPORATE AMERICA.
ENDURODYNE INDUSTRIAL WANTED A SLICE OF SUNRISE CITY, AND THEY WERE WILLING TO FUND JD'S SECRET SCIENCE PROJECTS TO GAIN THAT GROUND.
HIS IDEAS WERE SOLID, USING MODERN TECHNOLOGY AND CUTTING-EDGE PERFORMANCE ENHANCERS TO CREATE WHAT HE CALLED "THE ACHILLES CONFIGURATION"--
--A SECRET FORMULA FOR THE PERFECT SOLDIER.
COUNTLESS HUNGRY WANNABES VOLUNTEERED FOR THE PROGRAM...
...BUT NONE OF THEM DISPLAYED THE RESULTS JD WAS HOPING FOR.
SOMETHING IN THEIR DNA JUST WASN'T RIGHT.
MOST OF THEM REJECTED THE PROCESS IN SOME FORM OF CATASTROPHIC HEART FAILURE.
OTHERS JUST LIQUEFIED INTERNALLY IN THEIR SLEEP.
BUT THAT DIDN'T STOP HIM FROM REFINING THE FORMULA AND TRYING AGAIN. AND AGAIN. AND AGAIN.
LIFE WAS CHEAP, AND EVEN HIS FAILURES WERE CLEANING UP

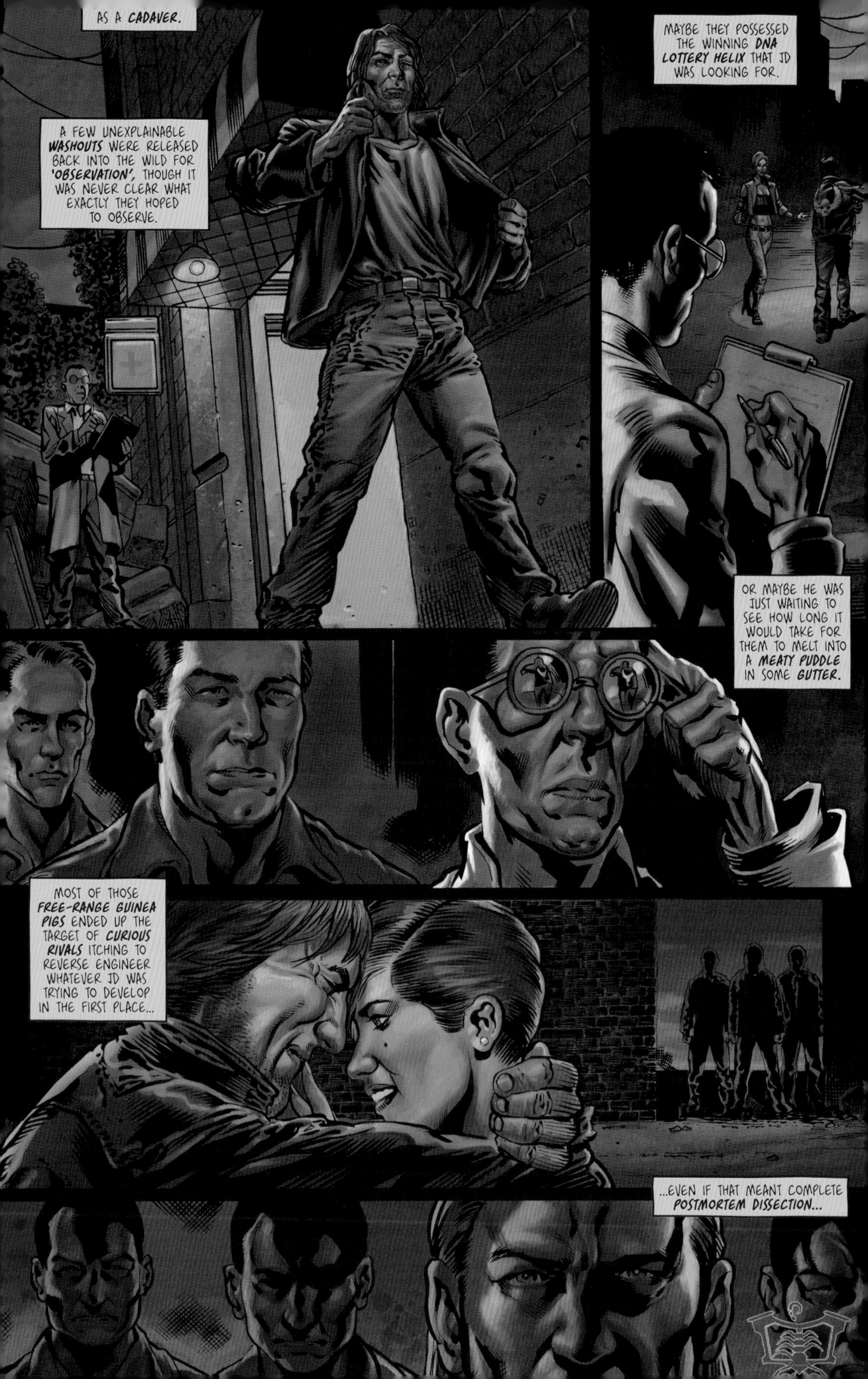
AS A CADAVER.
A FEW UNEXPLAINABLE WASHOUTS WERE RELEASED BACK INTO THE WILD FOR 'OBSERVATION', THOUGH IT WAS NEVER CLEAR WHAT EXACTLY THEY HOPED TO OBSERVE.
MAYBE THEY POSSESSED THE WINNING DNA LOTTERY HELIX THAT JD WAS LOOKING FOR.
OR MAYBE HE WAS JUST WAITING TO SEE HOW LONG IT WOULD TAKE FOR THEM TO MELT INTO A MEATY PUDDLE IN SOME GUTTER.
MOST OF THOSE FREE-RANGE GUINEA PIGS ENDED UP THE TARGET OF CURIOUS RIVALS ITCHING TO REVERSE ENGINEER WHATEVER JD WAS TRYING TO DEVELOP IN THE FIRST PLACE...
...EVEN IF THAT MEANT COMPLETE POSTMORTEM DISSECTION...

X Pilot is scourged and crowned with blood.

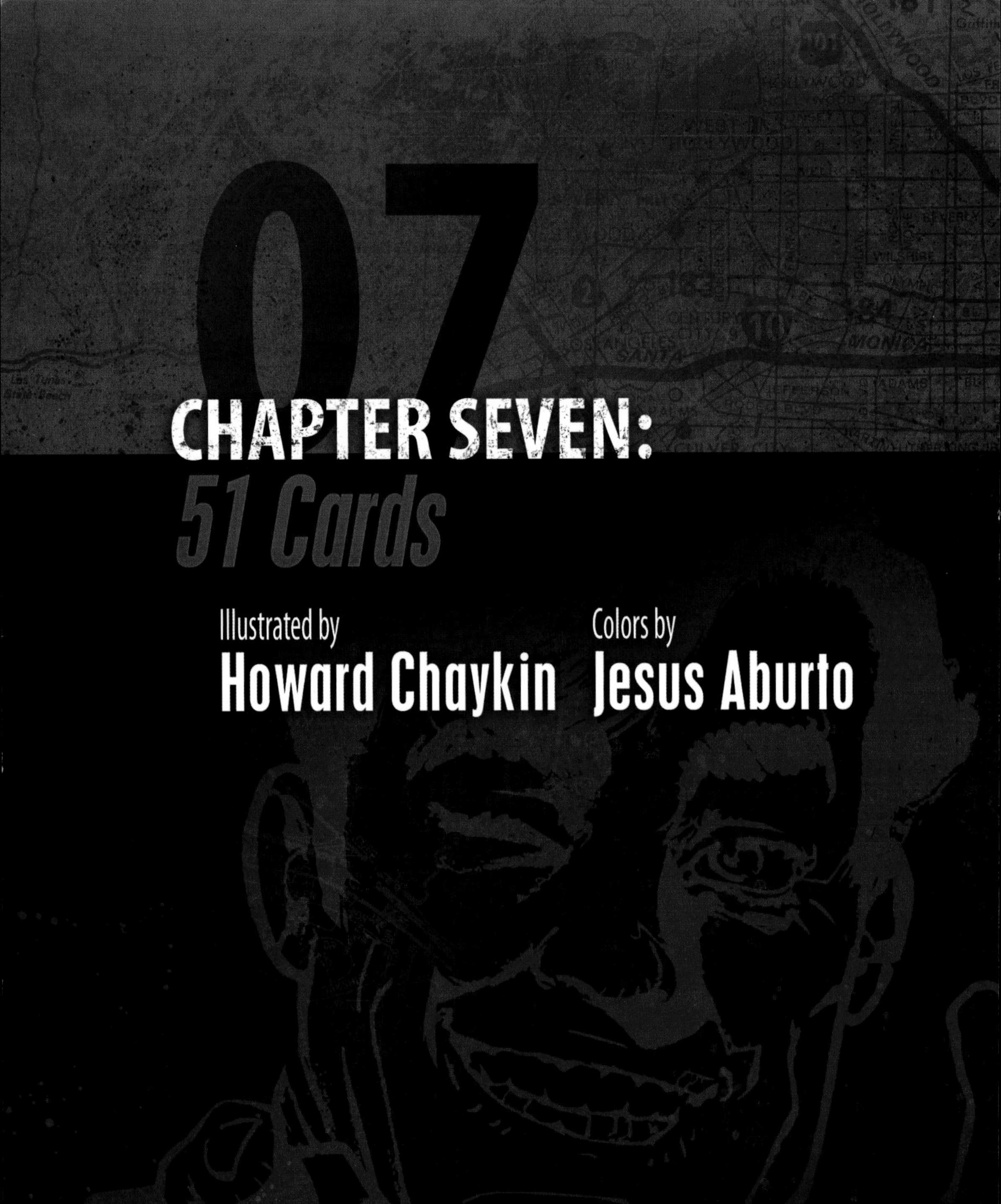

07

CHAPTER SEVEN:
51 Cards

Illustrated by
Howard Chaykin

Colors by
Jesus Aburto

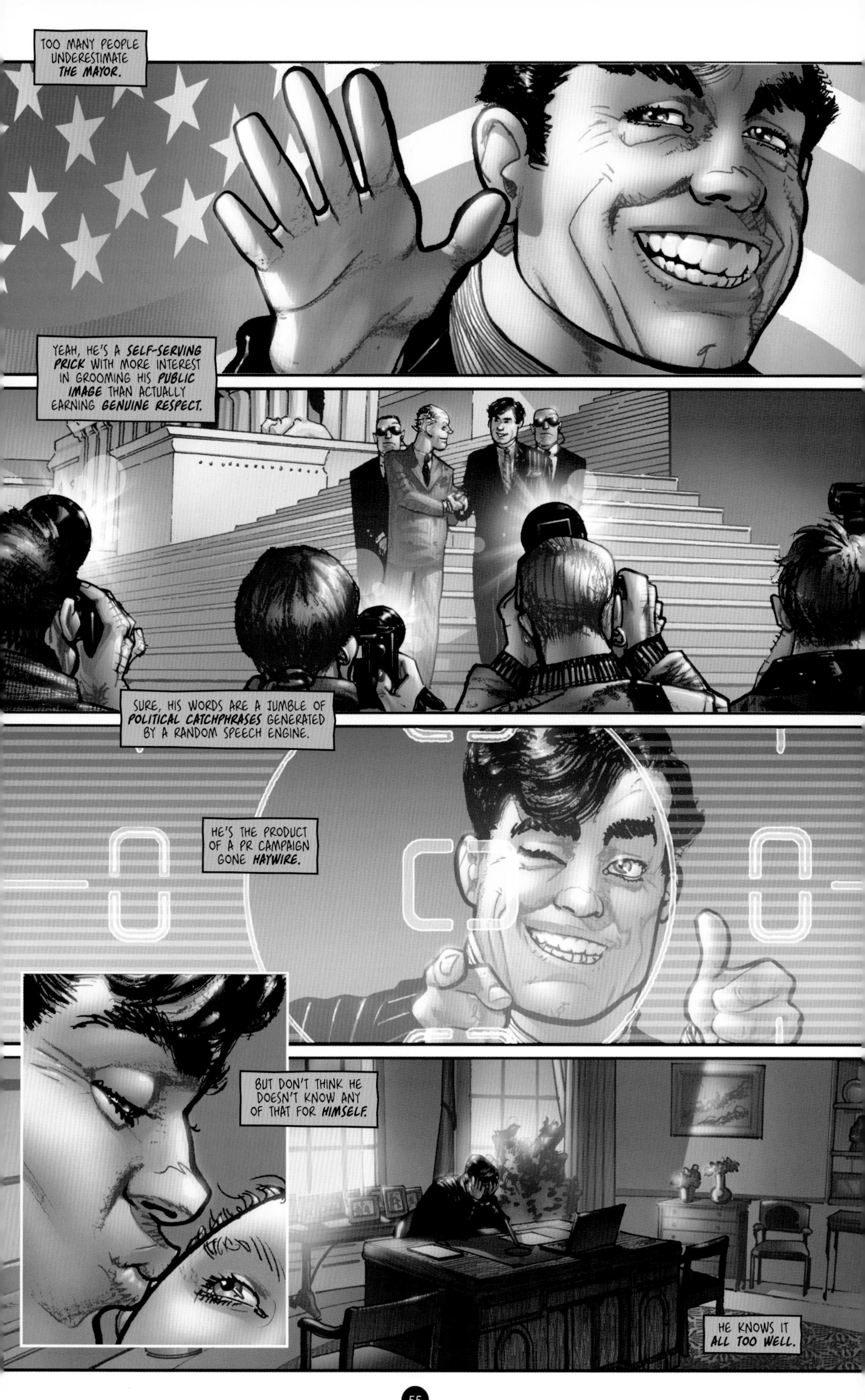
TOO MANY PEOPLE UNDERESTIMATE **THE MAYOR.**
YEAH, HE'S A **SELF-SERVING PRICK** WITH MORE INTEREST IN GROOMING HIS **PUBLIC IMAGE** THAN ACTUALLY EARNING **GENUINE RESPECT.**
SURE, HIS WORDS ARE A JUMBLE OF **POLITICAL CATCHPHRASES** GENERATED BY A RANDOM SPEECH ENGINE.
HE'S THE PRODUCT OF A PR CAMPAIGN GONE **HAYWIRE.**
BUT DON'T THINK HE DOESN'T KNOW ANY OF THAT FOR **HIMSELF.**
HE KNOWS IT **ALL TOO WELL.**

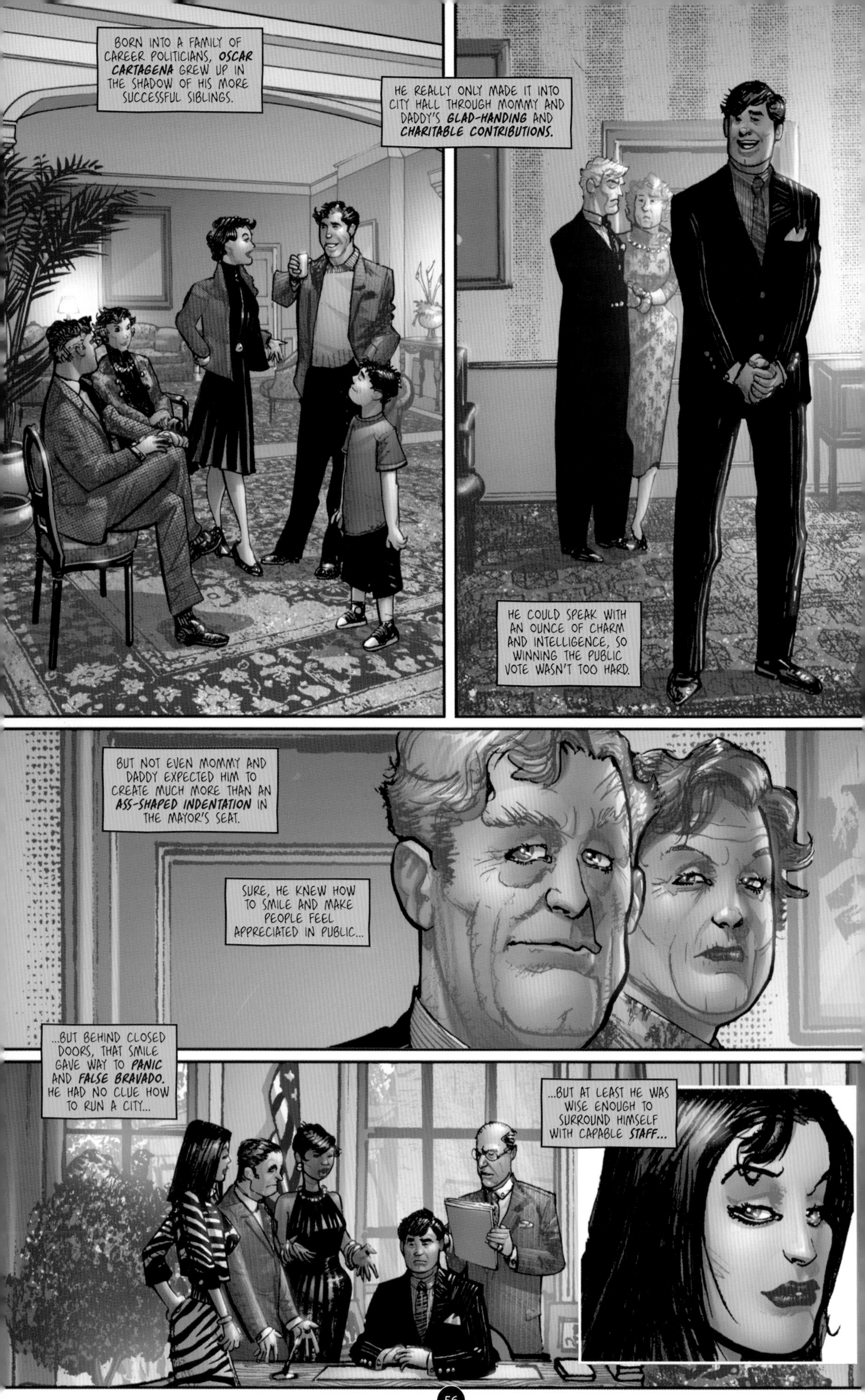
BORN INTO A FAMILY OF CAREER POLITICIANS, OSCAR CARTAGENA GREW UP IN THE SHADOW OF HIS MORE SUCCESSFUL SIBLINGS.
HE REALLY ONLY MADE IT INTO CITY HALL THROUGH MOMMY AND DADDY'S GLAD-HANDING AND CHARITABLE CONTRIBUTIONS.
HE COULD SPEAK WITH AN OUNCE OF CHARM AND INTELLIGENCE, SO WINNING THE PUBLIC VOTE WASN'T TOO HARD.
BUT NOT EVEN MOMMY AND DADDY EXPECTED HIM TO CREATE MUCH MORE THAN AN ASS-SHAPED INDENTATION IN THE MAYOR'S SEAT.
SURE, HE KNEW HOW TO SMILE AND MAKE PEOPLE FEEL APPRECIATED IN PUBLIC...
...BUT BEHIND CLOSED DOORS, THAT SMILE GAVE WAY TO PANIC AND FALSE BRAVADO. HE HAD NO CLUE HOW TO RUN A CITY...
...BUT AT LEAST HE WAS WISE ENOUGH TO SURROUND HIMSELF WITH CAPABLE STAFF...

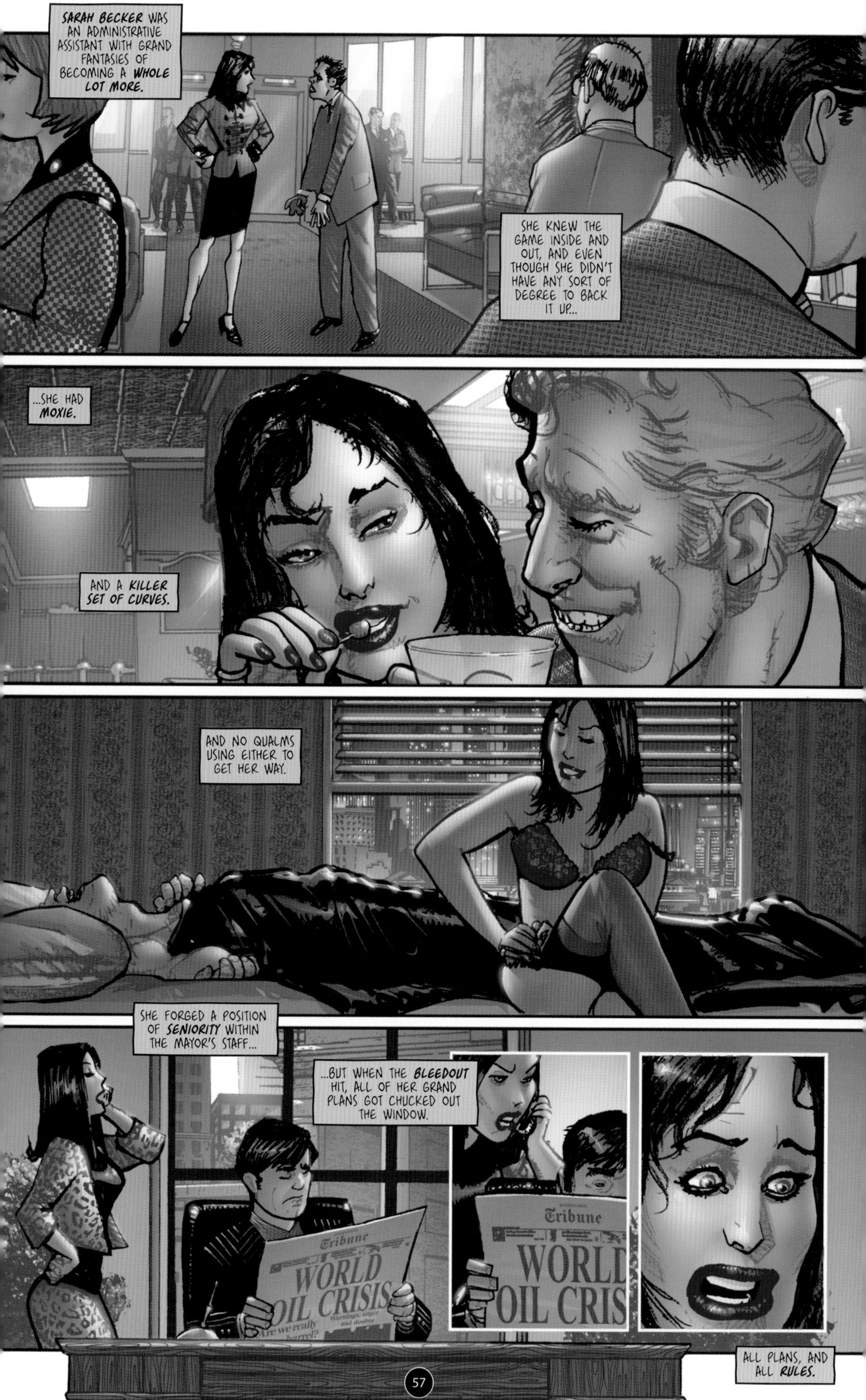
SARAH BECKER WAS AN ADMINISTRATIVE ASSISTANT WITH GRAND FANTASIES OF BECOMING A WHOLE LOT MORE.
SHE KNEW THE GAME INSIDE AND OUT, AND EVEN THOUGH SHE DIDN'T HAVE ANY SORT OF DEGREE TO BACK IT UP...
...SHE HAD MOXIE.
AND A KILLER SET OF CURVES.
AND NO QUALMS USING EITHER TO GET HER WAY.
SHE FORGED A POSITION OF SENIORITY WITHIN THE MAYOR'S STAFF...
...BUT WHEN THE BLEEDOUT HIT, ALL OF HER GRAND PLANS GOT CHUCKED OUT THE WINDOW.
Tribune
WORLD OIL CRISIS
Tribune
WORLD OIL CRIS
ALL PLANS, AND ALL RULES.

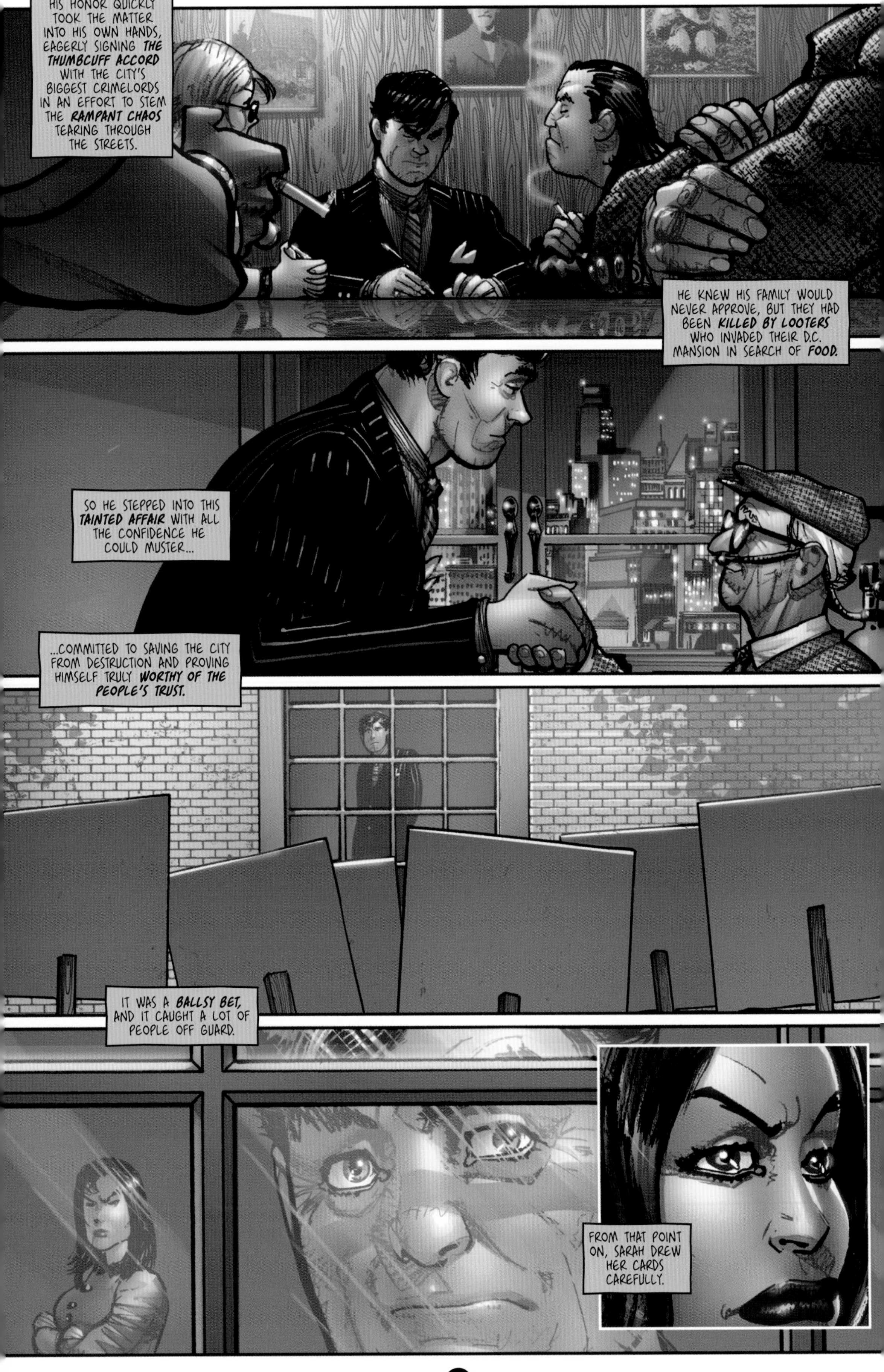
HIS HONOR QUICKLY TOOK THE MATTER INTO HIS OWN HANDS, EAGERLY SIGNING THE THUMBCUFF ACCORD WITH THE CITY'S BIGGEST CRIMELORDS IN AN EFFORT TO STEM THE RAMPANT CHAOS TEARING THROUGH THE STREETS.
HE KNEW HIS FAMILY WOULD NEVER APPROVE, BUT THEY HAD BEEN KILLED BY LOOTERS WHO INVADED THEIR D.C. MANSION IN SEARCH OF FOOD.
SO HE STEPPED INTO THIS TAINTED AFFAIR WITH ALL THE CONFIDENCE HE COULD MUSTER...
...COMMITTED TO SAVING THE CITY FROM DESTRUCTION AND PROVING HIMSELF TRULY WORTHY OF THE PEOPLE'S TRUST.
IT WAS A BALLSY BET, AND IT CAUGHT A LOT OF PEOPLE OFF GUARD.
FROM THAT POINT ON, SARAH DREW HER CARDS CAREFULLY.

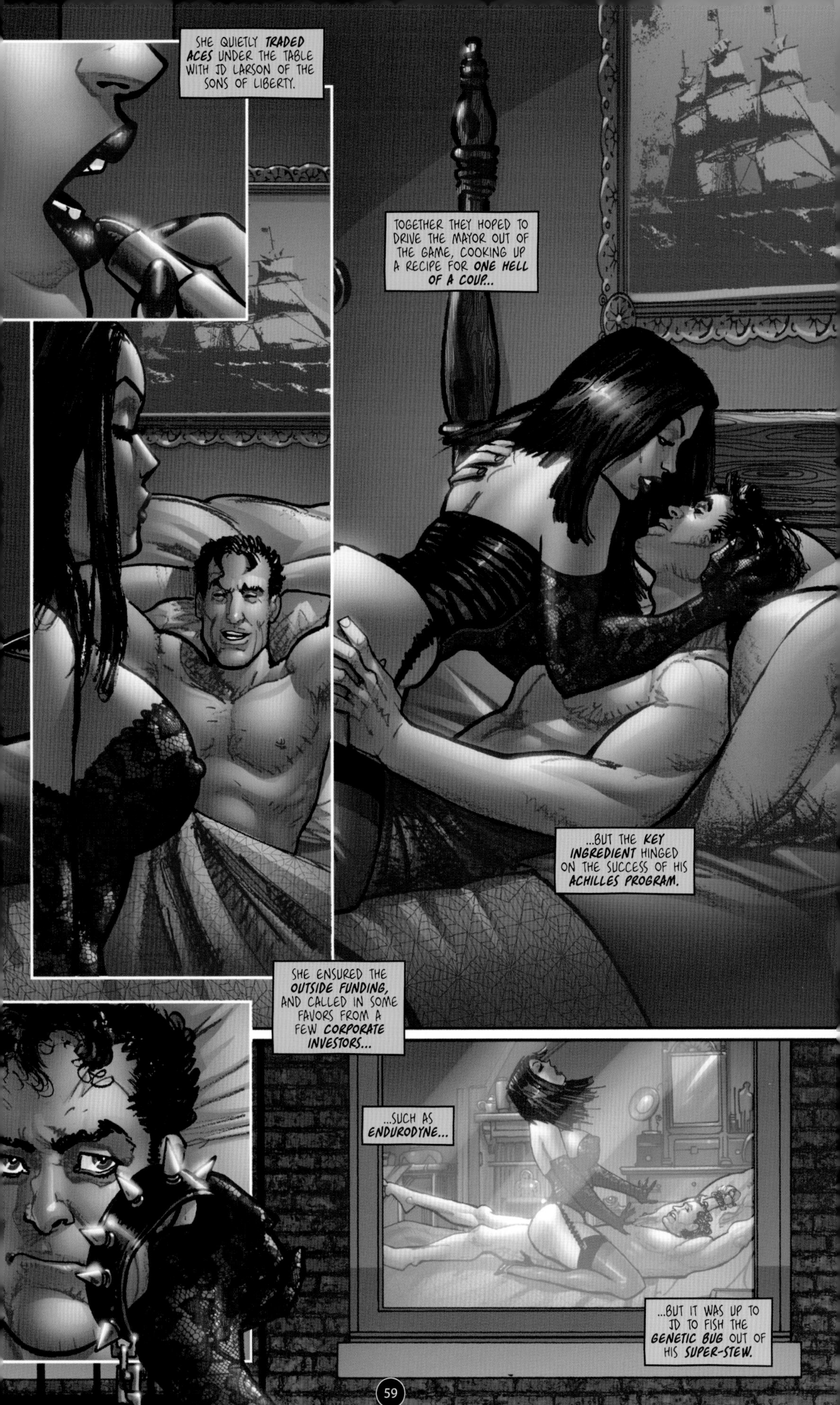
SHE QUIETLY TRADED ACES UNDER THE TABLE WITH JD LARSON OF THE SONS OF LIBERTY.
TOGETHER THEY HOPED TO DRIVE THE MAYOR OUT OF THE GAME, COOKING UP A RECIPE FOR ONE HELL OF A COUP...
...BUT THE KEY INGREDIENT HINGED ON THE SUCCESS OF HIS ACHILLES PROGRAM.
SHE ENSURED THE OUTSIDE FUNDING, AND CALLED IN SOME FAVORS FROM A FEW CORPORATE INVESTORS...
...SUCH AS ENDURODYNE...
...BUT IT WAS UP TO JD TO FISH THE GENETIC BUG OUT OF HIS SUPER-STEW.

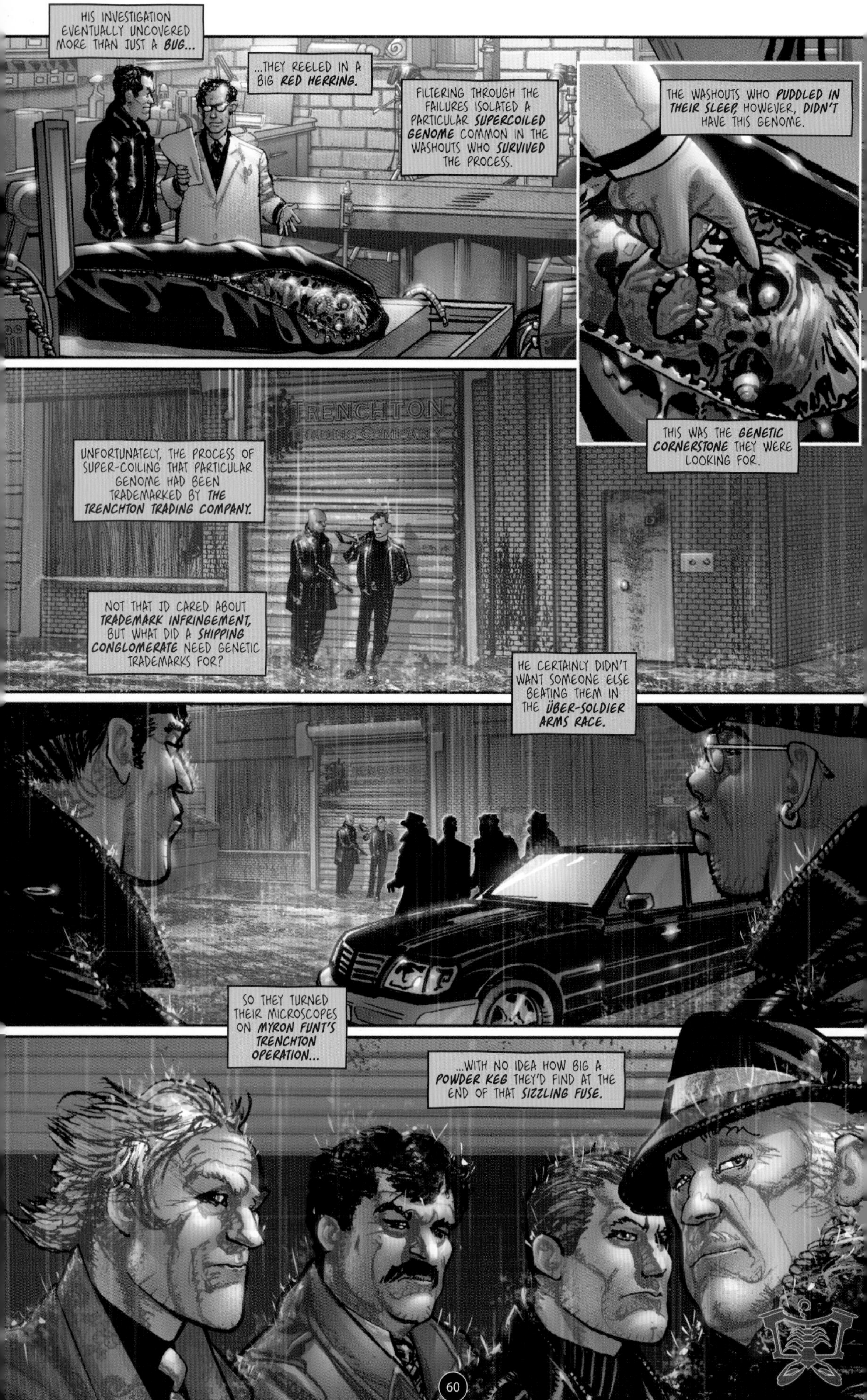
HIS INVESTIGATION EVENTUALLY UNCOVERED MORE THAN JUST A BUG...
...THEY REELED IN A BIG RED HERRING.
FILTERING THROUGH THE FAILURES ISOLATED A PARTICULAR SUPERCOILED GENOME COMMON IN THE WASHOUTS WHO SURVIVED THE PROCESS.
THE WASHOUTS WHO PUDDLED IN THEIR SLEEP, HOWEVER, DIDN'T HAVE THIS GENOME.
THIS WAS THE GENETIC CORNERSTONE THEY WERE LOOKING FOR.
TRENCHTON TRADING COMPANY
UNFORTUNATELY, THE PROCESS OF SUPER-COILING THAT PARTICULAR GENOME HAD BEEN TRADEMARKED BY THE TRENCHTON TRADING COMPANY.
NOT THAT JD CARED ABOUT TRADEMARK INFRINGEMENT, BUT WHAT DID A SHIPPING CONGLOMERATE NEED GENETIC TRADEMARKS FOR?
HE CERTAINLY DIDN'T WANT SOMEONE ELSE BEATING THEM IN THE ÜBER-SOLDIER ARMS RACE.
SO THEY TURNED THEIR MICROSCOPES ON MYRON FUNT'S TRENCHTON OPERATION...
...WITH NO IDEA HOW BIG A POWDER KEG THEY'D FIND AT THE END OF THAT SIZZLING FUSE.

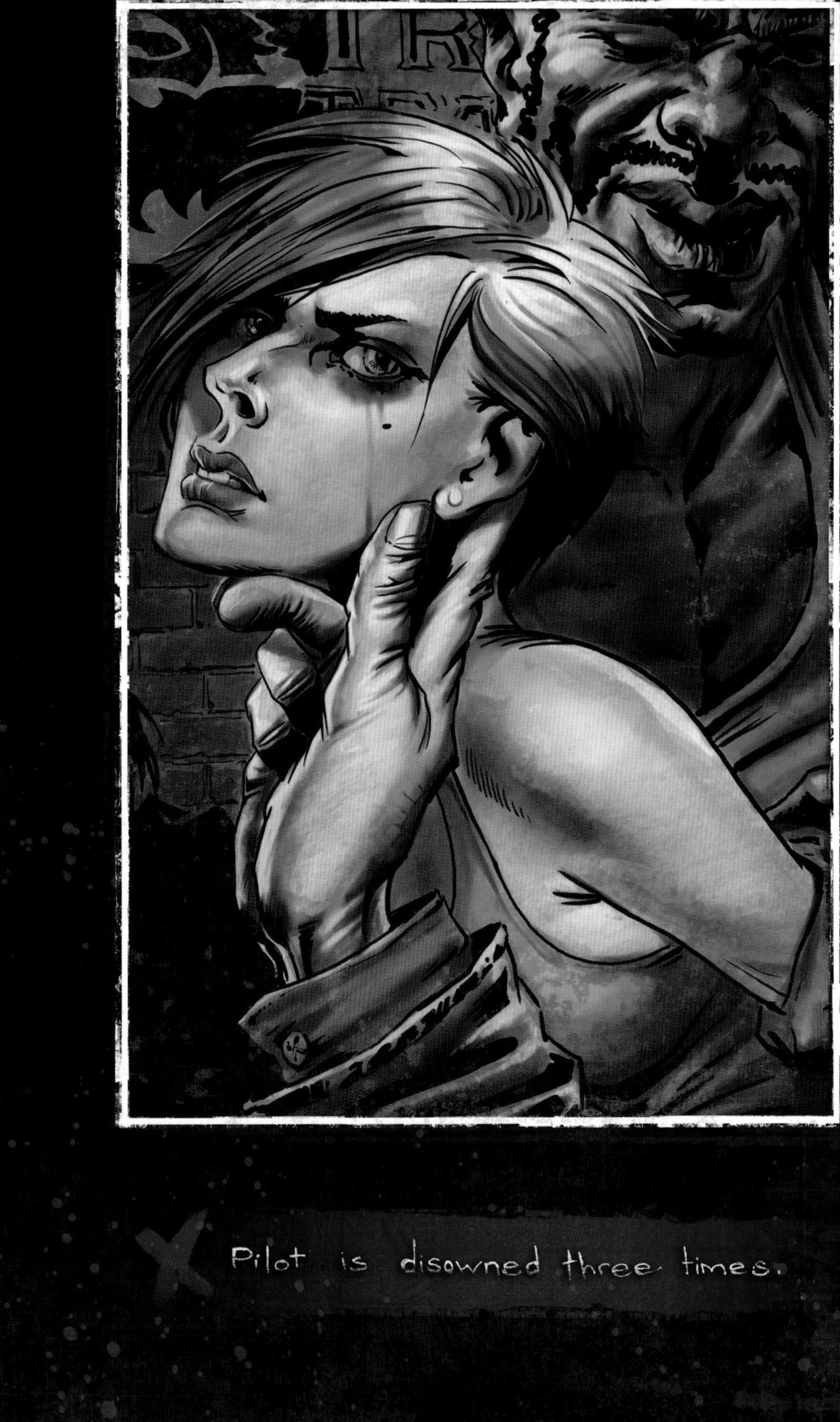

Pilot is disowned three times.

08

CHAPTER EIGHT:
Contingency Theory

Illustrated by
Glenn Fabry

Colors by
Andrey Shcherbak

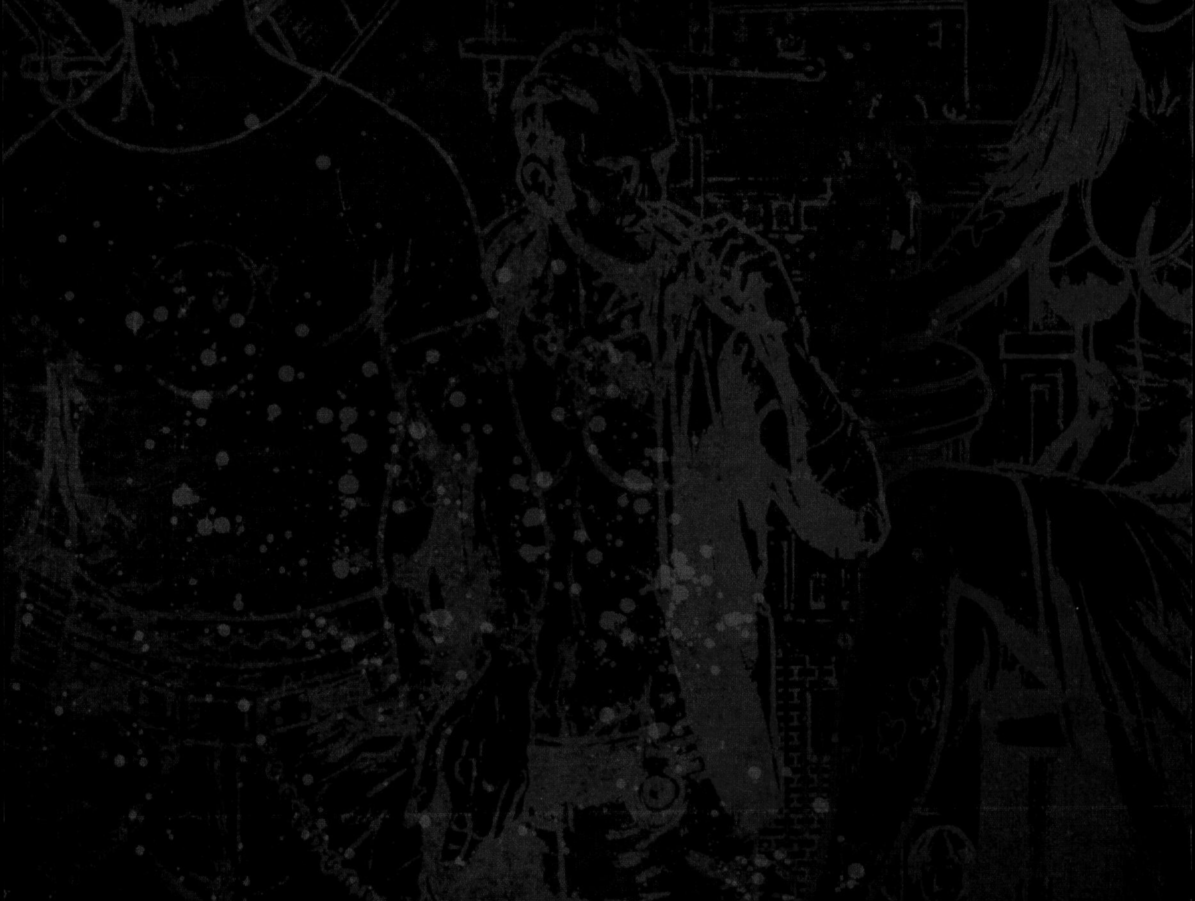

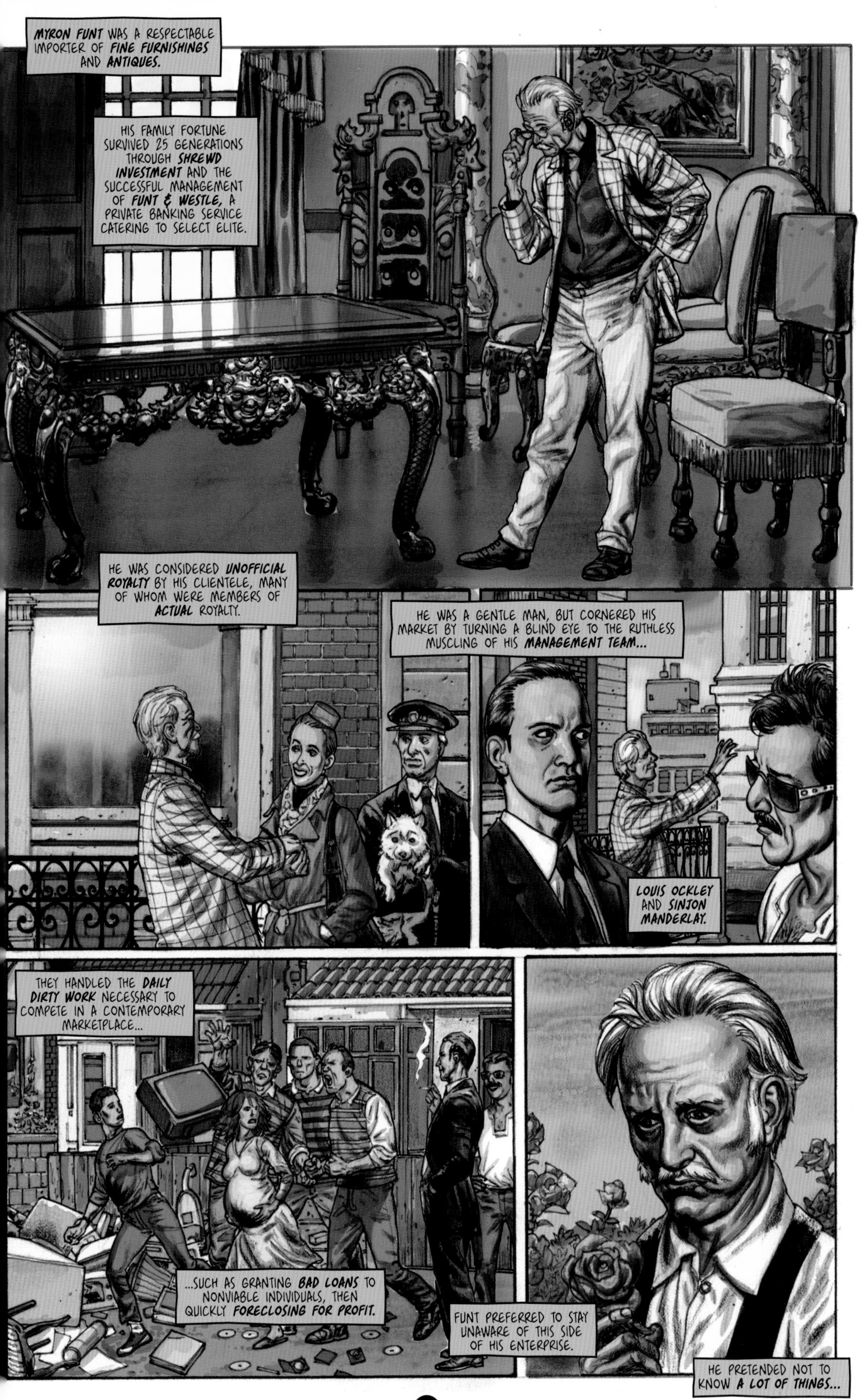
MYRON FUNT WAS A RESPECTABLE IMPORTER OF FINE FURNISHINGS AND ANTIQUES.
HIS FAMILY FORTUNE SURVIVED 25 GENERATIONS THROUGH SHREWD INVESTMENT AND THE SUCCESSFUL MANAGEMENT OF FUNT & WESTLE, A PRIVATE BANKING SERVICE CATERING TO SELECT ELITE.
HE WAS CONSIDERED UNOFFICIAL ROYALTY BY HIS CLIENTELE, MANY OF WHOM WERE MEMBERS OF ACTUAL ROYALTY.
HE WAS A GENTLE MAN, BUT CORNERED HIS MARKET BY TURNING A BLIND EYE TO THE RUTHLESS MUSCLING OF HIS MANAGEMENT TEAM...
LOUIS OCKLEY AND SINJON MANDERLAY.
THEY HANDLED THE DAILY DIRTY WORK NECESSARY TO COMPETE IN A CONTEMPORARY MARKETPLACE...
...SUCH AS GRANTING BAD LOANS TO NONVIABLE INDIVIDUALS, THEN QUICKLY FORECLOSING FOR PROFIT.
FUNT PREFERRED TO STAY UNAWARE OF THIS SIDE OF HIS ENTERPRISE.
HE PRETENDED NOT TO KNOW A LOT OF THINGS...

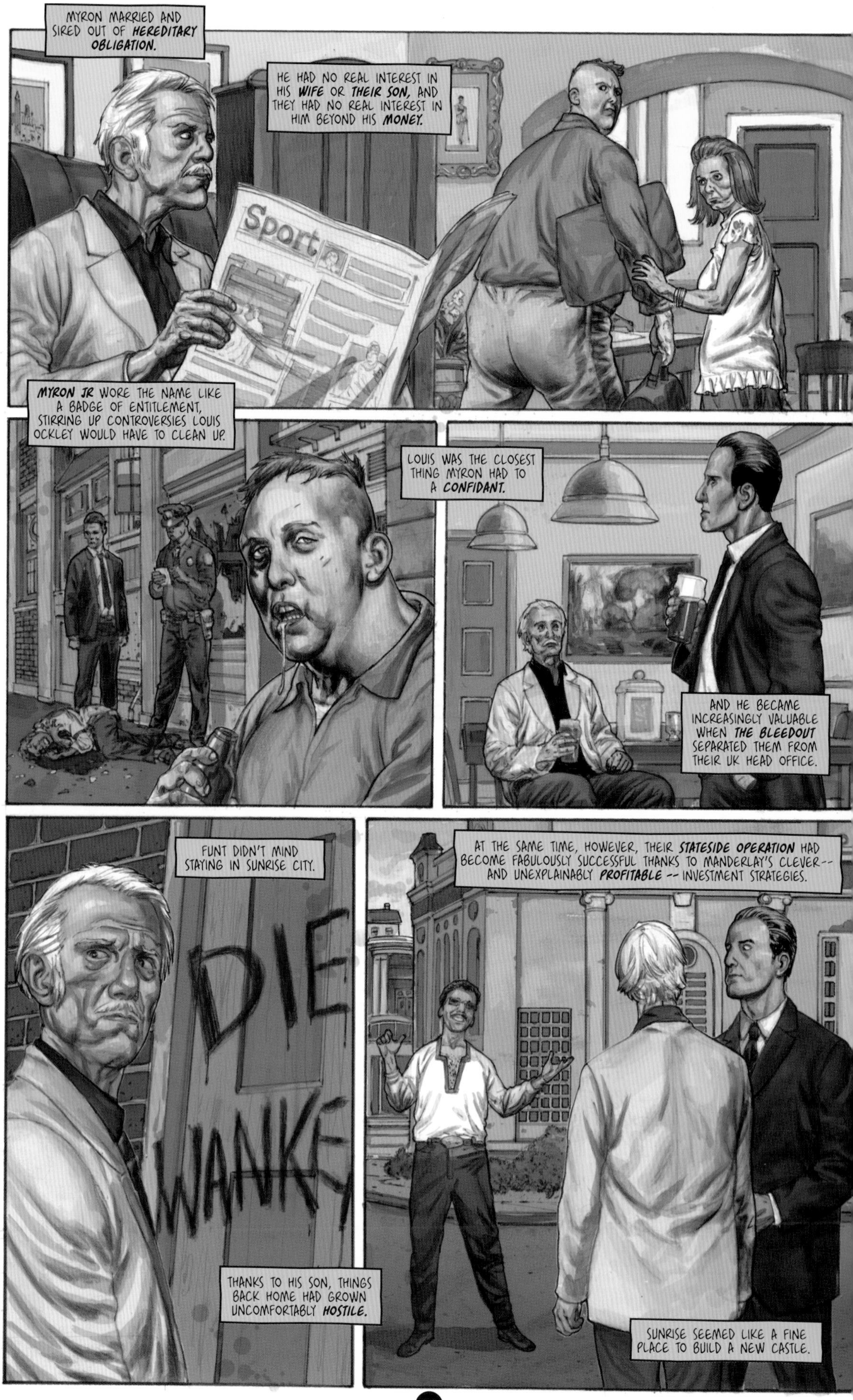
MYRON MARRIED AND SIRED OUT OF HEREDITARY OBLIGATION.
HE HAD NO REAL INTEREST IN HIS WIFE OR THEIR SON, AND THEY HAD NO REAL INTEREST IN HIM BEYOND HIS MONEY.
Sport
MYRON JR WORE THE NAME LIKE A BADGE OF ENTITLEMENT, STIRRING UP CONTROVERSIES LOUIS OCKLEY WOULD HAVE TO CLEAN UP.
LOUIS WAS THE CLOSEST THING MYRON HAD TO A CONFIDANT.
AND HE BECAME INCREASINGLY VALUABLE WHEN THE BLEEDOUT SEPARATED THEM FROM THEIR UK HEAD OFFICE.
FUNT DIDN'T MIND STAYING IN SUNRISE CITY.
DIE
WANKE
THANKS TO HIS SON, THINGS BACK HOME HAD GROWN UNCOMFORTABLY HOSTILE.
AT THE SAME TIME, HOWEVER, THEIR STATESIDE OPERATION HAD BECOME FABULOUSLY SUCCESSFUL THANKS TO MANDERLAY'S CLEVER-- AND UNEXPLAINABLY PROFITABLE -- INVESTMENT STRATEGIES.
SUNRISE SEEMED LIKE A FINE PLACE TO BUILD A NEW CASTLE.

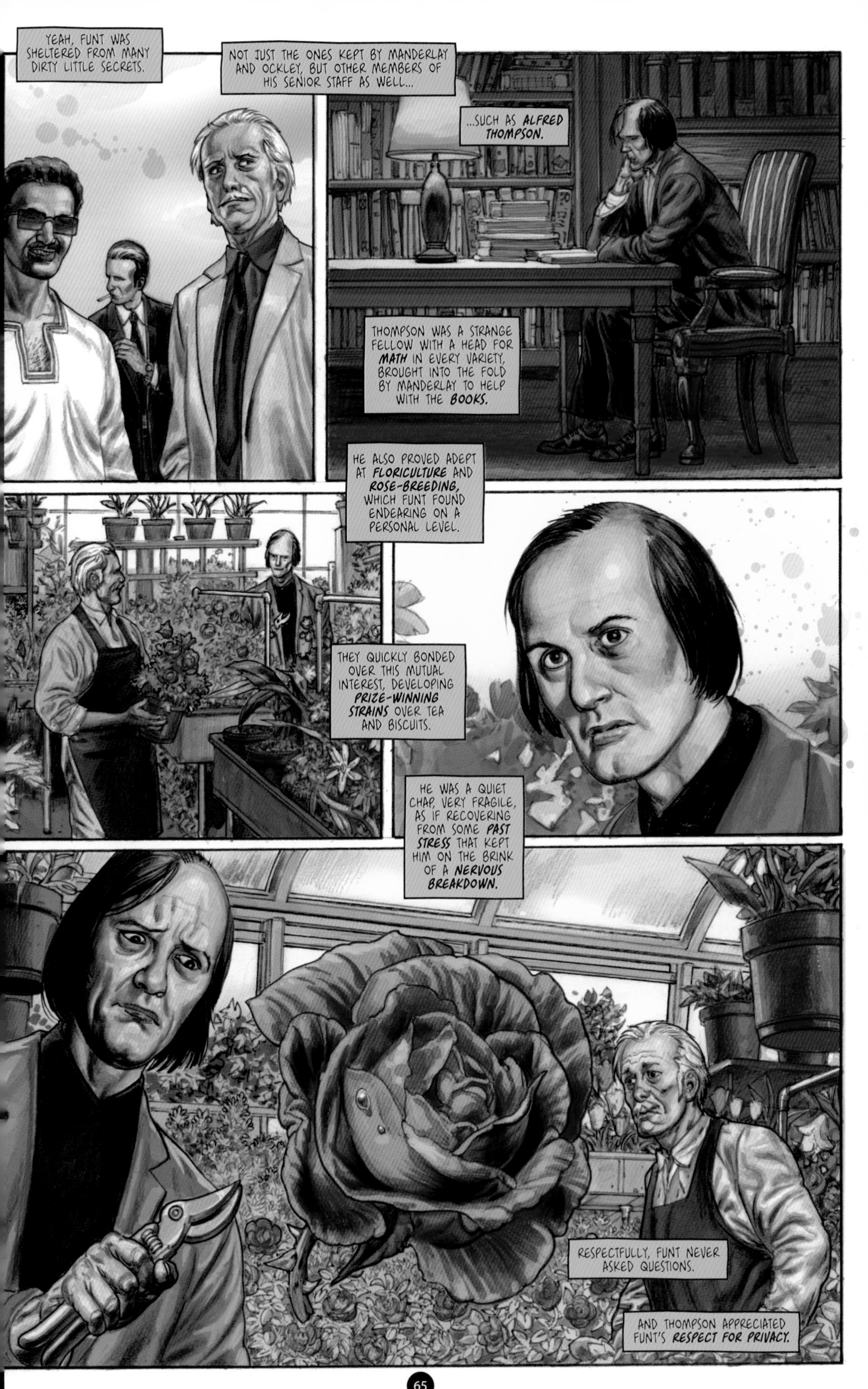
YEAH, FUNT WAS SHELTERED FROM MANY DIRTY LITTLE SECRETS.
NOT JUST THE ONES KEPT BY MANDERLAY AND OCKLEY, BUT OTHER MEMBERS OF HIS SENIOR STAFF AS WELL...
...SUCH AS ALFRED THOMPSON.
THOMPSON WAS A STRANGE FELLOW WITH A HEAD FOR MATH IN EVERY VARIETY, BROUGHT INTO THE FOLD BY MANDERLAY TO HELP WITH THE BOOKS.
HE ALSO PROVED ADEPT AT FLORICULTURE AND ROSE-BREEDING, WHICH FUNT FOUND ENDEARING ON A PERSONAL LEVEL.
THEY QUICKLY BONDED OVER THIS MUTUAL INTEREST, DEVELOPING PRIZE-WINNING STRAINS OVER TEA AND BISCUITS.
HE WAS A QUIET CHAP, VERY FRAGILE, AS IF RECOVERING FROM SOME PAST STRESS THAT KEPT HIM ON THE BRINK OF A NERVOUS BREAKDOWN.
RESPECTFULLY, FUNT NEVER ASKED QUESTIONS.
AND THOMPSON APPRECIATED FUNT'S RESPECT FOR PRIVACY.

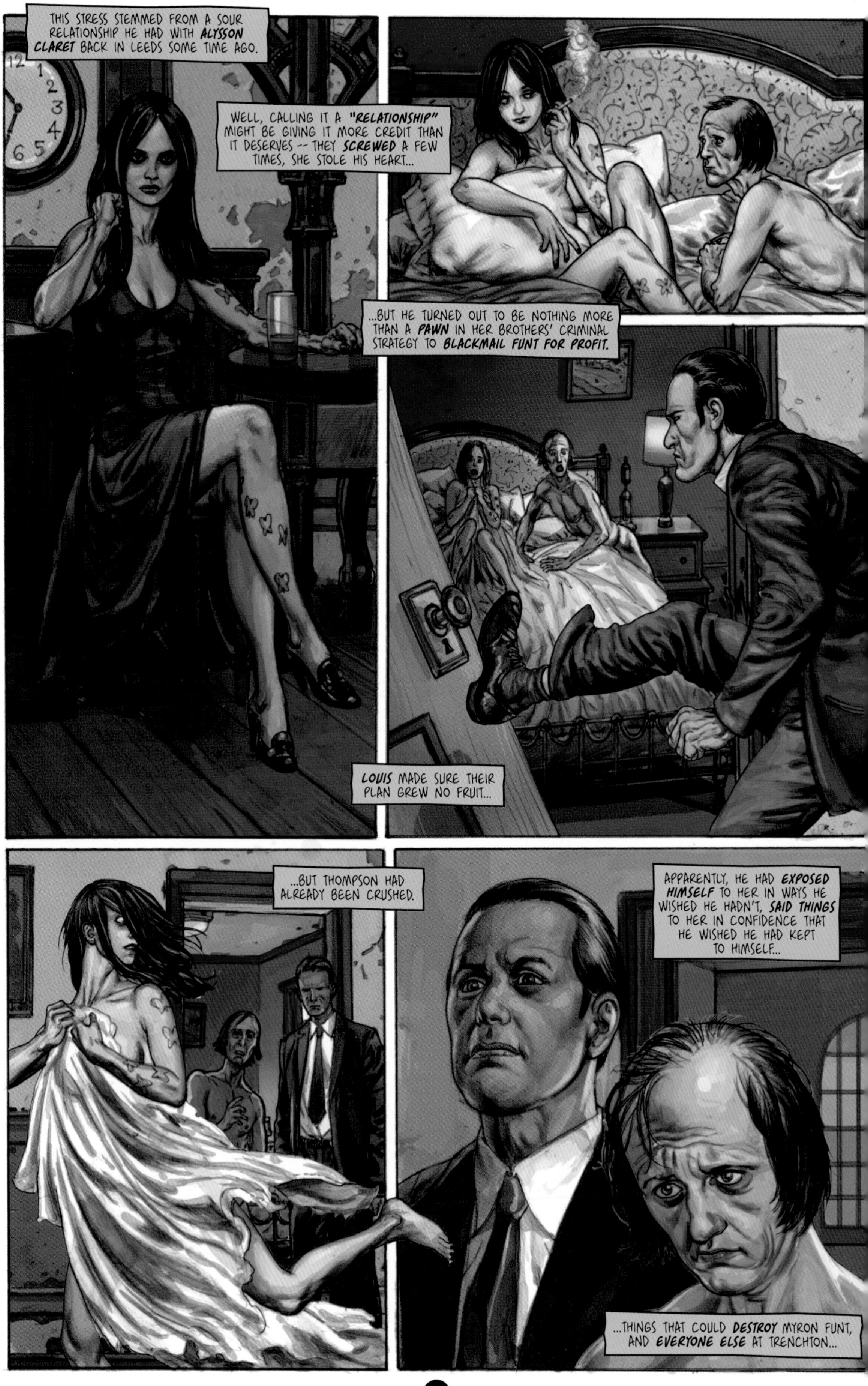

THIS STRESS STEMMED FROM A SOUR RELATIONSHIP HE HAD WITH ALYSSON CLARET BACK IN LEEDS SOME TIME AGO.
WELL, CALLING IT A "RELATIONSHIP" MIGHT BE GIVING IT MORE CREDIT THAN IT DESERVES -- THEY SCREWED A FEW TIMES, SHE STOLE HIS HEART...
...BUT HE TURNED OUT TO BE NOTHING MORE THAN A PAWN IN HER BROTHERS' CRIMINAL STRATEGY TO BLACKMAIL FUNT FOR PROFIT.
LOUIS MADE SURE THEIR PLAN GREW NO FRUIT...
...BUT THOMPSON HAD ALREADY BEEN CRUSHED.
APPARENTLY, HE HAD EXPOSED HIMSELF TO HER IN WAYS HE WISHED HE HADN'T, SAID THINGS TO HER IN CONFIDENCE THAT HE WISHED HE HAD KEPT TO HIMSELF...
...THINGS THAT COULD DESTROY MYRON FUNT, AND EVERYONE ELSE AT TRENCHTON...

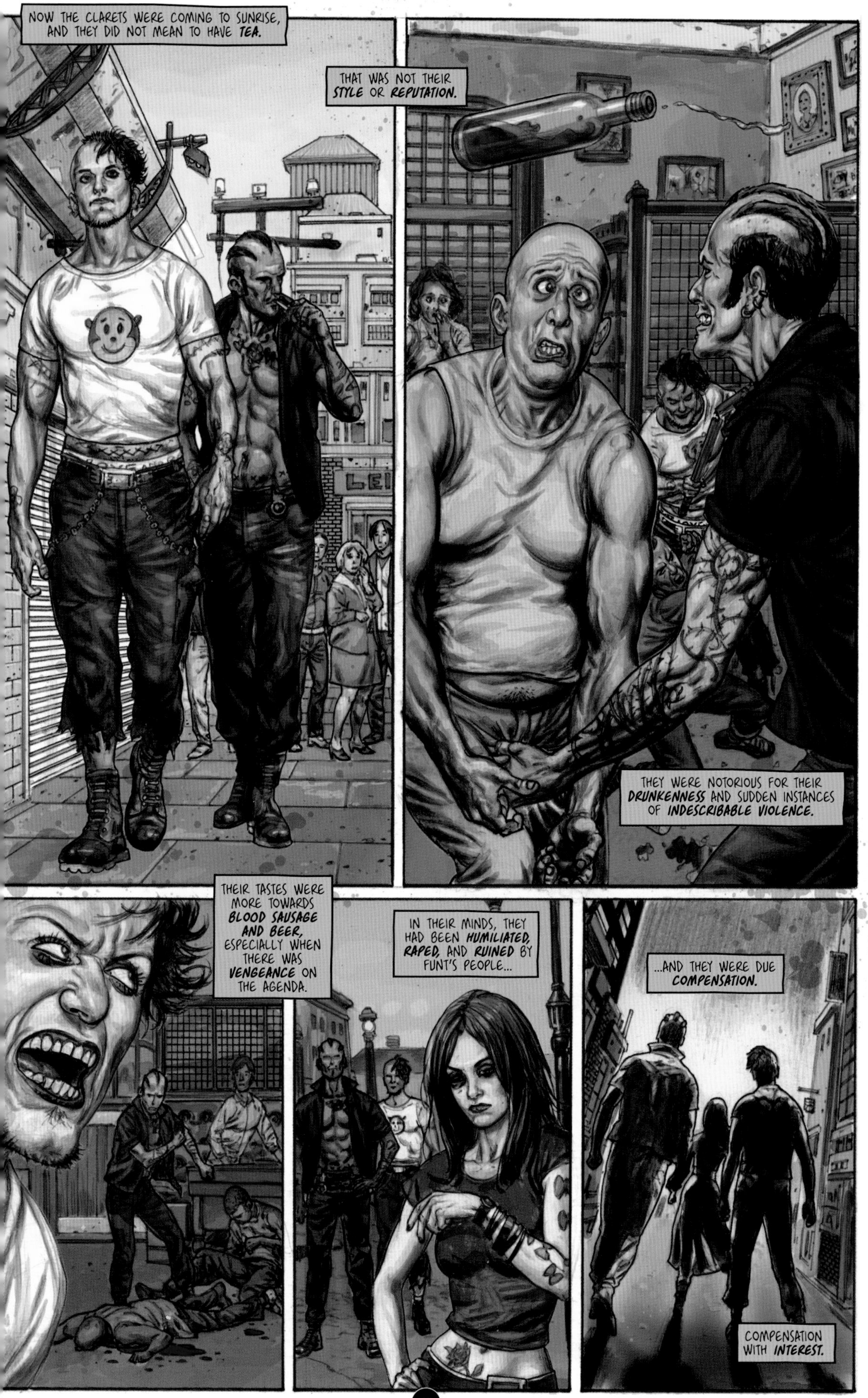
NOW THE CLARETS WERE COMING TO SUNRISE, AND THEY DID NOT MEAN TO HAVE TEA.
THAT WAS NOT THEIR STYLE OR REPUTATION.
THEY WERE NOTORIOUS FOR THEIR DRUNKENNESS AND SUDDEN INSTANCES OF INDESCRIBABLE VIOLENCE.
THEIR TASTES WERE MORE TOWARDS BLOOD SAUSAGE AND BEER, ESPECIALLY WHEN THERE WAS VENGEANCE ON THE AGENDA.
IN THEIR MINDS, THEY HAD BEEN HUMILIATED, RAPED, AND RUINED BY FUNT'S PEOPLE...
...AND THEY WERE DUE COMPENSATION.
COMPENSATION WITH INTEREST.

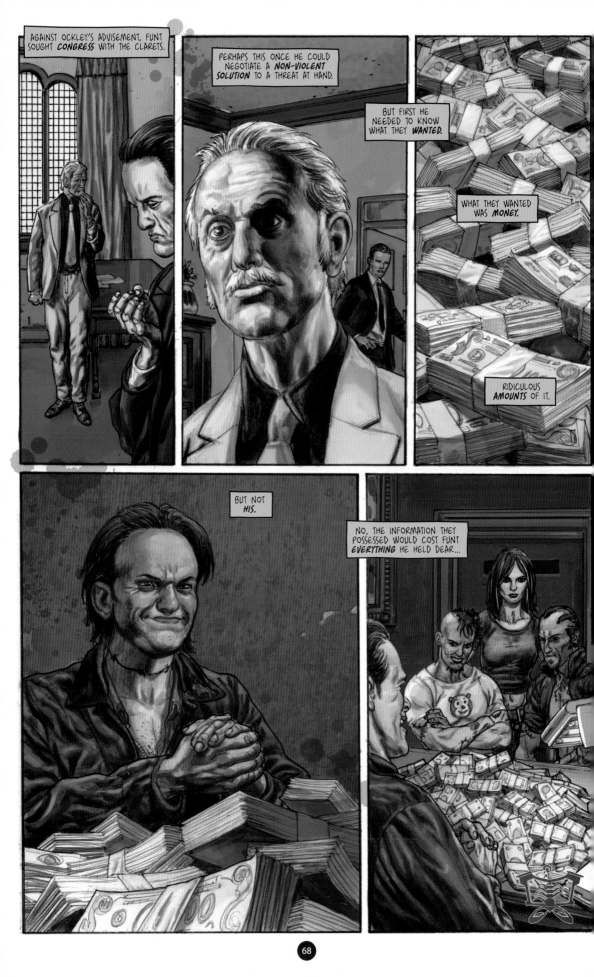

AGAINST OCKLEY'S ADVISEMENT, FUNT SOUGHT *CONGRESS* WITH THE CLARETS.

PERHAPS THIS ONCE HE COULD NEGOTIATE A *NON-VIOLENT SOLUTION* TO A THREAT AT HAND.

BUT FIRST HE NEEDED TO KNOW WHAT THEY *WANTED*.

WHAT THEY WANTED WAS *MONEY*.

RIDICULOUS *AMOUNTS* OF IT.

BUT NOT *HIS*.

NO, THE INFORMATION THEY POSSESSED WOULD COST FUNT *EVERYTHING* HE HELD DEAR...

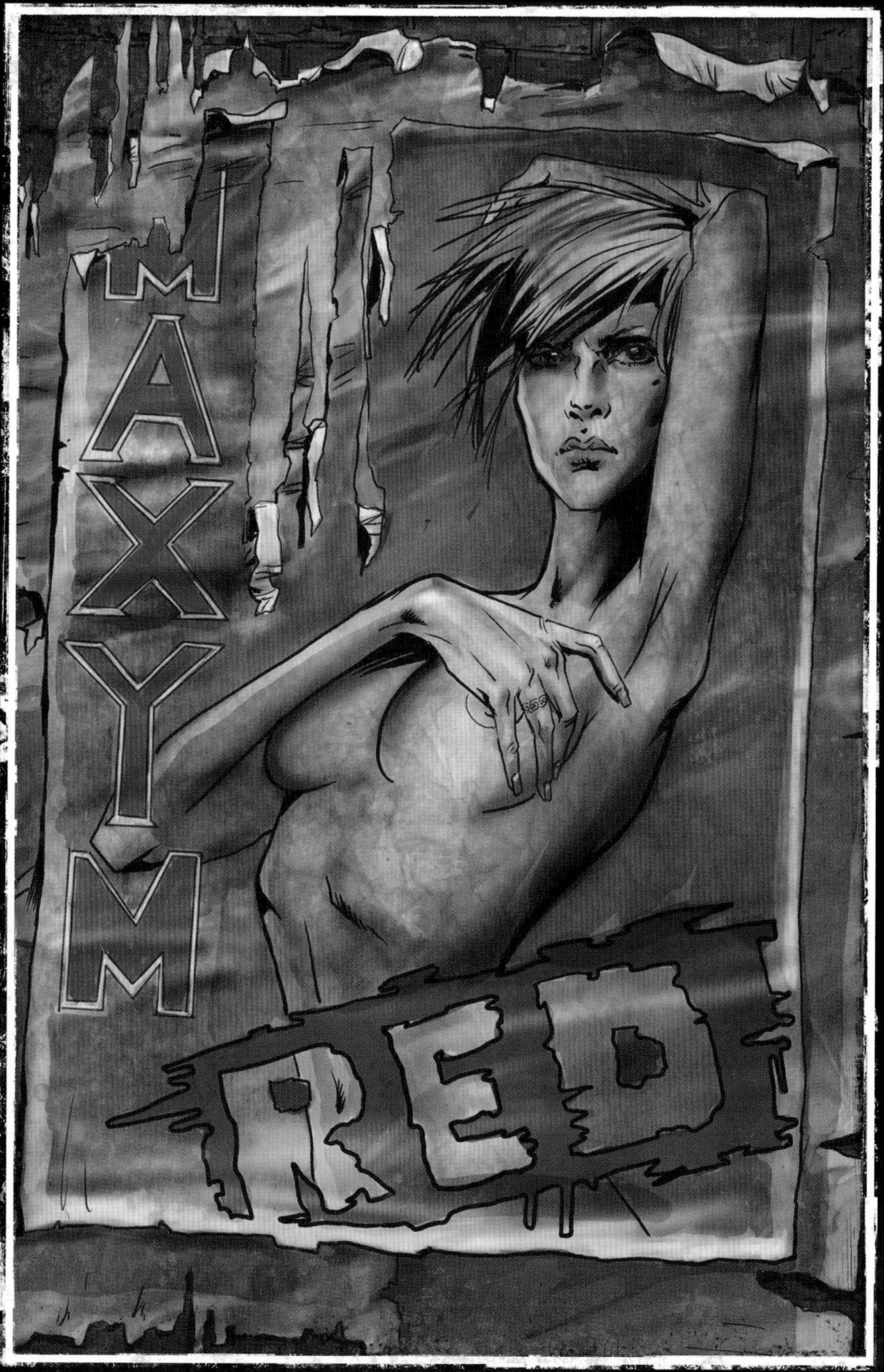
MAXYM
RED

Pilot entrusts his territory to the repentant.

CHAPTER NINE:
Tenax Propositi

Illustrated by
Vince Proce

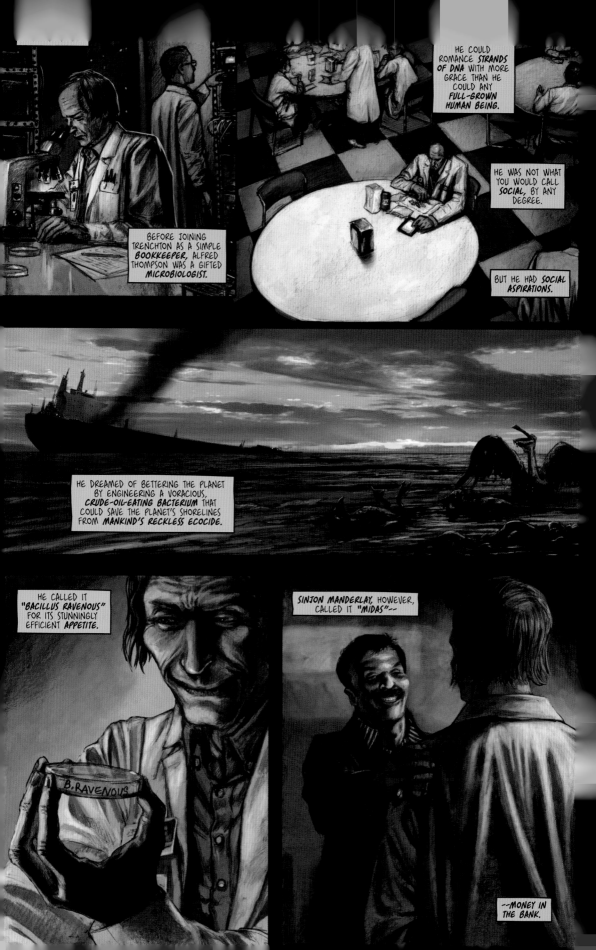

BEFORE JOINING TRENCHTON AS A SIMPLE *BOOKKEEPER*, ALFRED THOMPSON WAS A GIFTED *MICROBIOLOGIST*.

HE COULD ROMANCE *STRANDS OF DNA* WITH MORE GRACE THAN HE COULD ANY *FULL-GROWN HUMAN BEING*.

HE WAS NOT WHAT YOU WOULD CALL *SOCIAL*, BY ANY DEGREE.

BUT HE HAD *SOCIAL ASPIRATIONS*.

HE DREAMED OF BETTERING THE PLANET BY ENGINEERING A VORACIOUS, *CRUDE-OIL-EATING BACTERIUM* THAT COULD SAVE THE PLANET'S SHORELINES FROM *MANKIND'S RECKLESS ECOCIDE*.

HE CALLED IT *"BACILLUS RAVENOUS"* FOR ITS STUNNINGLY EFFICIENT *APPETITE*.

B.RAVENOUS

SINJON MANDERLAY, HOWEVER, CALLED IT *"MIDAS"*--

--MONEY IN THE BANK.

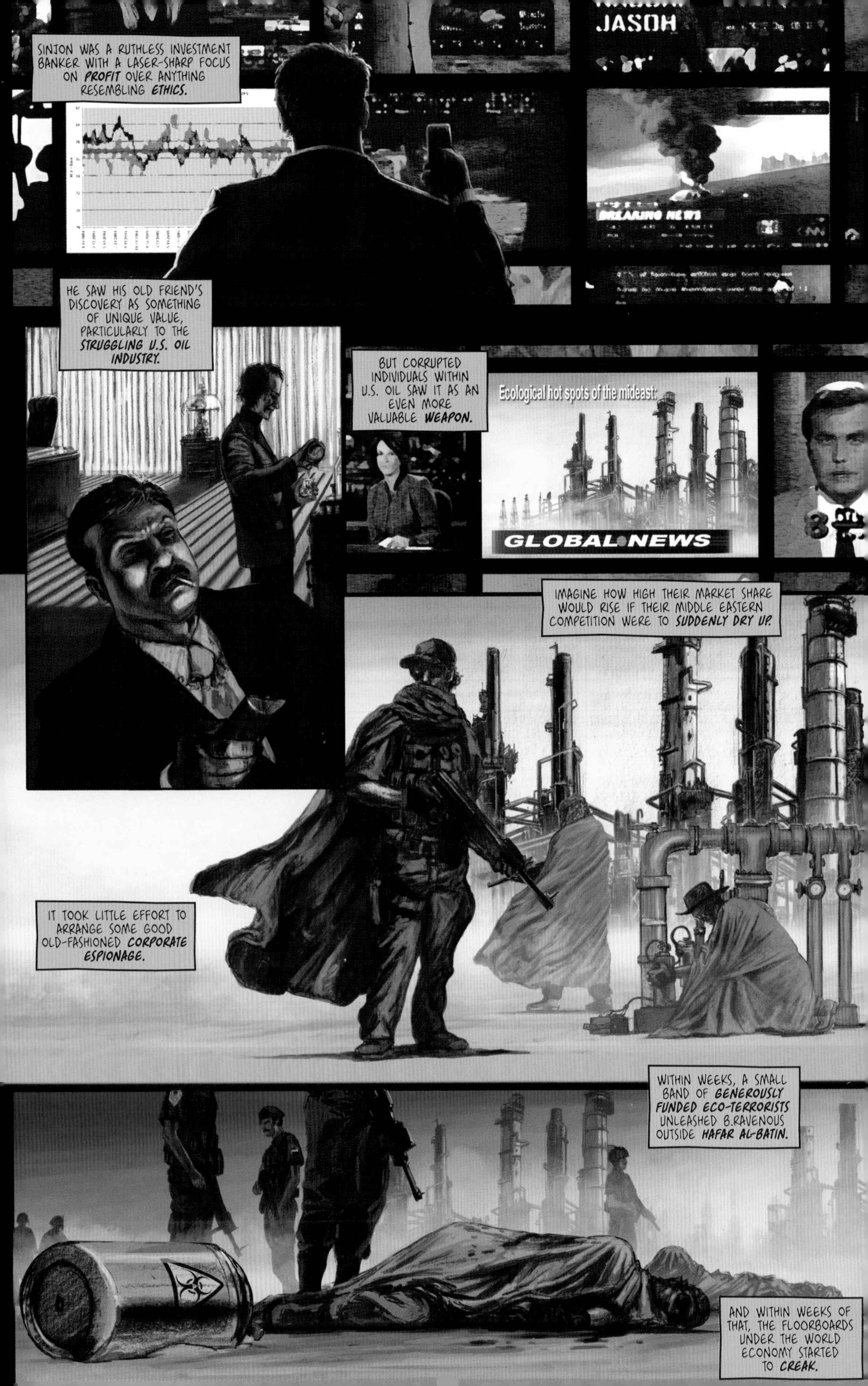
JASOH
SINJON WAS A RUTHLESS INVESTMENT BANKER WITH A LASER-SHARP FOCUS ON **PROFIT** OVER ANYTHING RESEMBLING **ETHICS.**
BREAKING NEWS
HE SAW HIS OLD FRIEND'S DISCOVERY AS SOMETHING OF UNIQUE VALUE, PARTICULARLY TO THE **STRUGGLING U.S. OIL INDUSTRY.**
BUT CORRUPTED INDIVIDUALS WITHIN U.S. OIL SAW IT AS AN EVEN MORE VALUABLE **WEAPON.**
Ecological hot spots of the mideast:
GLOBAL NEWS
IMAGINE HOW HIGH THEIR MARKET SHARE WOULD RISE IF THEIR MIDDLE EASTERN COMPETITION WERE TO **SUDDENLY DRY UP.**
IT TOOK LITTLE EFFORT TO ARRANGE SOME GOOD OLD-FASHIONED **CORPORATE ESPIONAGE.**
WITHIN WEEKS, A SMALL BAND OF **GENEROUSLY FUNDED ECO-TERRORISTS** UNLEASHED B.RAVENOUS OUTSIDE **HAFAR AL-BATIN.**
AND WITHIN WEEKS OF THAT, THE FLOORBOARDS UNDER THE WORLD ECONOMY STARTED TO **CREAK.**

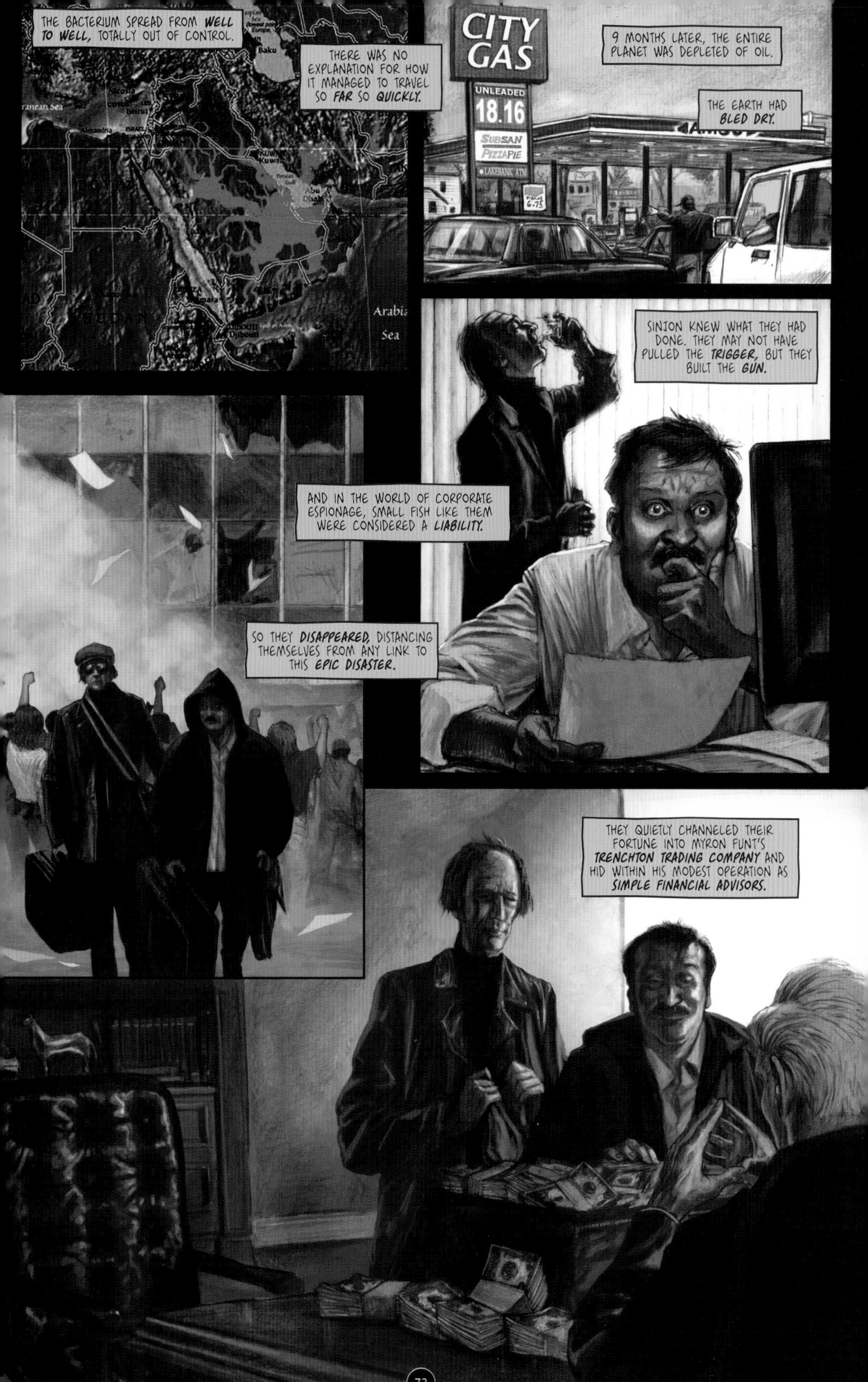
THE BACTERIUM SPREAD FROM WELL TO WELL, TOTALLY OUT OF CONTROL.
THERE WAS NO EXPLANATION FOR HOW IT MANAGED TO TRAVEL SO FAR SO QUICKLY.
Baku
Arabia
Sea
CITY GAS
UNLEADED
18.16
SUBSAN
PIZZA PIE
LAKEBANK ATM
9 MONTHS LATER, THE ENTIRE PLANET WAS DEPLETED OF OIL.
THE EARTH HAD BLED DRY.
SINJON KNEW WHAT THEY HAD DONE. THEY MAY NOT HAVE PULLED THE TRIGGER, BUT THEY BUILT THE GUN.
AND IN THE WORLD OF CORPORATE ESPIONAGE, SMALL FISH LIKE THEM WERE CONSIDERED A LIABILITY.
SO THEY DISAPPEARED, DISTANCING THEMSELVES FROM ANY LINK TO THIS EPIC DISASTER.
THEY QUIETLY CHANNELED THEIR FORTUNE INTO MYRON FUNT'S TRENCHTON TRADING COMPANY AND HID WITHIN HIS MODEST OPERATION AS SIMPLE FINANCIAL ADVISORS.

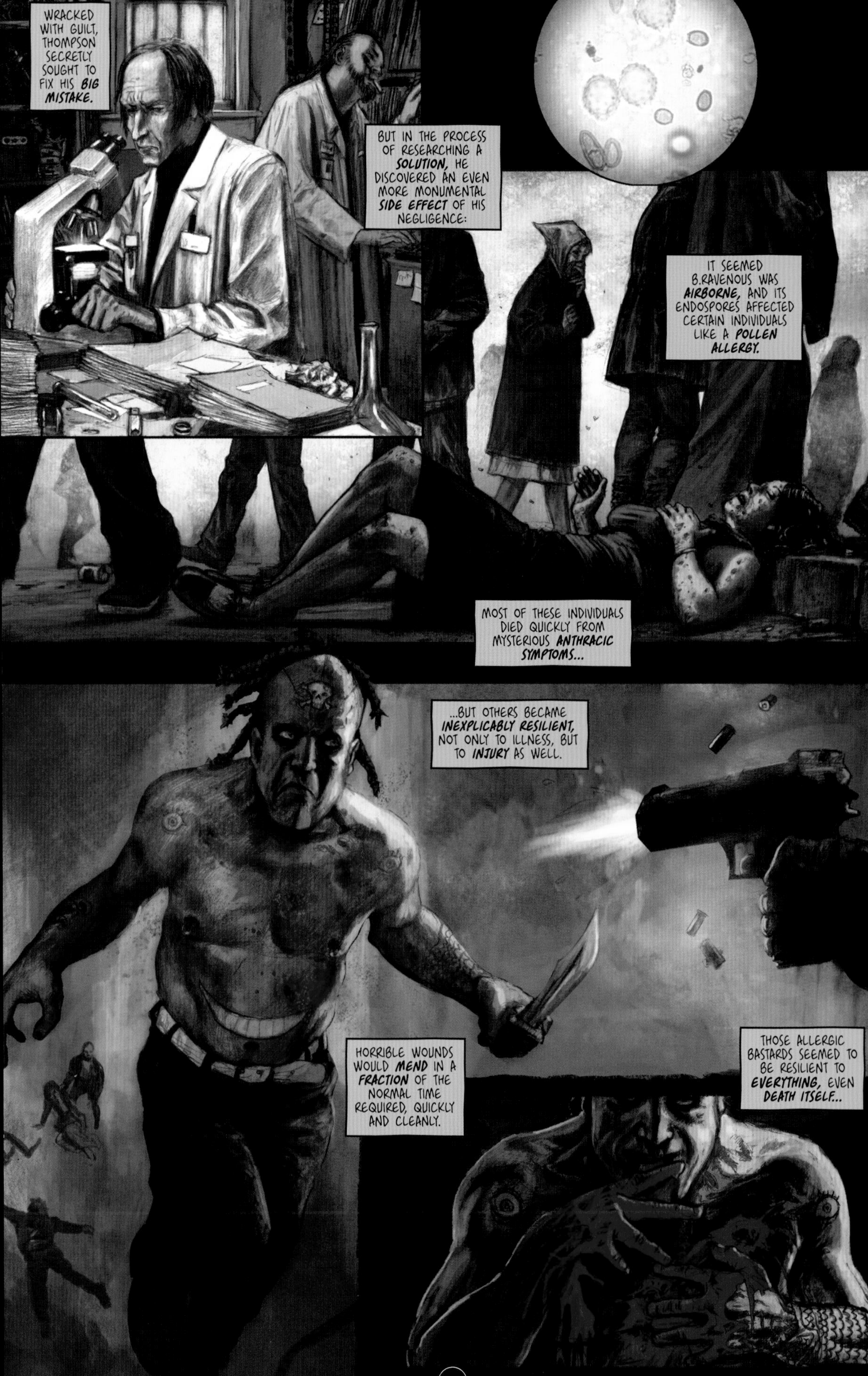
WRACKED WITH GUILT, THOMPSON SECRETLY SOUGHT TO FIX HIS BIG MISTAKE.
BUT IN THE PROCESS OF RESEARCHING A SOLUTION, HE DISCOVERED AN EVEN MORE MONUMENTAL SIDE EFFECT OF HIS NEGLIGENCE:
IT SEEMED B.RAVENOUS WAS AIRBORNE, AND ITS ENDOSPORES AFFECTED CERTAIN INDIVIDUALS LIKE A POLLEN ALLERGY.
MOST OF THESE INDIVIDUALS DIED QUICKLY FROM MYSTERIOUS ANTHRACIC SYMPTOMS...
...BUT OTHERS BECAME INEXPLICABLY RESILIENT, NOT ONLY TO ILLNESS, BUT TO INJURY AS WELL.
HORRIBLE WOUNDS WOULD MEND IN A FRACTION OF THE NORMAL TIME REQUIRED, QUICKLY AND CLEANLY.
THOSE ALLERGIC BASTARDS SEEMED TO BE RESILIENT TO EVERYTHING, EVEN DEATH ITSELF...

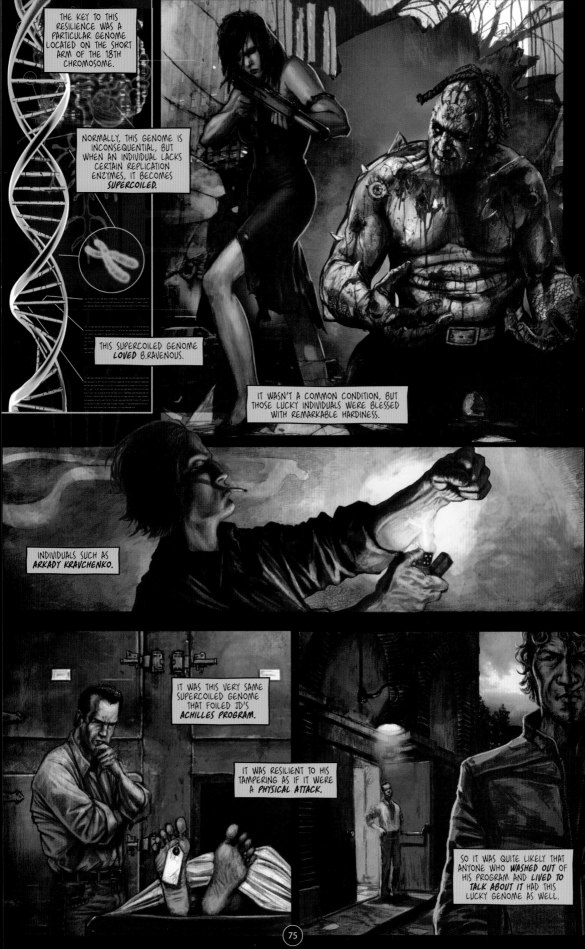

THE KEY TO THIS RESILIENCE WAS A PARTICULAR GENOME LOCATED ON THE SHORT ARM OF THE 18TH CHROMOSOME.

NORMALLY, THIS GENOME IS INCONSEQUENTIAL, BUT WHEN AN INDIVIDUAL LACKS CERTAIN REPLICATION ENZYMES, IT BECOMES *SUPERCOILED.*

THIS SUPERCOILED GENOME *LOVED B.RAVENOUS.*

IT WASN'T A COMMON CONDITION, BUT THOSE LUCKY INDIVIDUALS WERE BLESSED WITH REMARKABLE HARDINESS.

INDIVIDUALS SUCH AS *ARKADY KRAVCHENKO.*

IT WAS THIS VERY SAME SUPERCOILED GENOME THAT FOILED JD'S *ACHILLES PROGRAM.*

IT WAS RESILIENT TO HIS *TAMPERING* AS IF IT WERE A *PHYSICAL ATTACK.*

SO IT WAS QUITE LIKELY THAT ANYONE WHO *WASHED OUT* OF HIS PROGRAM AND *LIVED TO TALK ABOUT IT* HAD THIS LUCKY GENOME AS WELL.

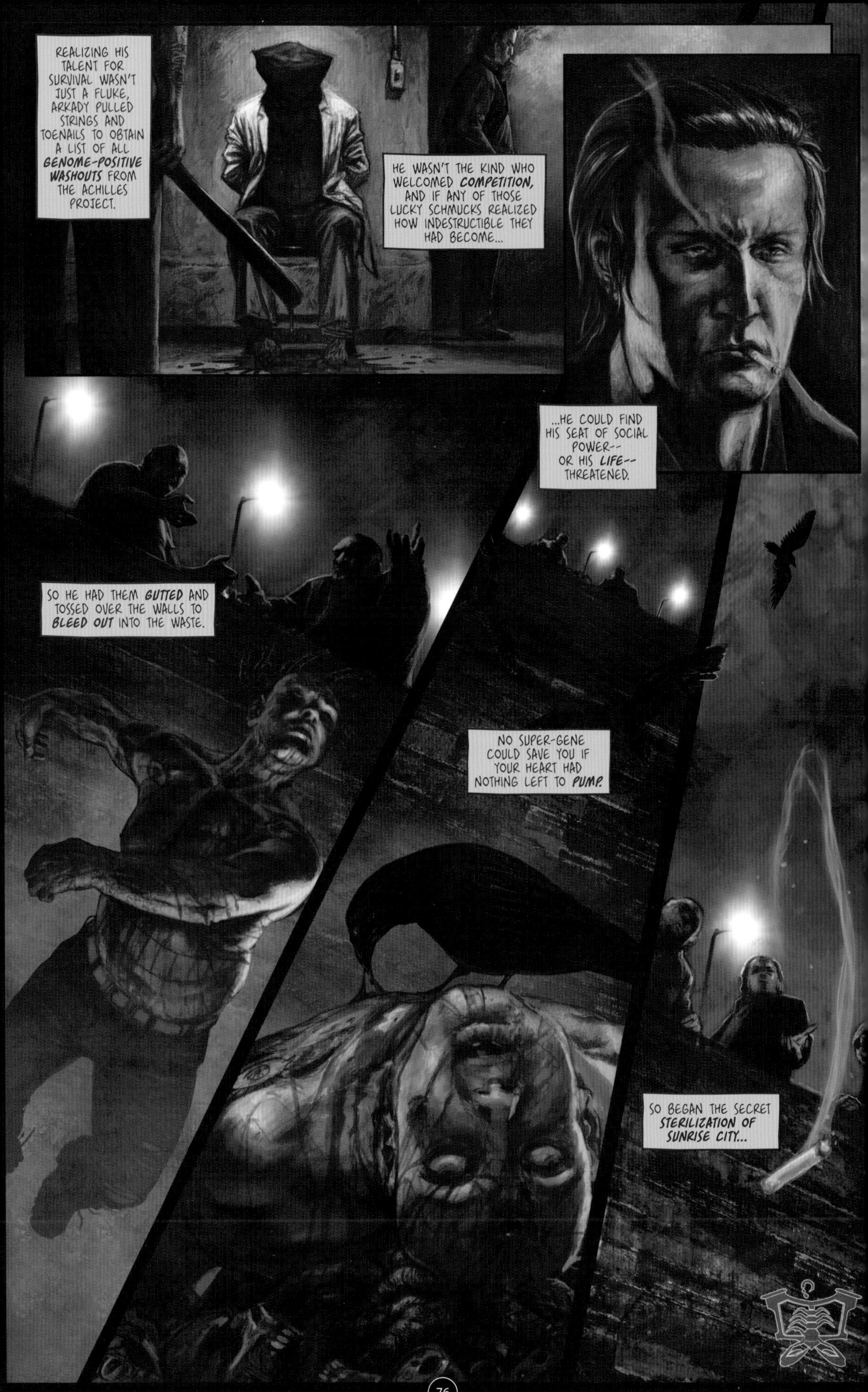
REALIZING HIS TALENT FOR SURVIVAL WASN'T JUST A FLUKE, ARKADY PULLED STRINGS AND TOENAILS TO OBTAIN A LIST OF ALL GENOME-POSITIVE WASHOUTS FROM THE ACHILLES PROJECT.
HE WASN'T THE KIND WHO WELCOMED COMPETITION, AND IF ANY OF THOSE LUCKY SCHMUCKS REALIZED HOW INDESTRUCTIBLE THEY HAD BECOME...
...HE COULD FIND HIS SEAT OF SOCIAL POWER-- OR HIS LIFE-- THREATENED.
SO HE HAD THEM GUTTED AND TOSSED OVER THE WALLS TO BLEED OUT INTO THE WASTE.
NO SUPER-GENE COULD SAVE YOU IF YOUR HEART HAD NOTHING LEFT TO PUMP.
SO BEGAN THE SECRET STERILIZATION OF SUNRISE CITY...

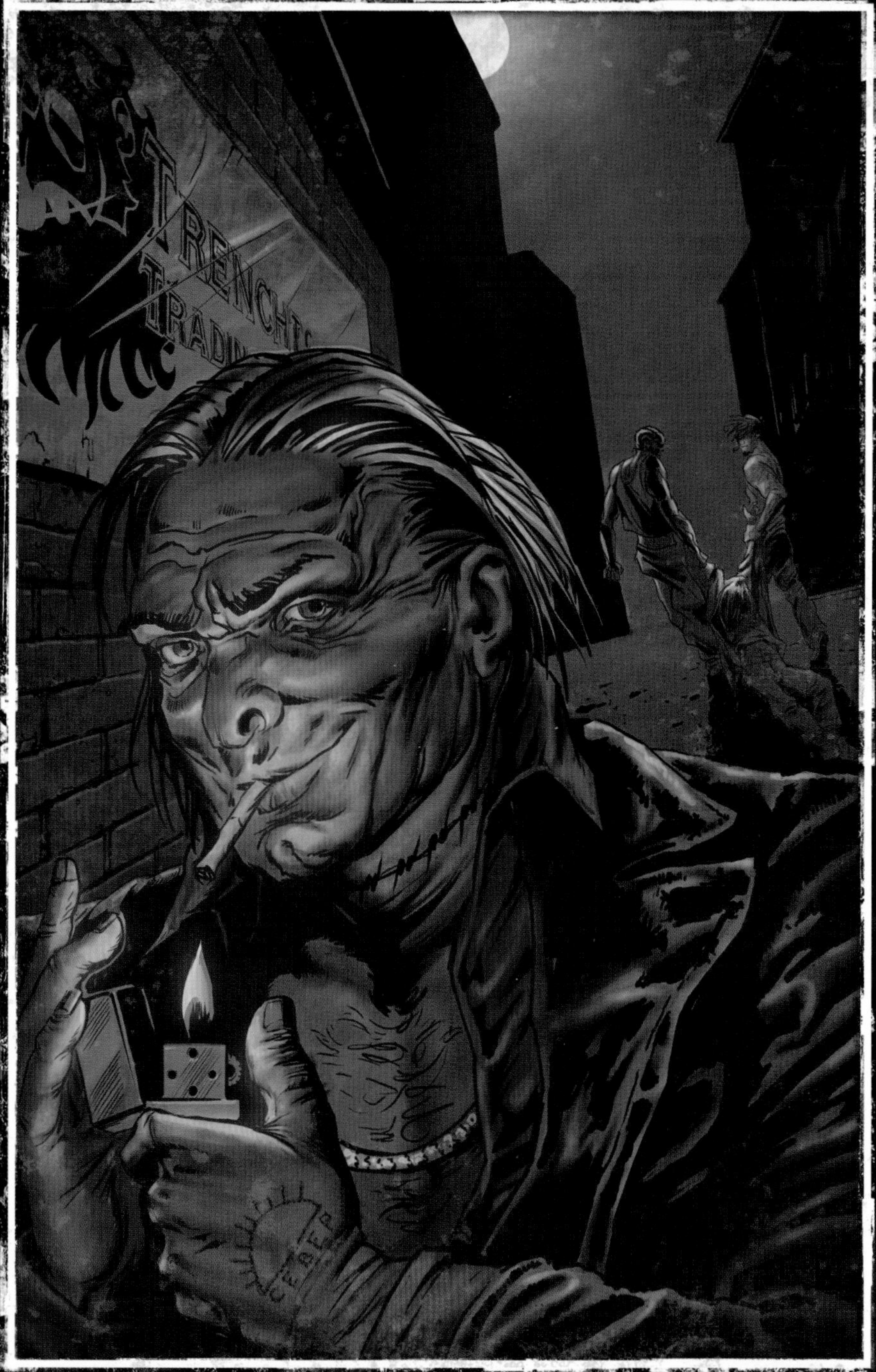

Pilot is laid in the tomb.

10

CHAPTER TEN: *Machtpolitik*

Illustrated by
Trevor Hairsine

Colors by
Alexey Sklarov

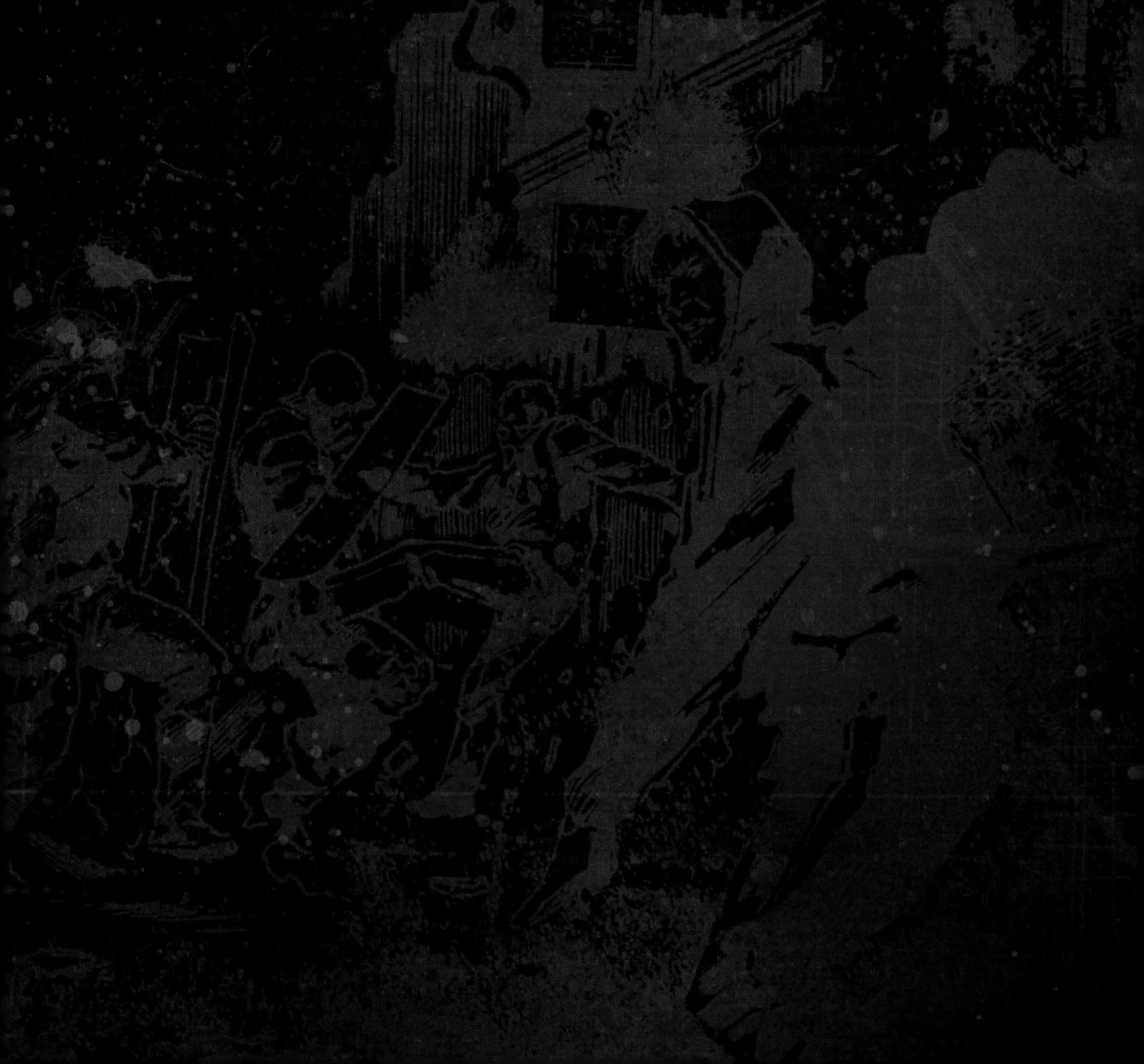

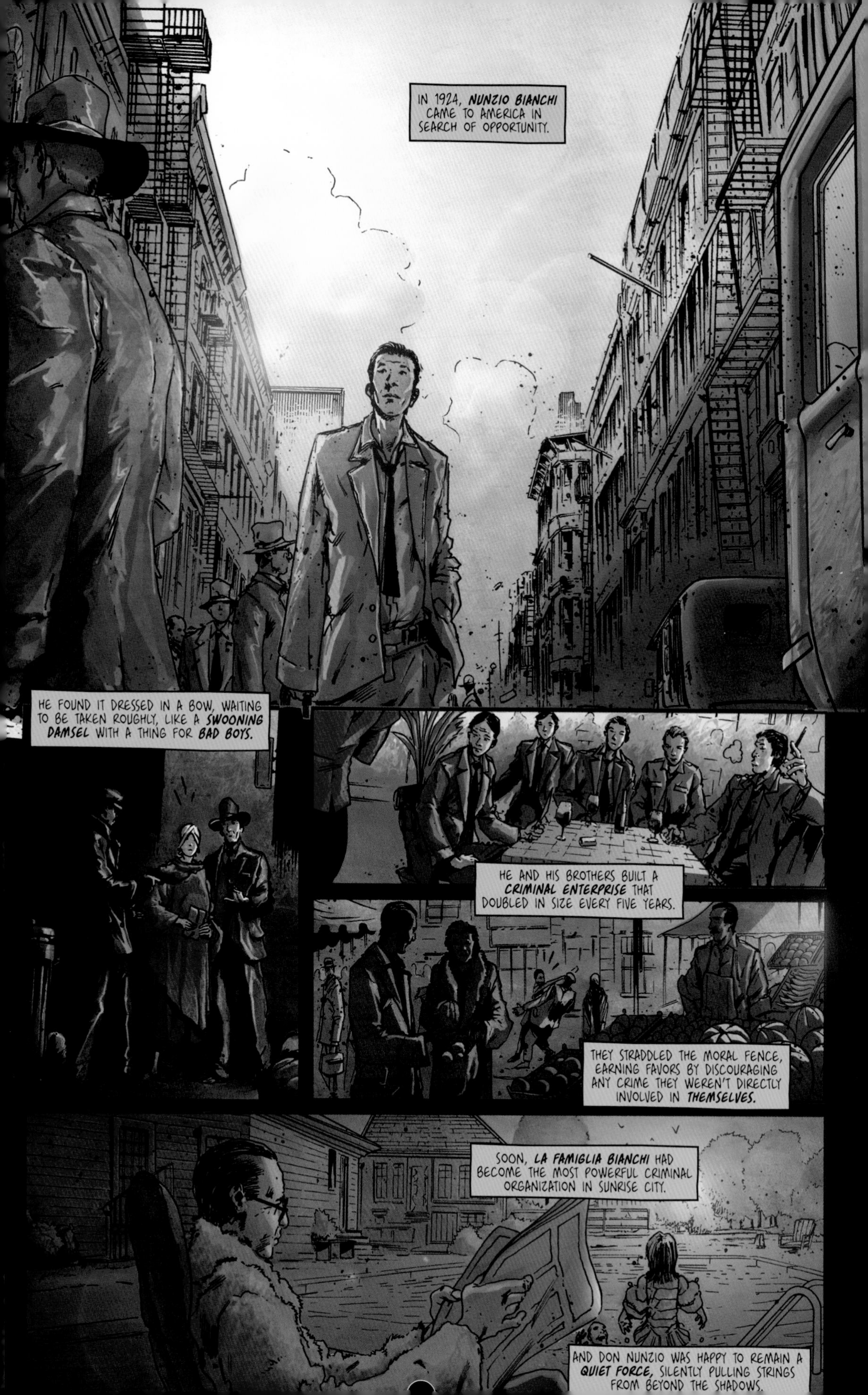
IN 1924, NUNZIO BIANCHI CAME TO AMERICA IN SEARCH OF OPPORTUNITY.
HE FOUND IT DRESSED IN A BOW, WAITING TO BE TAKEN ROUGHLY, LIKE A SWOONING DAMSEL WITH A THING FOR BAD BOYS.
HE AND HIS BROTHERS BUILT A CRIMINAL ENTERPRISE THAT DOUBLED IN SIZE EVERY FIVE YEARS.
THEY STRADDLED THE MORAL FENCE, EARNING FAVORS BY DISCOURAGING ANY CRIME THEY WEREN'T DIRECTLY INVOLVED IN THEMSELVES.
SOON, LA FAMIGLIA BIANCHI HAD BECOME THE MOST POWERFUL CRIMINAL ORGANIZATION IN SUNRISE CITY.
AND DON NUNZIO WAS HAPPY TO REMAIN A QUIET FORCE, SILENTLY PULLING STRINGS FROM BEYOND THE SHADOWS.

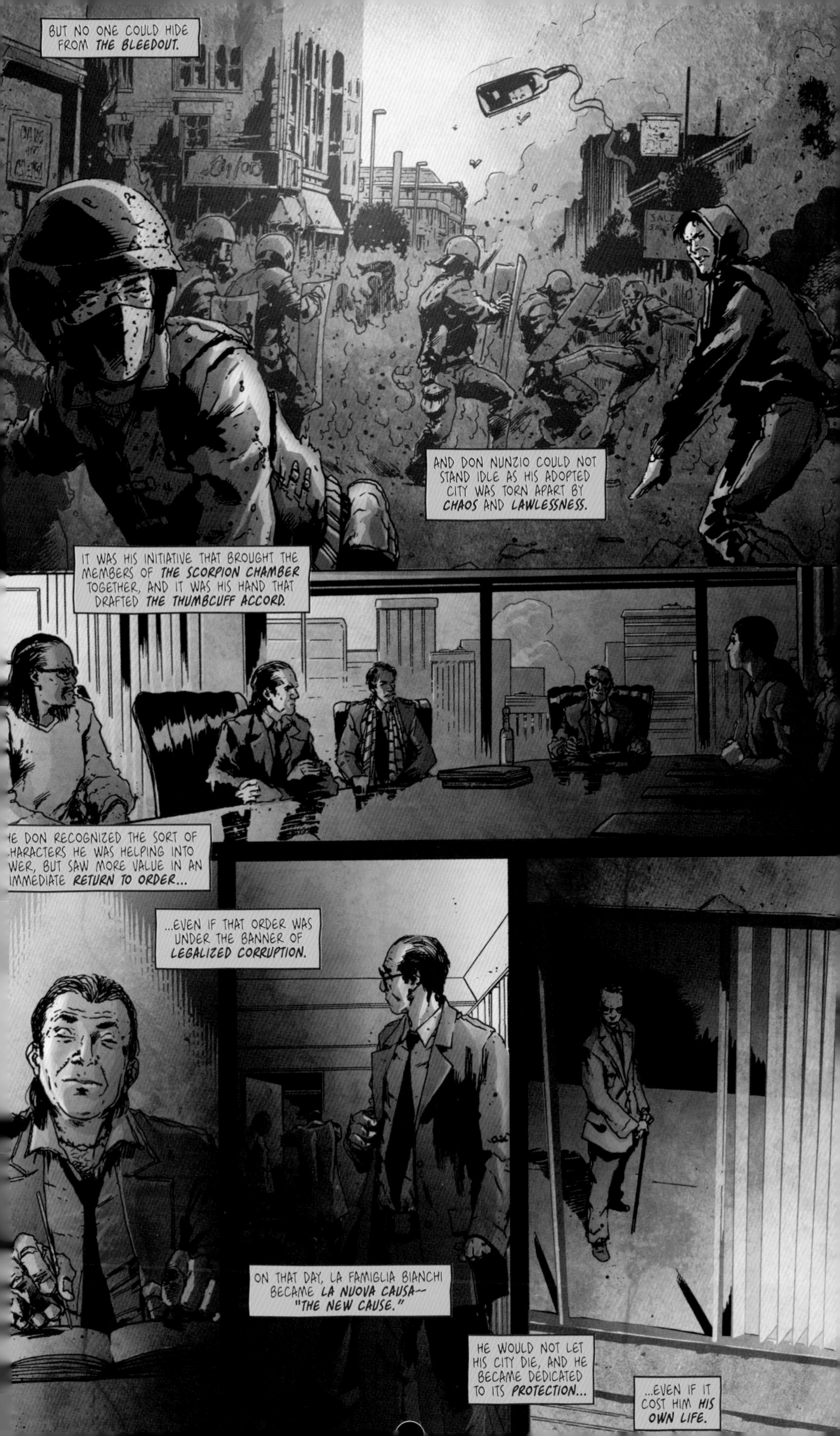

BUT NO ONE COULD HIDE FROM **THE BLEEDOUT.**
AND DON NUNZIO COULD NOT STAND IDLE AS HIS ADOPTED CITY WAS TORN APART BY **CHAOS** AND **LAWLESSNESS.**
IT WAS HIS INITIATIVE THAT BROUGHT THE MEMBERS OF **THE SCORPION CHAMBER** TOGETHER, AND IT WAS HIS HAND THAT DRAFTED **THE THUMBCUFF ACCORD.**
E DON RECOGNIZED THE SORT OF HARACTERS HE WAS HELPING INTO WER, BUT SAW MORE VALUE IN AN IMMEDIATE **RETURN TO ORDER...**
...EVEN IF THAT ORDER WAS UNDER THE BANNER OF **LEGALIZED CORRUPTION.**
ON THAT DAY, LA FAMIGLIA BIANCHI BECAME **LA NUOVA CAUSA--** **"THE NEW CAUSE."**
HE WOULD NOT LET HIS CITY DIE, AND HE BECAME DEDICATED TO ITS **PROTECTION...**
...EVEN IF IT COST HIM **HIS OWN LIFE.**

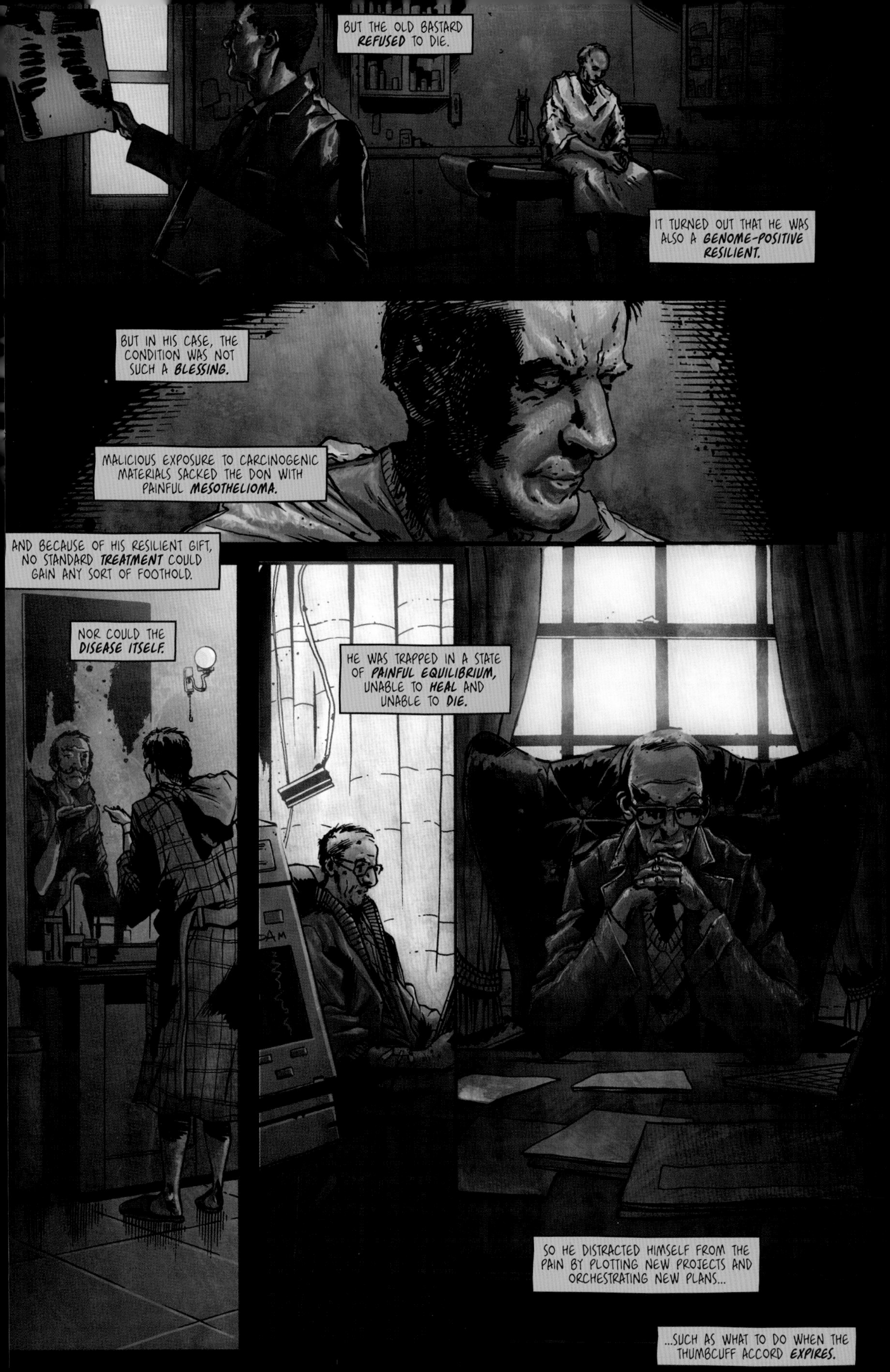
BUT THE OLD BASTARD REFUSED TO DIE.
IT TURNED OUT THAT HE WAS ALSO A GENOME-POSITIVE RESILIENT.
BUT IN HIS CASE, THE CONDITION WAS NOT SUCH A BLESSING.
MALICIOUS EXPOSURE TO CARCINOGENIC MATERIALS SACKED THE DON WITH PAINFUL MESOTHELIOMA.
AND BECAUSE OF HIS RESILIENT GIFT, NO STANDARD TREATMENT COULD GAIN ANY SORT OF FOOTHOLD.
NOR COULD THE DISEASE ITSELF.
HE WAS TRAPPED IN A STATE OF PAINFUL EQUILIBRIUM, UNABLE TO HEAL AND UNABLE TO DIE.
SO HE DISTRACTED HIMSELF FROM THE PAIN BY PLOTTING NEW PROJECTS AND ORCHESTRATING NEW PLANS...
...SUCH AS WHAT TO DO WHEN THE THUMBCUFF ACCORD EXPIRES.

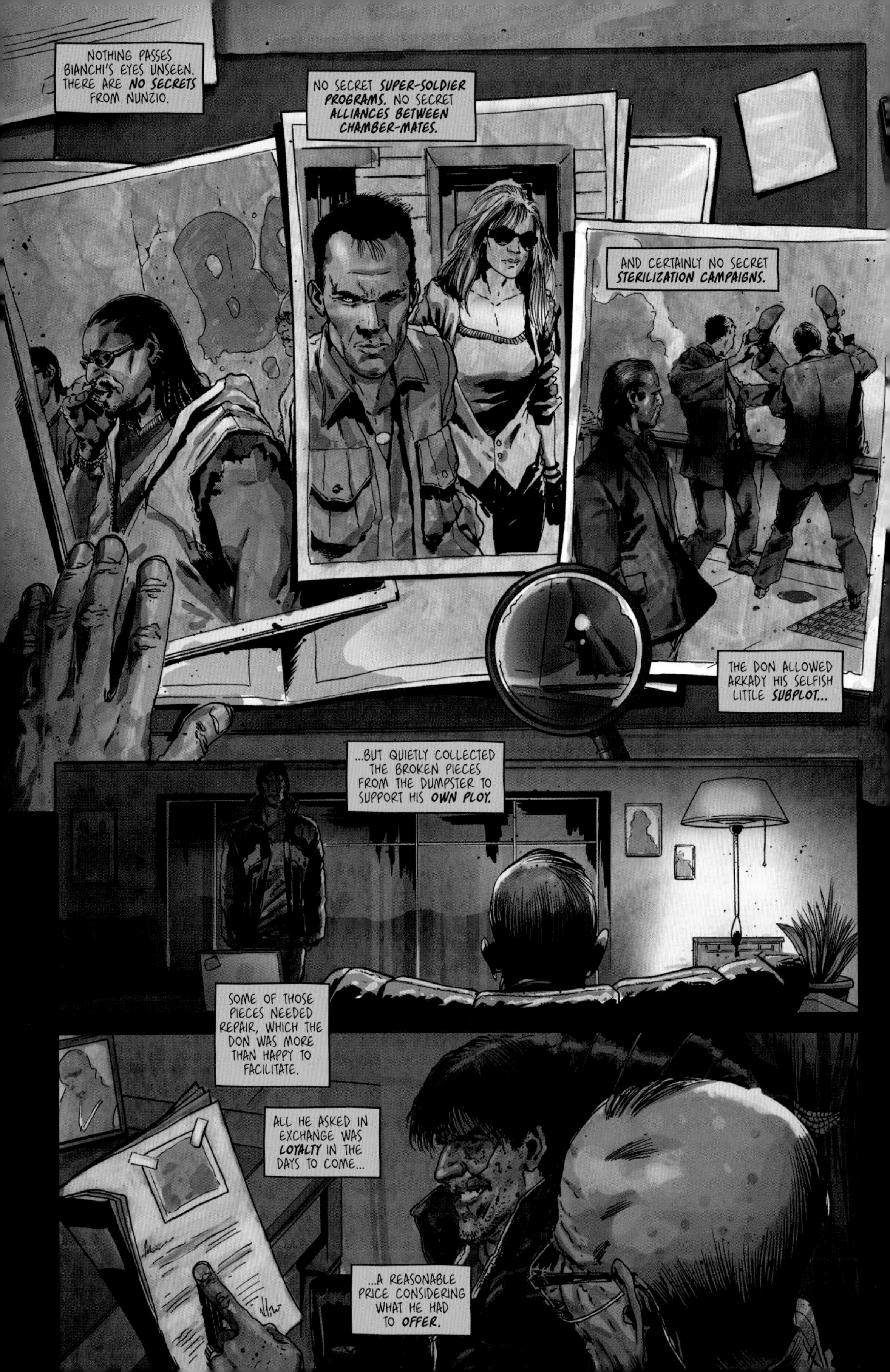
NOTHING PASSES BIANCHI'S EYES UNSEEN. THERE ARE NO SECRETS FROM NUNZIO.
NO SECRET SUPER-SOLDIER PROGRAMS. NO SECRET ALLIANCES BETWEEN CHAMBER-MATES.
AND CERTAINLY NO SECRET STERILIZATION CAMPAIGNS.
THE DON ALLOWED ARKADY HIS SELFISH LITTLE SUBPLOT...
...BUT QUIETLY COLLECTED THE BROKEN PIECES FROM THE DUMPSTER TO SUPPORT HIS OWN PLOY.
SOME OF THOSE PIECES NEEDED REPAIR, WHICH THE DON WAS MORE THAN HAPPY TO FACILITATE.
ALL HE ASKED IN EXCHANGE WAS LOYALTY IN THE DAYS TO COME...
...A REASONABLE PRICE CONSIDERING WHAT HE HAD TO OFFER.

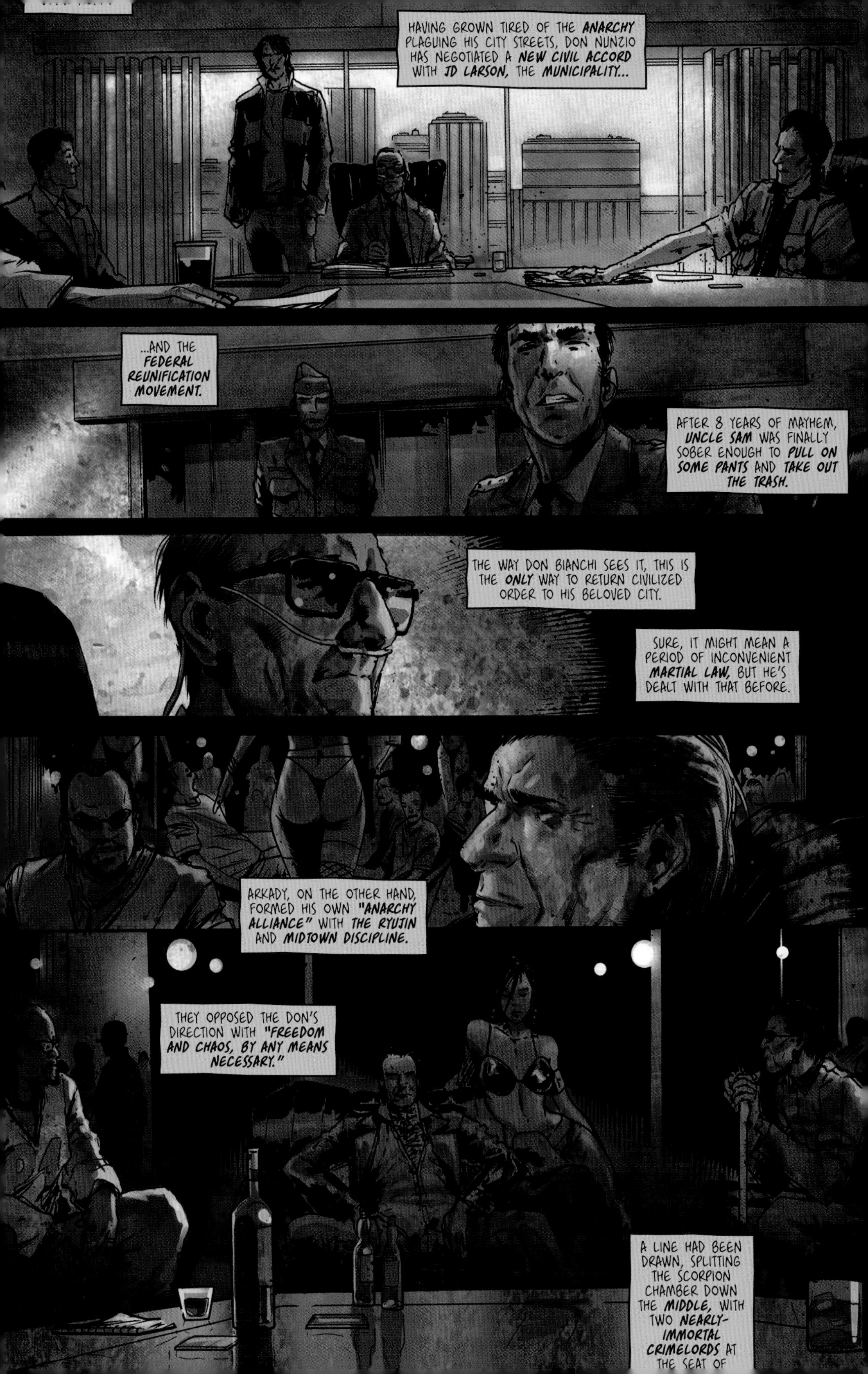
HAVING GROWN TIRED OF THE ANARCHY PLAGUING HIS CITY STREETS, DON NUNZIO HAS NEGOTIATED A NEW CIVIL ACCORD WITH JD LARSON, THE MUNICIPALITY...
...AND THE FEDERAL REUNIFICATION MOVEMENT.
AFTER 8 YEARS OF MAYHEM, UNCLE SAM WAS FINALLY SOBER ENOUGH TO PULL ON SOME PANTS AND TAKE OUT THE TRASH.
THE WAY DON BIANCHI SEES IT, THIS IS THE ONLY WAY TO RETURN CIVILIZED ORDER TO HIS BELOVED CITY.
SURE, IT MIGHT MEAN A PERIOD OF INCONVENIENT MARTIAL LAW, BUT HE'S DEALT WITH THAT BEFORE.
ARKADY, ON THE OTHER HAND, FORMED HIS OWN "ANARCHY ALLIANCE" WITH THE RYUJIN AND MIDTOWN DISCIPLINE.
THEY OPPOSED THE DON'S DIRECTION WITH "FREEDOM AND CHAOS, BY ANY MEANS NECESSARY."
A LINE HAD BEEN DRAWN, SPLITTING THE SCORPION CHAMBER DOWN THE MIDDLE, WITH TWO NEARLY-IMMORTAL CRIMELORDS AT THE SEAT OF

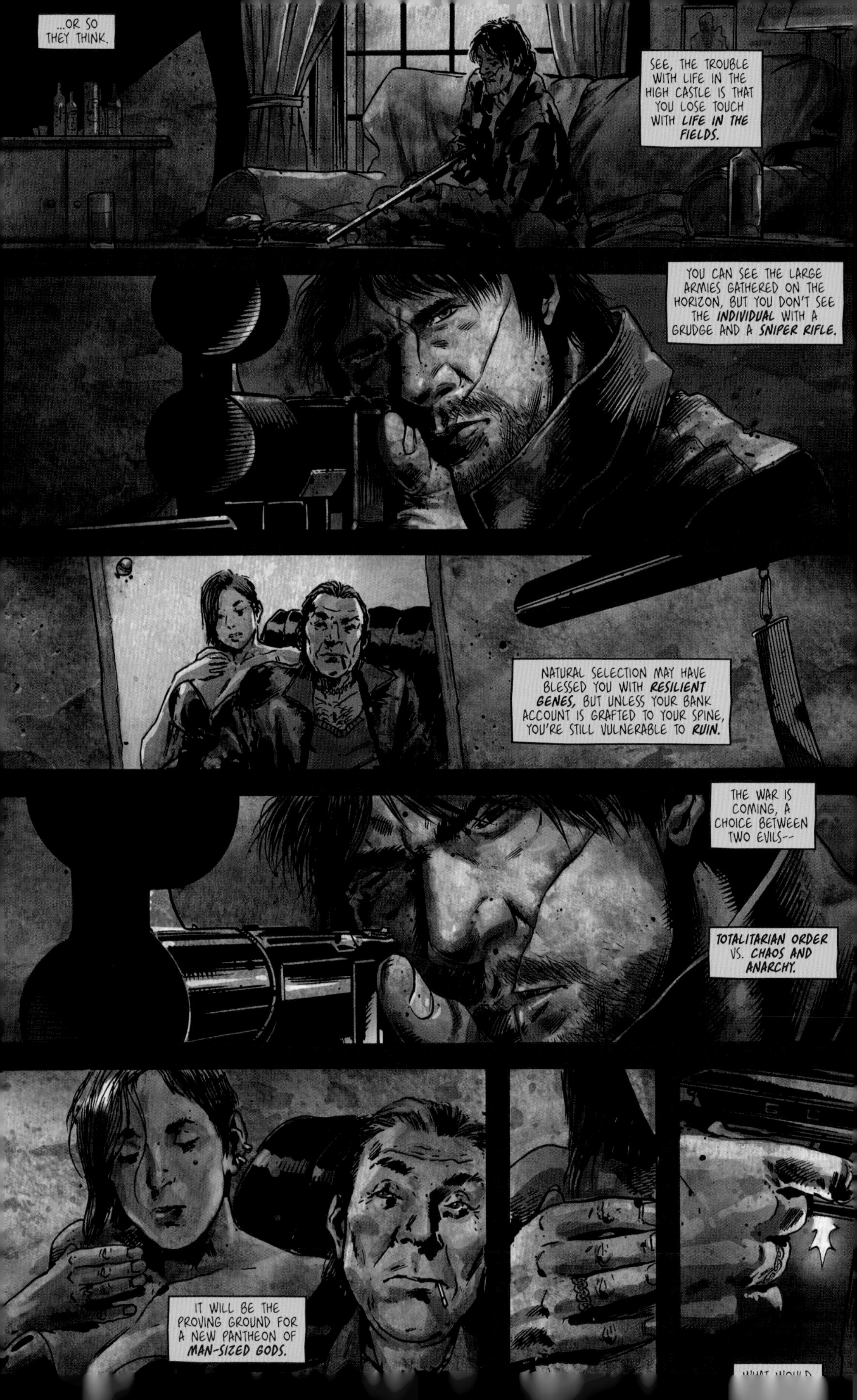
...OR SO THEY THINK.
SEE, THE TROUBLE WITH LIFE IN THE HIGH CASTLE IS THAT YOU LOSE TOUCH WITH ***LIFE IN THE FIELDS.***
YOU CAN SEE THE LARGE ARMIES GATHERED ON THE HORIZON, BUT YOU DON'T SEE THE ***INDIVIDUAL*** WITH A GRUDGE AND A ***SNIPER RIFLE.***
NATURAL SELECTION MAY HAVE BLESSED YOU WITH ***RESILIENT GENES,*** BUT UNLESS YOUR BANK ACCOUNT IS GRAFTED TO YOUR SPINE, YOU'RE STILL VULNERABLE TO ***RUIN.***
THE WAR IS COMING, A CHOICE BETWEEN TWO EVILS--
TOTALITARIAN ORDER VS. ***CHAOS AND ANARCHY.***
IT WILL BE THE PROVING GROUND FOR A NEW PANTHEON OF ***MAN-SIZED GODS.***

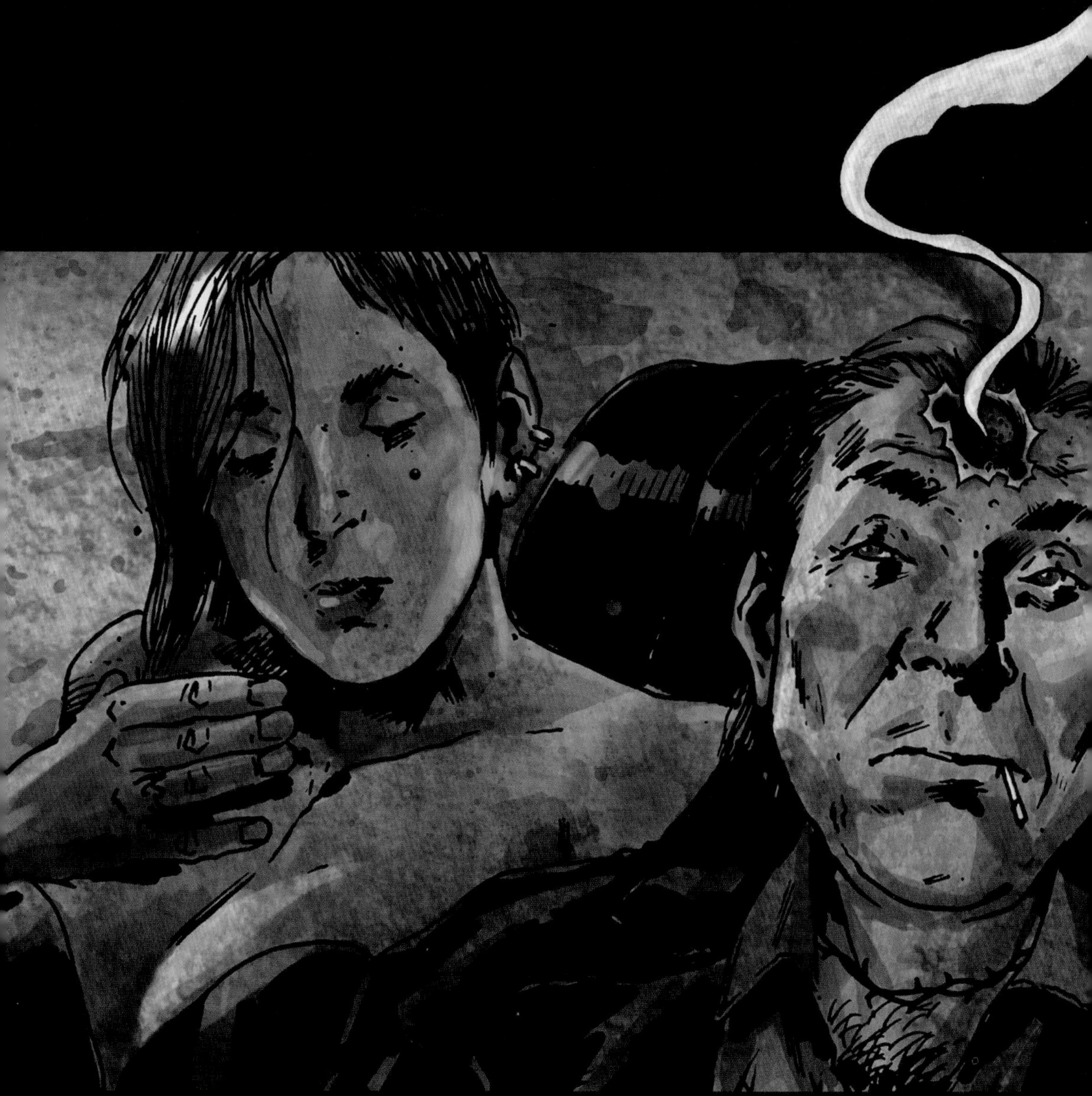

END BOOK ONE

THROUGH RUINATION

A Short Story

The following journal entries were collected from a series of loose sheets and notebooks discovered in an abandoned apartment building during the construction of the inner security walls containing downtown Sunrise City. Despite unspecific dates and missing pages, the entries have been arranged to suit the most logical sequence of events.

December 23rd

I think Connie knows about Meghan, or at the very least suspects something. She's been extra bitchy lately, especially whenever I mention stopping off at Eric's bar, where Meghan happens to work. She's been on edge ever since her brother's luxury car dealership closed down. I told her that in this economy, it was bound to happen -- on the necessity/comfort/luxury scale, luxury is the first thing to go. It's not like anyone *NEEDS* a 100k car when an 18k car can get you there just as well. She asked what my job as a web developer would be considered. I told her it's a comfort -- when times are tight, people need an affordable escape from their worries, and these days the Internet is the quickest and most affordable distraction. Except for drugs and alcohol, she pointed out, but I reminded her how well Eric's bar is doing these days. That ended the conversation dead.

February 10th

Joey had a little scare at school today. No one bothered to inform the substitute of Joey's diabetes, and he couldn't help himself when one of the other kids passed out birthday cupcakes to the class. About an hour later, he passed out on his way to the bathroom. The school nurse knew to check his blood sugar and administer a correction, but there was a little concern that he might have damaged his pump in the fall. He's fine now, but Connie is a wreck. She still votes for homeschooling, but I don't want a shut-in for a son. We have this same argument once a week, it seems.

March 2nd

Everybody is talking about the North Sea tsunamis like it's the end of the world or something. Gas prices spiked because of the many oil rigs that were severed by the initial quake and subsequent waves. They say the spill is worse than the Gulf disaster. I have to reassure Connie that the planet is not falling apart. She asked what we'd do if something like that were to hit our city. I told her that's a crazy thing to worry about, and that I'd rather not live in fear of the ridiculous. She got pissed and threw a wine glass at me, so I left the house. At least Meghan doesn't drag a black cloud around with her everywhere.

May 16th

Gas prices are still going up, even though the whole North Sea spill was months ago. It's affecting everything – airline tickets, our utility bills, postage rates, even groceries seem to be costing an arm and a leg each week. I understand that it takes gas to get those goods to the shelf, but all this price-jacking seems to be a little out of control.

June 3rd

I just spent $5.97 for regular unleaded today -- almost $85 to fill the tank! Donald next door says he spent over $100 filling up his SUV yesterday, and he does that once a week! I'm no fan of federal regulation, but Washington needs to do something. We're being held hostage by rich Middle Eastern billionaires who think they can just lead us around like a hungry mule with a carrot on a string. They need to realize we can grow our own goddamn carrots.

July 27th

We lost another client today. From what I understand, they had to do some "restructuring" that included about 350 layoffs. That's two big clients in three weeks. I've even heard rumors that our investors are looking to sell the studio but haven't been able to find any interested buyers. Reminder to self: check the status of our 401k. And update the resume.

August 9th

Shit. Pink slip. Me and forty-three others in this office. I hear they completely closed the studio in Singapore. Connie is going to freak. But hey -- at least we don't live in Singapore. The economy over there is even worse than over here.

November 16th

Three months and four recruiters and not even a follow-up phone interview. No one is hiring. In fact, most places are laying people off. Connie has no idea how tight things are getting. I haven't even told my parents, not after the airline cancelled their anniversary tickets because of 'route consolidation'. Man, Christmas is going to suck this year.

January 2nd

Things just took a surreal turn. Just as gas prices were about to hit a ridiculous $10 per gallon, ten OPEC nations declared critical financial issues because -- get this -- "New oil has become prohibitively difficult to find." Apparently, they've been exporting from their reserves for the past six months, and they claim those reserves are nearly depleted. I'm not sure how that's possible, considering the billions of barrels they supposedly had stored away, but that's what they're claiming. And that's why the world economy has been in such a terrible nosedive -- the rising gas prices aren't a *symptom* of the global recession, they are the *cause*. Nobody's really sure what this means right now, but the President put FEMA on alert and issued a price freeze on all goods across the board. I should have bought that hybrid when I could still afford it.

January 12th

Russia, China, South America, and Canada have now stepped forward to claim similar oil production issues, but US oil remains tight-lipped, of course. Other than a few earthquakes in the Middle East, things have been eerily quiet. The streets are growing more and more deserted as people start conserving gas. Public transit is still running, but only because of government imposed stability measures while the real extent of the situation is investigated. FEMA calls it "preparedness," but it feels like the calm before a storm. Connie has started popping Ambien with wine. Even Meghan has started to freak out a bit. We spend more time hypothesizing emergency scenarios than doing anything intimate. I have started stockpiling Joey's insulin, though, just in case.

February 16th

You know that moment of silence right before an explosion, like time itself is holding its breath? Well that moment just ended. According to some global committee of geologists, the planet has indeed been "bled dry" -- their words. Somehow, without warning or explanation, all of the accessible oil has disappeared. All that's left is what remains in reserve storage, and even that is practically evaporating despite impractically high prices. They aren't offering any explanations, just scads of data showing where they thought we were in terms of accessible volume and where we seem to actually be today. The bar graph looks like the downside of Mt. Everest. As hard as the situation is to comprehend, it didn't take long for panic riots to rip through the streets. I was at Eric's bar when the report came out, and it was all I could do to get back home in one piece. It's like everyone lost their mind at the exact same time. It was crazy, like a zombie movie, only everyone was still alive, and terrified of… shit, I don't know. The future? Each other? Apparently, the same thing happened in pretty much every city on the planet. The world went absolutely insane for six straight days.

The streets look like they've been ripped apart by a tidal wave -- storefronts smashed, trash and debris everywhere, some cars are still on fire... Eric's bar was burned to the ground by looters, so he asked if he could move in with us until he gets things straightened out with the insurance company. That could be months, if ever, but to my surprise, Connie insisted yes. I guess not everyone is devolving into savagery.

February 18th

Eric's situation got me thinking about our own cash. I canceled our insurance -- what's the point of paying for some future emergency when we're facing one right now? Besides, two of the biggest national insurance providers declared bankruptcy just last week, along with a handful of banks. I tried to cash in our retirement funds, but the global stock market has pretty much tanked. I feel sick thinking about how much money I sank into those funds over the years. I should have stuffed it in a goddamn mattress instead.

March

Executive Order 11921 has officially been issued, giving FEMA control over just about everything -- all methods of production and distribution, all energy sources, all wages, salaries, credit, and the flow of every single dollar in the country. Seriously. The President won't use the actual phrase, but it's martial law on a national scale. Every single registered guardsman and soldier on the books has been deployed to lock down the domestic chaos, all 2.8 million of them. But it's still not enough to secure the other 320 million Americans terrified by their own shadow. They're just too spread out, barely able to keep things quiet after dark, when the looting is at its worst.

Well, patience pays off, sorta -- I finally found a job. FEMA started recruiting able-bodied workers to help install solar panels and turbines on the rooftops to compensate for the reduced output from the city's coal-based region of the grid. Without sufficient diesel to run the mining equipment, coal production has dropped, which has affected nearly half of the nation's electrical supply. Right now, we've got barely enough power to keep lights and electricity on for rationed hours. There's some concern over the manufacturing costs of the solar panels and turbine parts, but as long as FEMA keeps food on my table, that's not my problem.

More and more stores and restaurants are closing because of produce shortages, and for every one of them, ten new rooftop gardens and bathtub stills pop up. Mostly home-brewed beer, but there have already been a number of fires and explosions from amateur biodiesel stills. FEMA is really cracking down on those lunatics, much harder than the bootleggers.

Another long train of people leaving the city on foot today. It's like a scene out of the Bible. Connie wants to leave too, but she's not thinking it through. I told her with no gas for the car, we'd only be able to take what we can carry. Is she really ready to abandon everything we own? She said she doesn't care, that we should sell it all, but nobody's buying anything other than food these days. I think she believes I only want to stay around for Meghan. I'd tell her how ridiculous that was, if she'd just come out and say it. I pulled Eric aside, and he told me Meghan moved in with her brother,

Raphael. He's a dick, but he runs a garage full of thugs and ex-cons, the kind of people who are rarely messed with. In fact, they're usually the ones causing the trouble. I'm pretty sure I can check her off my list of worries.

April

The military has been rationing food pretty tightly lately. People have been orderly so far, but as soon as their looted stockpiles start running out, things might not remain so calm. Apartment security has been difficult to maintain, and we've had to really keep an eye on our own neighbors. The whole building is stressed -- one guy downstairs has been blasting "The End" by The Doors on infinite loop for two days now, and he won't answer no matter how loud we knock and scream.

TV options have boiled down to 24-hour news or reruns. Networks are even starting to drop off the air as staff is reduced due to lack of advertising dollars. Physical mail is still running, but it isn't at all reliable. No one is allowed to send any sort of goods for the time being. Phone service works, but cell tower traffic has been capped by FEMA. Even internet access has become limited because of all the bankrupt ISPs, brown outs, and increased traffic. Airports around the world have become battle zones and refugee camps as people try in vain to reach somewhere safe to settle. There seem to be a million theories speculating on what happened to the oil, but no one knows, and no one has the means of effectively investigating. "What happened?" isn't quite as important today as "What do we do now?"

Someone finally kicked in the door downstairs to shut up that goddamn music, only to find the occupant had committed suicide days earlier. Now the whole building smells like death.

FEMA started rationing water today. Apparently, one of the main lines broke somewhere underground, but it has been a massive, expensive task to dig through the pavement to make the repair. All of that frustrating road work that had once been so common is now suddenly a monumental catastrophe. They would have had this fixed in a day before the Bleedout, but now they won't even tell us how long it will be before rationing is lifted.

Dead vehicles are starting to clutter the city. Cars are becoming makeshift homes for people who can no longer pay rent. Parking lots are becoming camp grounds. FEMA may have restricted all pending eviction processes, but a lot of angry landowners aren't making it comfortable for deadbeat tenants, ignoring upkeep costs and repairs, leaving those complications to the very tenants who can't afford to fix them. Many apartment buildings are reverting back to bank ownership, but they're no better landlords. The whole city is becoming a slum.

That's it -- I'm completely broke. Zero cash. I used to live a credit-based, virtual-money lifestyle, and now I've got no actual cash to show for it. All of my investments dried up months ago. Banks have been capping withdrawals at $200 per week, but even those accounts are empty. The only functional credit cards are those whose banks haven't closed, but those come with outrageous 40% interest rates. We're now living completely off of FEMA rations and what useless possessions we still own. I've been trading books and DVDs for extra food tickets, but I'm down to crap no one wants.

May

Mom called today. Looters invaded the farm and Dad was injured. She didn't go into any detail, but said he hasn't been able to get out of bed since. She sounded worried, so I told Connie and Joey to pack their bags -- we're moving to the farm.

What used to be a three hour drive took two-and-a-half days on foot. We might have made better time, but we had to monitor Joey's exercise, diet, and dosage. Eric and I took shifts carrying him on our backs, which slowed us down a bit, but honestly, it was a nice trek. I might even say "fun," like an overdue camping trip. I even saw Connie smile once or twice, but I think she was just happy to be out of the city.

Mom was very happy to see us. Dad even hobbled out of bed to greet us at the door. Apparently, some meth addicts from a nearby trailer park broke into the house and stabbed him in the leg when he tried to scare them off with a golf club. I asked why he didn't scare them off with a shotgun, and he said he had accidentally left it in the hen house that day. I told him the hens shouldn't need that much motivation to lay eggs.

June

Even out here in the sticks, life is adjusting to the Bleedout. Aside from the occasional pillaging, most of the surrounding farms have had to scale back production to what little they can harvest by hand. All their fancy tilling machines and tools that helped them cover acres at a time are now derelicts resting in the barn. Dad said they've been able to fire a couple up on biodiesel, but the problem is distilling the biodiesel in large enough quantities. There's one guy fourteen miles east who mills and sells soy-fuel, but it's incredibly expensive and strictly distributed by FEMA. So they travel on horseback and farm by hand, selling what they can't store to local shops. It really is a return to the Old West. And frankly, it doesn't seem like too bad a life...

Today, Mom hosted a potluck for ten of our closest neighbors, who are actually spread out over a four mile radius. They're good people, each growing a different crop so that everyone has a nice variety of goods to barter. There's a pretty good head of livestock available, and the river offers some good fishing. The local sheriff even comes out from town eight miles away to occasionally check on things, but it's a good twenty-minute gallop on horseback, so the neighbors are trusted to defend themselves. Good old frontier justice.

Fall

We found Joey passed out in the cornfield yesterday. At some point, his pump had failed, code A33, and God only knows how long he had been going without a dose. We gave him a correction, but he's still pretty sick. Lucille from the next farm down has some nursing experience, and she says she can help normalize him, but we'll either need a new pump or more syringes. The closest FEMA health station is a few hours away, so Eric and I will head out on horseback.

The clinic was a madhouse. I've seen crowded downtown emergency rooms, but never thought a small town hospital could be so busy. One of the orderlies explained that their supply convoy had been hijacked, and they were already running low on stuff, including insulin and syringes. He gave me a handful of needles and one vial of long-acting formula, but said that's all he could spare. I asked where I could get more, and he suggested venturing back into the city. After all, they're the ones who've been hijacking the shipments in the first place.

I told Eric to take the syringes back to the farm while I ride into the city. I've gotten a few messages from Meghan since we relocated, and she says things have stabilized a bit downtown since we left. Maybe her brother can help me get what Joey needs. It might take a couple of days to get there and back, so Eric will have to watch out for the farm in the meantime. He asked what he should tell Connie. I said to tell her I'm doing what needs to be done. Just leave out the part about seeing Meghan.

It only took a day to get to the city on horseback. Navigating the suburbs was like touring a long-forgotten warzone -- barred windows, burnt out gas stations, etc. It's amazing how much damage a wave of panic and violence can leave behind when no one can afford to make repairs. Entering the city itself was like stepping closer to ground zero -- the degree of ruin grew exponentially the closer I got to downtown. Yet it was strangely abandoned and quiet. At one point, I was stopped at some sort of police checkpoint and asked my business. I told them I was trying to reach Raphael's Garage on 9th and they waved me right through. I guess Raphael's reputation has grown.

Raphael's Garage stands in the center of the block like a fortress of hope in a field of blackened decay. The thug watching the front door tried to spook me off the horse at gunpoint, but Meghan stepped out to yank his leash. She looked fantastic, clearly weathering the Bleedout without much worry. She said they have plenty to eat, and don't have to worry about looters any more. Most people know better than to invade the Garage. She took me inside to see Raphael, nodding approval to each of the thugs and cons we passed along the way. Raphael greeted me with a sneer, but welcomed me into his den of well-off criminals. He explained how the laws here have changed, and how gangs like his got together to boot FEMA out of town, paving the way for a new government of the fittest, strongest, and most heartless. There is a degree of order here, but it is based on fear. Fortunately, he told me that as long as Meghan vouched for me, I wouldn't have to worry about any of that. Thank God.

Meghan and I stayed up late catching up on the months past. I forgot how much I missed her. Pretty soon we ran out of things to talk about, but that just led to physical reminiscing. She felt as good as the first time I laid hands on her.

Raphael arranged a meeting with a pharmacist who might be able to get me a new pump and more syringes. I asked what he might want in return, but Raphael said not to worry about it, he's got it covered. Friends help friends, right?

Today I discovered where my limits fall. I'm not even sure I remember it all clearly, to be honest. We went to meet the pharmacist in what must have been the shadiest alley in the city, just me, Raphael, and one of Raphael's thugs, a huge guy named Cooz. I wasn't gonna ask where he picked up that nickname, but I wouldn't have remembered anyway. Somebody in the alley started shooting at us as soon as we showed up, and Cooz was dead before he even hit the ground. There was so much blood coming out of his body, it looked like he was shrinking, like a leaky waterbed. Raphael pulled me behind a dumpster for cover, but someone was already there waiting. I remember staring down the barrel of the stranger's handgun, thinking about Joey slipping into a coma because I never came home with his medicine. And then, apparently, I shit my pants and flipped out on the guy.

I remember roaring like a monster and wrestling the stranger for the gun. It felt like forever, but Raphael says it was only a minute long struggle that ended when the gun went off. I remember thinking the guy had simply surrendered, but his eyes had rolled back in his head and my hands were wet with his blood. Raphael says I threw up on him, but I don't remember that part. He had to carry me back to the Garage like a drunk.

The real pharmacist showed up at the Garage a few hours later. He was just some strung-out tweaker who apologized profusely for running away when he heard the gunshots. I was still pretty shaken up, but he gave me a brand new pump, two months worth of cartridges, and replacement batteries as restitution. I think he was more afraid of Raphael's wrath than mine, but I took the stuff gratefully.

Meghan thought I should stay another night to get my head on straight, but I told her I was already four days overdue, with another day's ride ahead. Joey needed this stuff a week ago. Before I could head out, Raphael made me a business offer: he'd pay nicely for fresh goods from the farm in exchange for ample medical supplies and hard-to-get goods from the city. My mind was still all over the place at that point, so I told him I'd have to think about it. I guess that was cool with him, since he just smiled and handed me the mugger's handgun, reloaded with fresh rounds. He said to ride safe -- I knew where to find him.

The ride home was quick, but not quick enough. Joey's condition became full-blown DKA and he slipped into a coma two days after I left. He stopped breathing six hours before I got home.

Winter

More snow today. River is starting to freeze. Should cover the rowboat.

Eric built a little greenhouse by the porch. It's nice.

Spring

Dad says he's going to set up a little biodiesel still in the barn, not enough to till the whole field, but enough to run the car in case of another emergency, maybe even enough to shuttle some goods to market and back.

Connie cleans Joey's room every day, as if waiting for him to come back from day camp. I can't stay in the house when she's like that.

I should have acted more surprised when I caught Eric and Connie in bed together. I don't even think they realized I was standing there in the doorway. They just kept going. I still don't think they know.

Dad's diesel still seems to work well enough that he invested in an old expeller press to make his own vegetable oil. It needs some work and parts, which he can't seem to find. I told him I might know a guy in the city who can help.

Summer

The landscape back to Raphael's Garage has grown even more ruined since my last visit. The streets and alleys are now clogged with junk and car wreckage, like makeshift barricades. I had to go a couple of miles out of my way to find an opening, and it was guarded by some rough-looking cops who weren't nearly as welcoming this time around. I'm not even sure they were real cops. They made me answer a million questions and told me I'd have to leave the horse. Somehow I'm not sure it will still be here when I get back.

I almost didn't recognize Raphael's place, now surrounded by concrete dividers and barbed wire, like some sort of prison facility. Fortunately, the guy out front recognized me this time and called Raph and Meghan out to meet me. Her smile was like a hit of laughing gas; I couldn't help but smile back. It's funny. Despite the depressing environment, I kinda felt like I was home again.

I told Raphael about Dad's unlicensed biodiesel still. He said he can get the parts I need, in exchange for a cut of the product. I told him the still probably wouldn't produce more than 10 gallons a week, but he asked what it would take to turn that into 100 gallons. I explained that it wasn't about the still, it was about growing the soy, and how much land that would take away from food crops. I also told him that by law we were only allowed 10 gallons for personal use, and that anything more than that could be subject to seizure by FEMA. We could even be arrested for intent to sell and distribute a federally controlled substance. Raphael laughed and said he knew all about the "Fascist Empire Masquerading as America" – those stupid laws are exactly why they tossed FEMA out of the city in the first place. I asked how we'd even get that much fuel there from the farm without being noticed. FEMA is pretty strict on licensed vehicle operation. Raph just chuckled and asked how many horses we've got. It's clear he isn't going to take no for an answer. He insisted I take an armed escort back with me for my protection, but I'm pretty sure they're to protect his own interests.

I was really hoping for some of Mom's usual hospitality when we got back to the farm, but it was clear our armed guests were there for no good reason. I explained Raphael's offer to Dad, and tried to convince him how valuable it could be to have a resource in the city, but he said we'd have to focus 100% of our effort on that fuel crop, which, he reminded me, was regulated by FEMA. We'd be breaking the law. I jokingly reminded him about Grandad's liquor stills during Prohibition, and how this kind of thing is in our blood, but he reminded me of how Grandad died in a speakeasy brawl trying to collect what he was owed. He eventually agreed to make a single large batch, as a thankful gesture, but that would have to be it.

We took 96 gallons back to the city by horse cart, but when we got there, the three escorts explained to Raphael that we had enough land to produce 200 gallons of fuel a week, easy. Apparently, that's why they were sent: to evaluate our setup. I told him that's crazy, we'd have to dedicate most of our field to that crop, and that there wouldn't be enough land left for food. Plus, we'd need three times as much manpower to harvest a crop that big. But Raphael just shrugged and said he'd throw in a couple extra cans of tuna fish each week. I told him that's not gonna help the rest of the community, but he said he didn't care. He said I should be thinking about my family, especially now that he knows where they live. End of discussion.

I asked Meghan if she had any suggestions for reasoning with her brother, but she said whatever sense of reason he used to have, which was never much, had gone out the window with the rest of the world. He had killed total strangers for less gain than what is at stake here. This biodiesel could put him in charge of a good number of city blocks. She thinks I should just do what he says and take advantage of the good pay, because honestly, as long as those three guys can lead Raphael back to the farm, my family is not safe. I asked if she would help me, but she just got dressed and left the bedroom.

Dad wasn't too happy to see me show up with armed escorts again, or to hear that our arrangement with Raphael was still in place. I told him he has no idea what kind of man Raphael is, or what kind of violence he can bring to this community. This biodiesel is liquid gold, and he doesn't care if he's gotta hurt or kill to get it. These three escorts aren't here to protect us from looters or FEMA, they're here to make sure we hold up our end of the bargain. And as long as Raphael knows where the farm is, nobody's safe. But I don't think Dad heard any of that. He gave me that disappointed look I've always hated. Goddammit.

At 2:00 am, I woke up to the worst racket out in the barn. Dad was taking the expeller press apart with a sledgehammer. I tried to get him to stop, but he figured that without the press, Raphael would be shit-out-of-luck. I told him Raphael wouldn't see it that way, but he wasn't listening to me. Unfortunately, he wouldn't listen to the escorts either, even when they showed up with guns in hand. One of them pulled out a cell phone to call Raphael, and that's when things got blurry. I don't know what got into his head, but Dad took a swing at one of them with the sledgehammer. Another one shot at him, which made me pull out the pistol Raphael gave me. I think I shot one, but the others started shooting back. I kept shooting, everyone was running and shooting. It sounded like a Chinese New Year parade for about twelve seconds. When the noise stopped, all three escorts were dead, I was out of bullets, and Eric was standing on the porch in his pajamas with a smoking shotgun in his hands. Dad was hit in the chest, too, still breathing, but with effort. I picked up the dead escort's cell phone to call nurse Lucille, but there was already a call in progress – Raphael was on the other end, and he heard the whole thing. I told him his guys were dead; too bad he doesn't know where the farm is now. I could almost hear him growl from the chest. All he said was, "Google maps, you dumb fuck," before hanging up.

At that moment, only one thought echoed through my brain --

"How could I have handled this situation differently?"

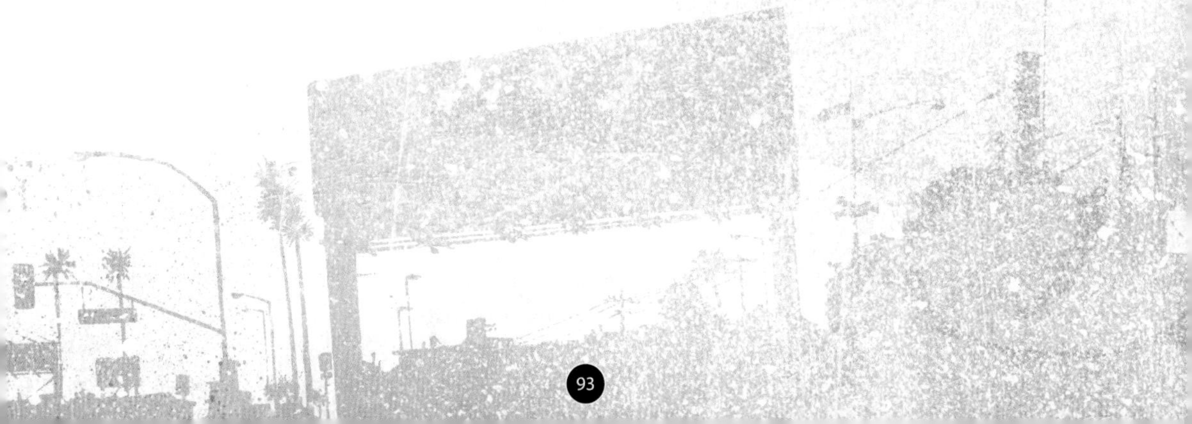

BLOOD ON THE STREET
Concept Art Gallery

Bleedout was created to provide back story for **CrimeCraft**, a free-to-play online video game in which players create characters, form gangs, and engage in fast-paced shootouts for cash and bragging rights. As an action-MMO, **CrimeCraft** exists as a persistent online world, offering a constantly changing experience to players from around the globe every day, 24/7. Players can live out their fantasies in this ever evolving virtual world, engaging in activities that would probably get them arrested in real life (hence the game's title). But these experiences needed a clear setting and story to give the players context and purpose.

As a major expansion to **CrimeCraft**, **Bleedout** addresses the key question driving the game's original design: "How did the world come to be like this?" From that single question, the creative vision flowed like an open wound. The story is delivered as a weekly episodic series, like an interactive television show, and runs for ten consecutive weeks.

Of the many challenges a video game producer faces every day, one of the most satisfying tasks is assembling and aligning the key talent to deliver the creative vision. We were creating a gritty world filled with heroes and villains, and in the case of Bleedout, that creative vision was truly a global endeavor. The development team resided in the Ukraine, while the production team worked in the United States, with additional artists contracted worldwide. It started with a producer and a writer, and then expanded to the art directors, concept artists, comic artists, game designers, line producers, sound designers and engineers, with everyone working toward a single vision and unified goal. The following pages contain just a small portion of the creative vision that went into designing the game.

Bleedout premiered online in December 2010, shattering our previous in-game population records, and the population of virtual criminals has continued to grow ever since.

—Michael Mendheim
*Executive Producer, **Bleedout***

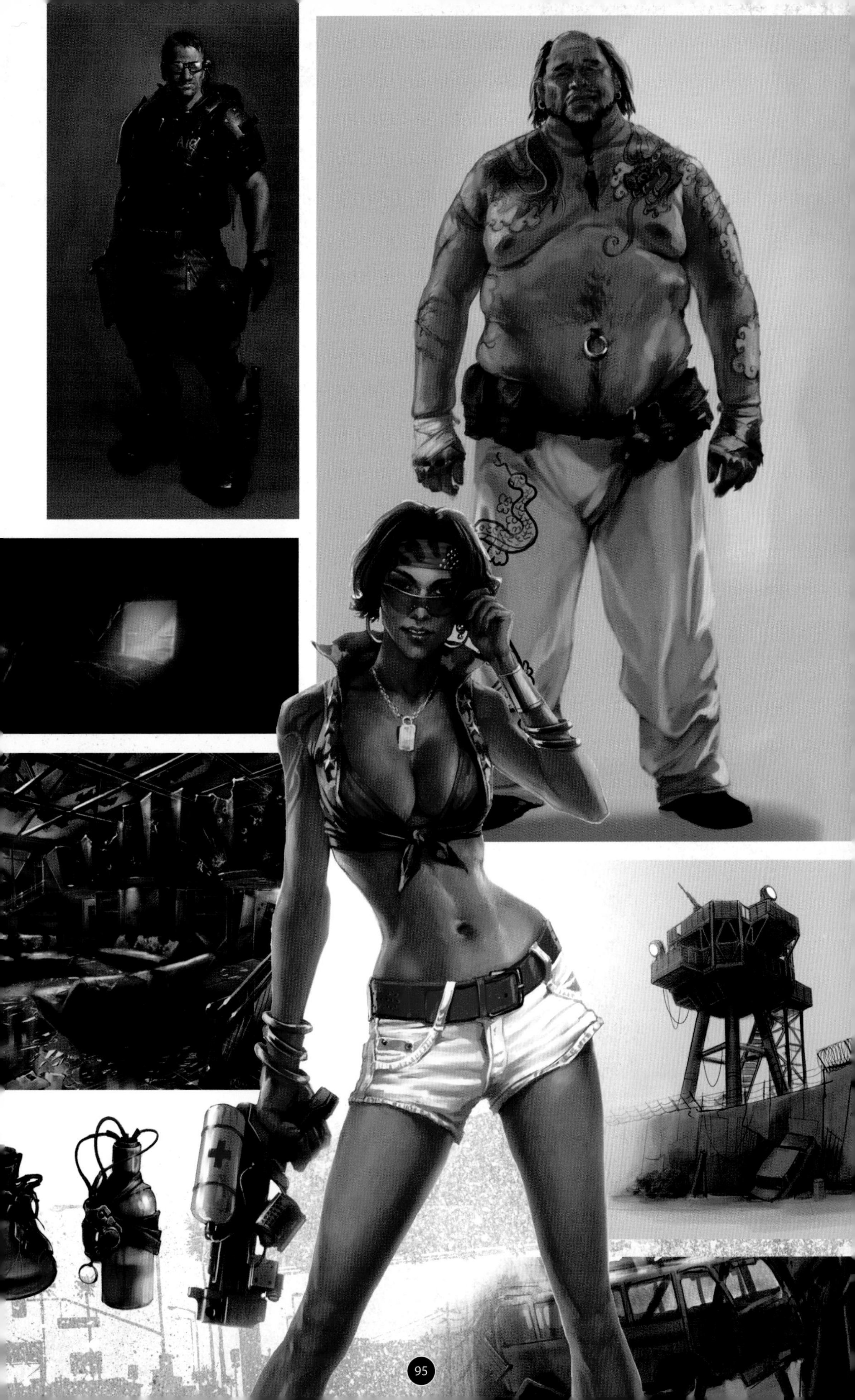

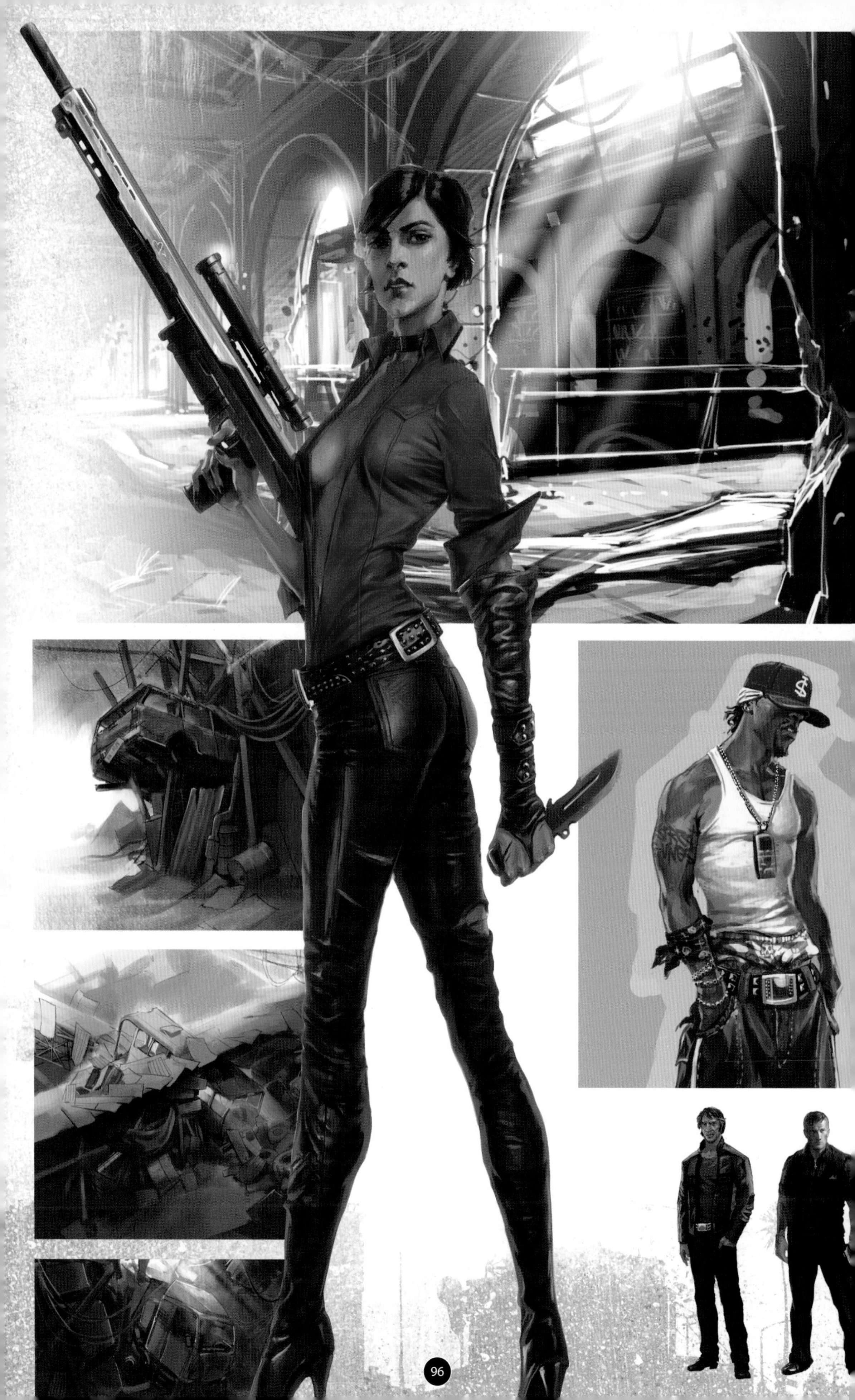

style

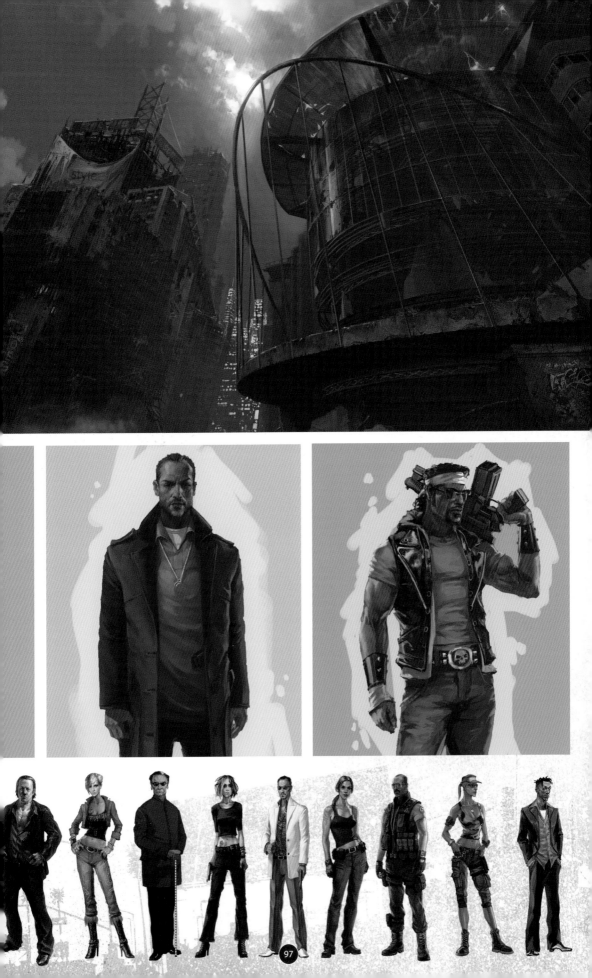

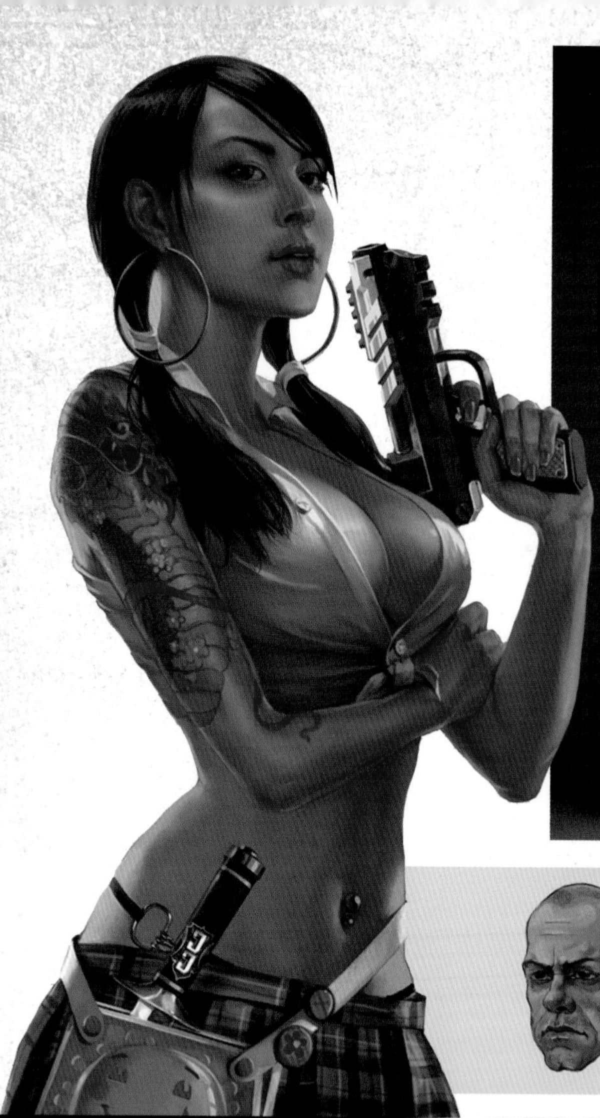

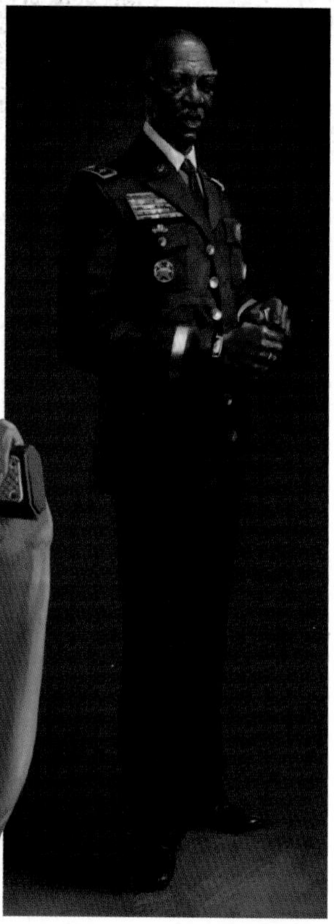

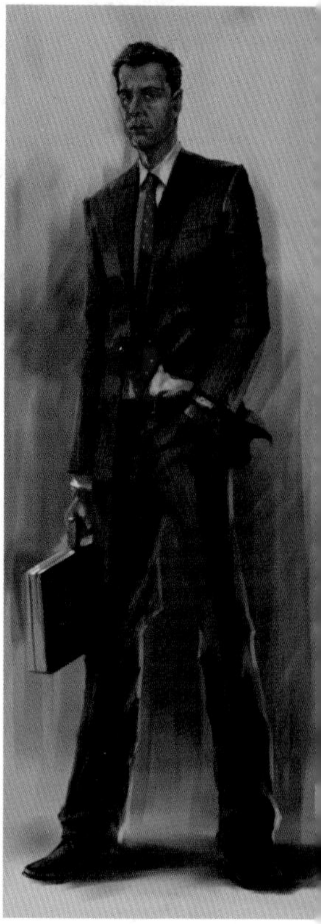

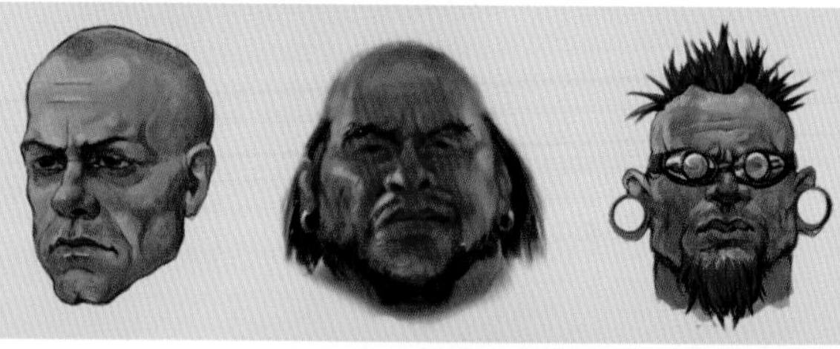

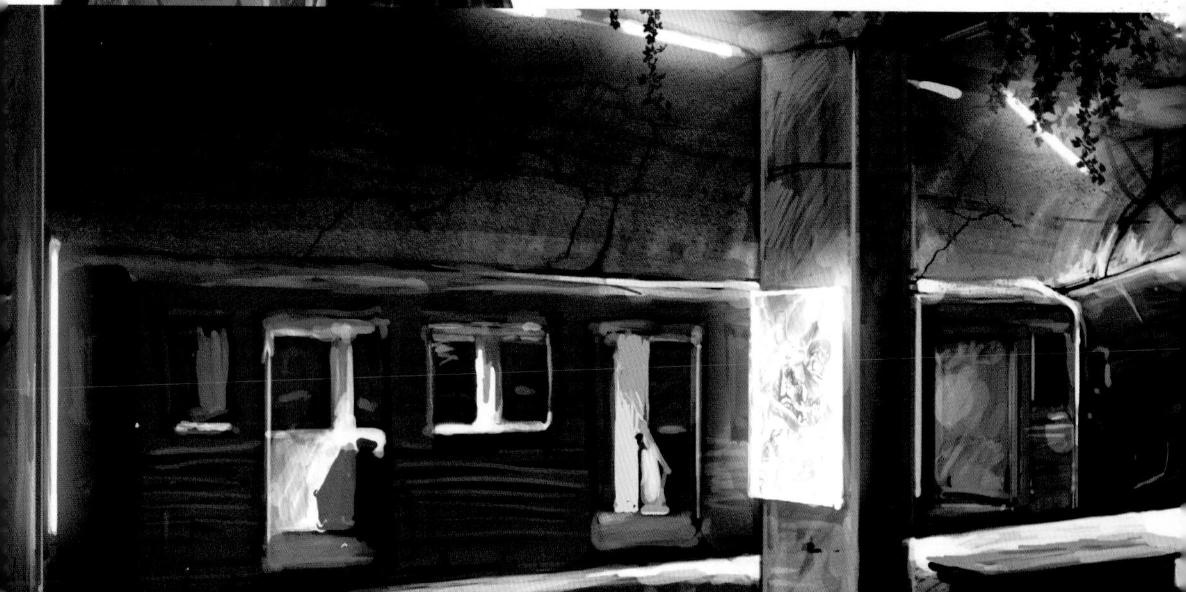

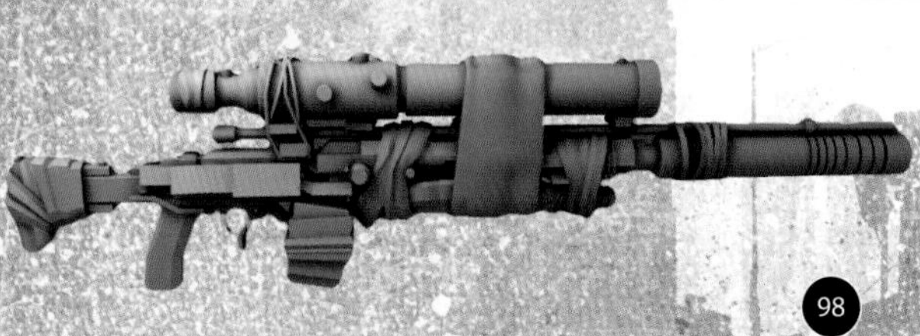

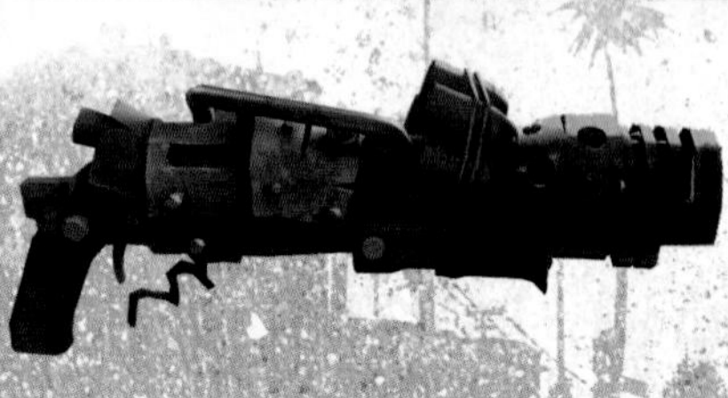

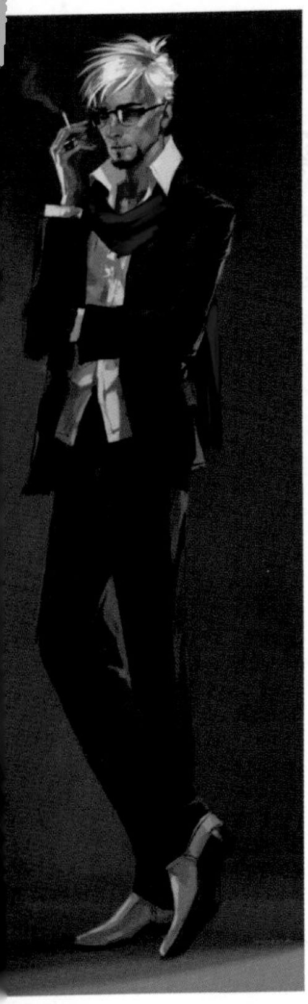
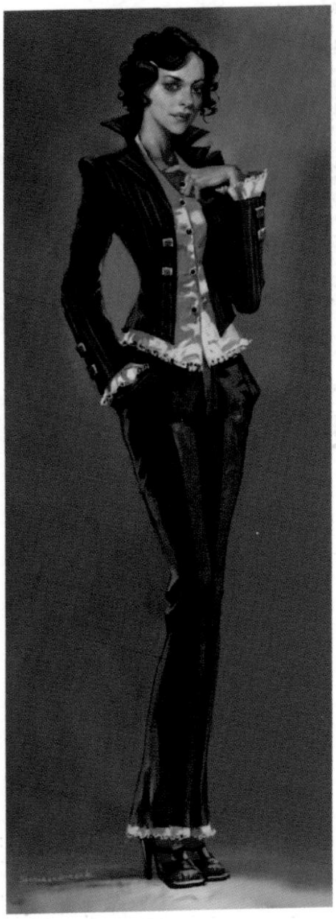
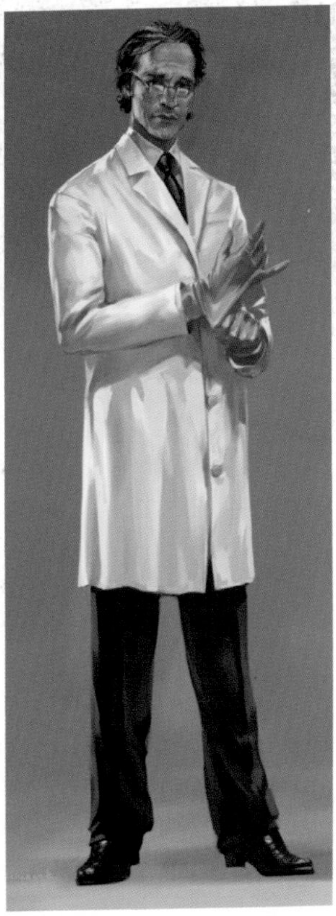
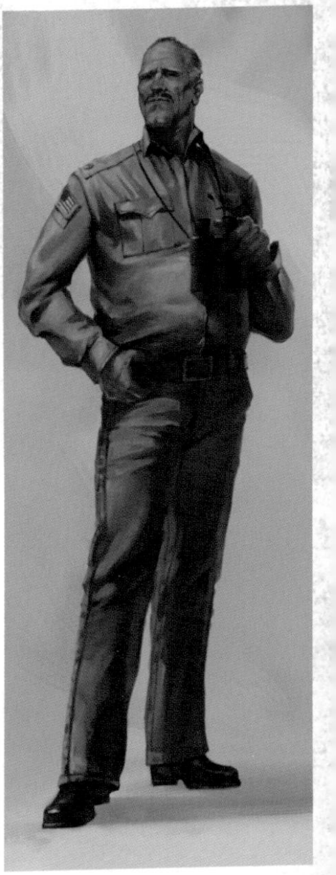
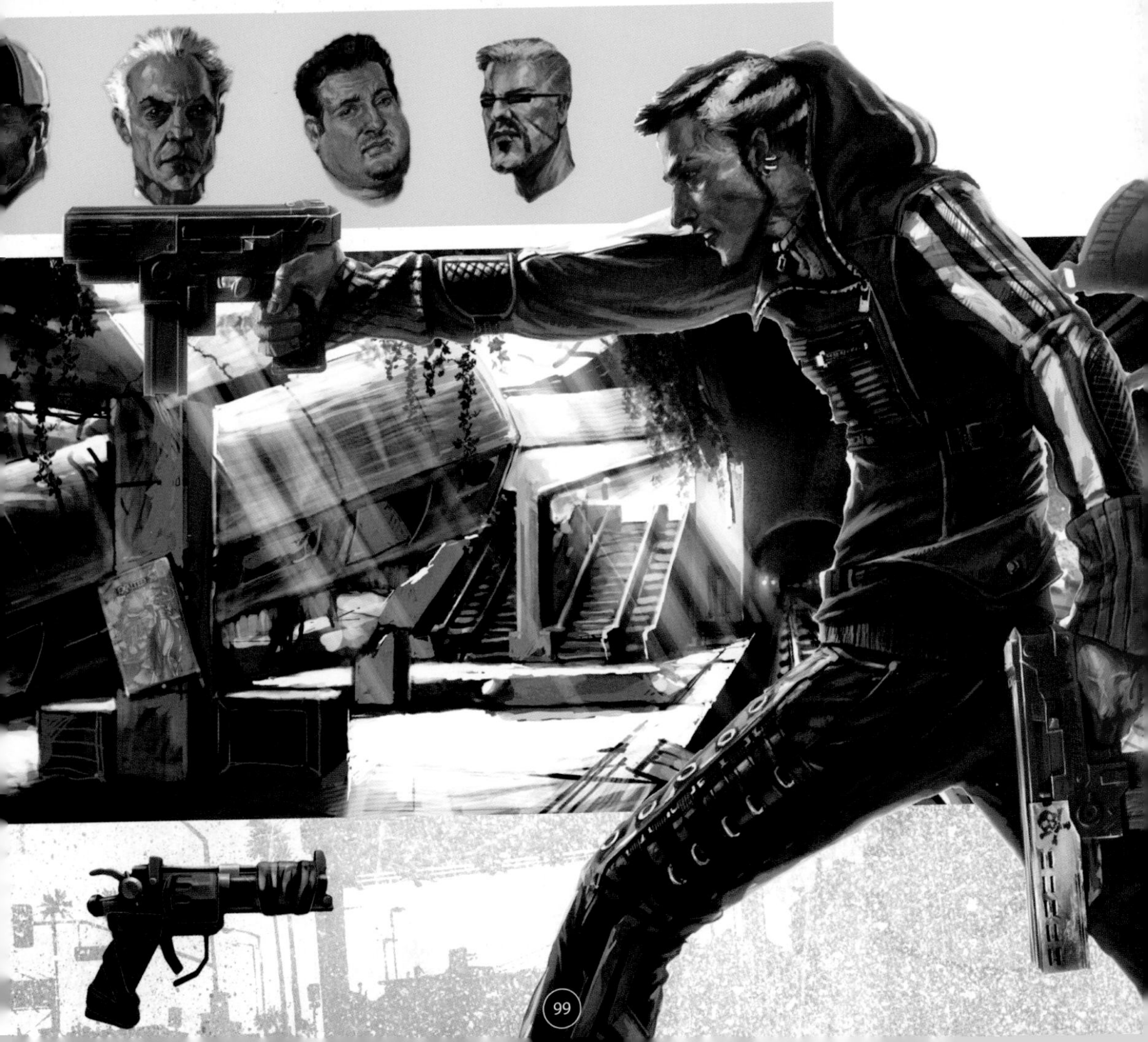

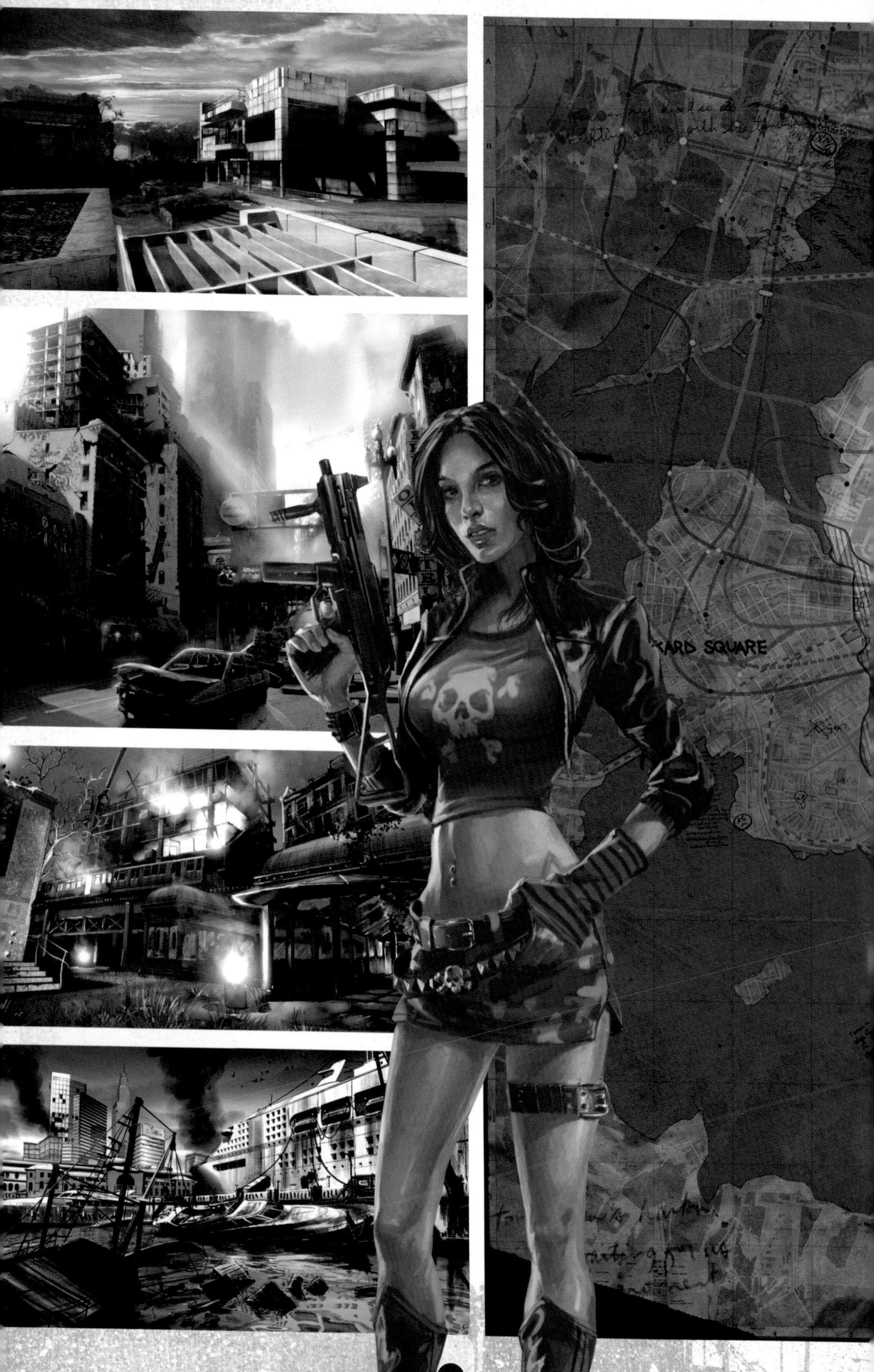
KARD SQUARE

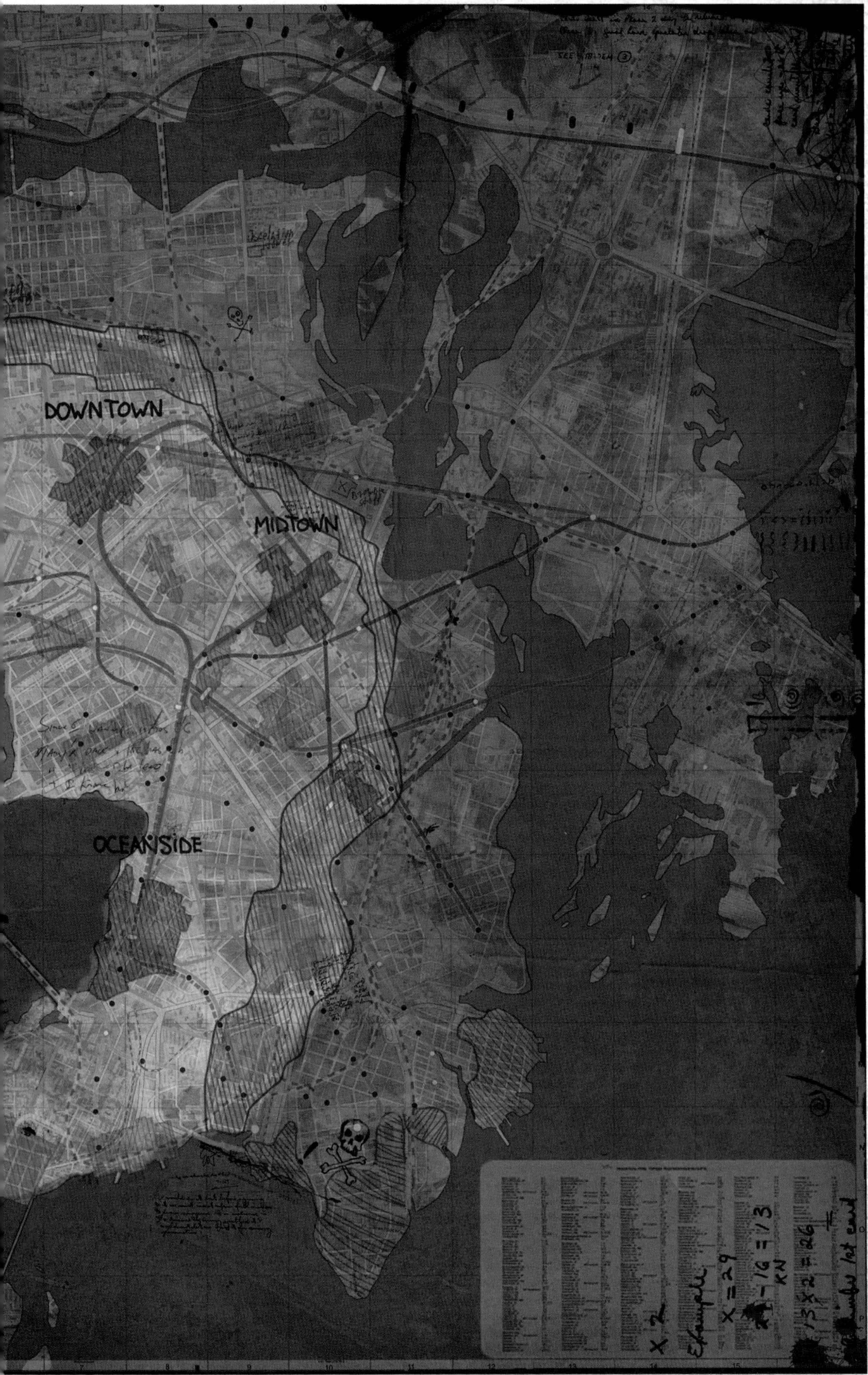
DOWNTOWN
MIDTOWN
OCEANSIDE

ABOUT THE AUTHORS

Mike Kennedy *www.neurobellum.com*

Mike has spent the last 20 years writing and producing original video games for Electronic Arts, Namco, Activision, 3DO, and most recently Vogster Entertainment, defining original properties such as **Dead to Rights**, **Def Jam: Icon**, **Unbound Saga**, and the **Army Men** series. His first professional comic gig was writing the adventures of Dark Horse's sexy, spectral vigilante heroine, **Ghost**, followed by a **Ghost/Batgirl** crossover with DC comics. This led to a number of **Star Wars** books, including **Underworld** and **The Aurorient Express**, and the creation of **Lone Wolf 2100**, a futuristic re-imagining of the classic Japanese samurai series Lone Wolf and Cub, created in full cooperation with the legendary Kazuo Koike. Other notable titles include **Aeon Flux** for Dark Horse and MTV, various **Alien vs. Predator** titles for Dark Horse and Fox, and **Superman: Infinite City**, a hardcover graphic novel from DC created with the late Carlos Meglia.

Nathan Fox *www.foxnathan.com*

Nathan Fox was raised with an early addiction to cartoons, commercials and video games. In the hopes of making such an addiction his full time job, Nathan attended the Kansas City Art Institute, where his eyes were opened to Anime, Yoshitoshi's Yukiyo-e Prints, Sideshows, and comics, which would lead him down the happily twisted path he still follows today. Nathan has been freelancing full time as an illustrator and storyteller ever since. His work has appeared in **The New York Times**, **Interview**, **The New Yorker**, **Rolling Stone**, **Wired**, **ESPN Magazine**, **Spin**, **MAD Magazine**, and many other publications. Noted works include **DMZ: Friendly Fire**, **Pigeons From Hell**, and **Flourescent Black**.

Zach Howard *www.zachhoward.com*

Zach Howard has been toiling in the industry since 2002, and has worked for pretty much every company at some point during that time. Although his heart is anchored to creator owned projects, you can often find him doing small stints on mainstream books, such as **Shaun of the Dead**, **Aliens: More Than Human**, and **Outer Orbit**. He both pencils and inks, but occasionally embarrasses himself with some writing.

Ben Templesmith *www.templesmith.com*

Ben Templesmith is a **New York Times** best-selling artist and writer most widely known for his work in the comic book industry, where he has received multiple nominations for the International Horror Guild Awards as well as the industry's top prize, the Eisner Award. As a creator, his most notable works have been **30 Days of Night** (which spawned a major motion picture) and **Fell**. His other projects include the critically acclaimed serial **Wormwood: Gentleman Corpse**, as well as **Welcome to Hoxford**, and **Singularity 7**, all of which he also wrote.

Sanford Greene *www.sanfordgreene.com*

Sanford Greene has worked in comics and related industries for over 9 years. His clients include DC Comics, SEGA, Nickelodeon, Hasbro, Warner Brothers, Fox, and Marvel Comics. Titles include **Wondergirl**, **Killer 7**, and **The Batman Strikes!** He is currently working on a graphic album for Humanoid Publishing, as well as a **Spider-Man** children's book for Harper Collins/Marvel Publishing. In his free time, he continues to develop his creator owned project, **1000**.

David Williams *brohawk.deviantart.com*

David Williams has been in the comics industry for over 20 years, illustrating for every major comic company and many in between. His first break into comics came by the way of Darick Robertson (**Transmetropolitan**, **The Boys**), before graduating to DC Comics with the help of comic book legend, superstar, and friend Dave Stevens. Williams took an 8 year break from comics to work in animation, honing his skills for a fresh new comeback to comics. He has since worked on popular titles such as **Wolverine: First Class**, **Incredible Hercules**, **Marvel Adventures**, and **G.I. Joe**.

Glenn Fabry

Glenn Fabry has been illustrating comics since 1985, where he began his career illustrating **Slaine** for 2000AD. He is most noted for his painted works and award-winning covers for such notable series as **Hellblazer** and **Preacher**. He has since illustrated stories in **The Authority**, **Thor**, Neil Gaiman's **Endless Nights**, and **Neverwhere**.

Vince Proce www.vincentproce.com

Vince Proce has created concept art and illustration for numerous popular video games, including **Mortal Kombat**, **Stranglehold**, and **Psi Ops**. He has provided painted works for Wizards of the Coast products, such as **Dungeons & Dragons** and **Magic: The Gathering**. His work has also been featured in several volumes of the acclaimed **Spectrum** series.

Howard Chaykin

Howard Chaykin has been a mainstay in the comic industry since the 70's, writing and illustrating some of the most recognized books to hit the shelves. He illustrated the first adaptation of **Star Wars** for Marvel Comics before setting off to create **American Flagg!**, which established his influential style for years to come. His sharp dialogue and sexy pulp adventure led to the reinvention of classic DC characters, such as **Blackhawk** and **The Shadow**. His most recent works include **Hawkgirl**, **Blade**, **Wolverine**, **Punisher War Journal**, and **Immortal Iron Fist**.

Gary Erskine www.garyerskine.com

Gary Erskine has been illustrating comic books for over twenty years, with published titles from Marvel, DC, Vertigo, Wildstorm, Dark Horse, Panini, Classical Comics, and Titan Books. Titles include **Dan Dare**, **Star Wars**, **Terminator**, **Transformers**, **Starman**, **Warheads**, **Captain America: Theater of War**, **The Filth** with Grant Morrison, and he is co-creator of **City of Silence** with Warren Ellis. He has also contributed character designs and storyboards for the games industry, as well as film and television work. When he is not drawing, he teaches workshops at libraries and schools around the UK.

Trevor Hairsine

Trevor Hairsine began his career at 2000AD in the mid-nineties, illustrating characters such as **Strontium Dog** and **Judge Dredd**. He went on to illustrate **Cla$$war** for Com.X before being declared one of Marvel Comic's "Young Guns" in 2005, which led to stints on **Captain America**, **Ultimate Six**, **Ultimate Nightmare**, **Wisdom**, and **X-Men: Deadly Genesis**. He has also provided artwork for **Dungeons & Dragons Miniatures** and **Magic: The Gathering**.

Tim Bradstreet timbradstreet.typepad.com

Artist/Designer, Tim Bradstreet has been riding the edge of genre illustration for nearly a quarter century. His stark, highly stylized work helped to launch both **Shadowrun**, and **Vampire: The Masquerade** into RPG nirvana, and further propelled him in to Comics, where during the last 20 years he has become one of the go-to visionaries for cover illustration and design. His take on **The Punisher** and **John Constantine: Hellblazer** helped redefine those characters for a new generation and was instrumental in attracting filmmakers to the properties. Bradstreet has also contributed to the film world through concept design for films such as **Blade II**, **The Punisher** (2004), and the 2007 film, **Dark Country**, starring Thomas Jane. 2009 saw the publication of Robert E. Howard's **El Borak and Other Desert Adventures**, featuring over 60 Bradstreet illustrations, as well as **Archetype**, a 312 page retrospective of his career. Currently, Tim is working on his own illustrated novel, **Red Sky Diary**, as well as providing covers for **Iron Man: The Rapture**, several **Punisher** one-shots, **Iron Siege**, and **Rogue Angel**.

Michael Mendheim

Michael Mendheim has worked as an Executive Producer and Creative Director in the videogame industry for over fifteen years with published titles by, Electronic Arts, Activision, 3DO and Vogster Entertainment. Michael graduated from Art Center College of Design in Pasadena and started his career in advertising illustration and overtime transitioned into videogames. Some of the projects he has Created/Produced include the #1 hit, **Mutant League Football** (which spawned a syndicated animated series and toy line) and the hugely successful, **Army Men** series. Other projects include **BattleTanx**, **Def Jam: Icon** and the critically acclaimed **Robocalypse**. Michael's latest creation is his dream project, an epic graphic novel illustrated by Simon Bisley. The title will be announced later this year.

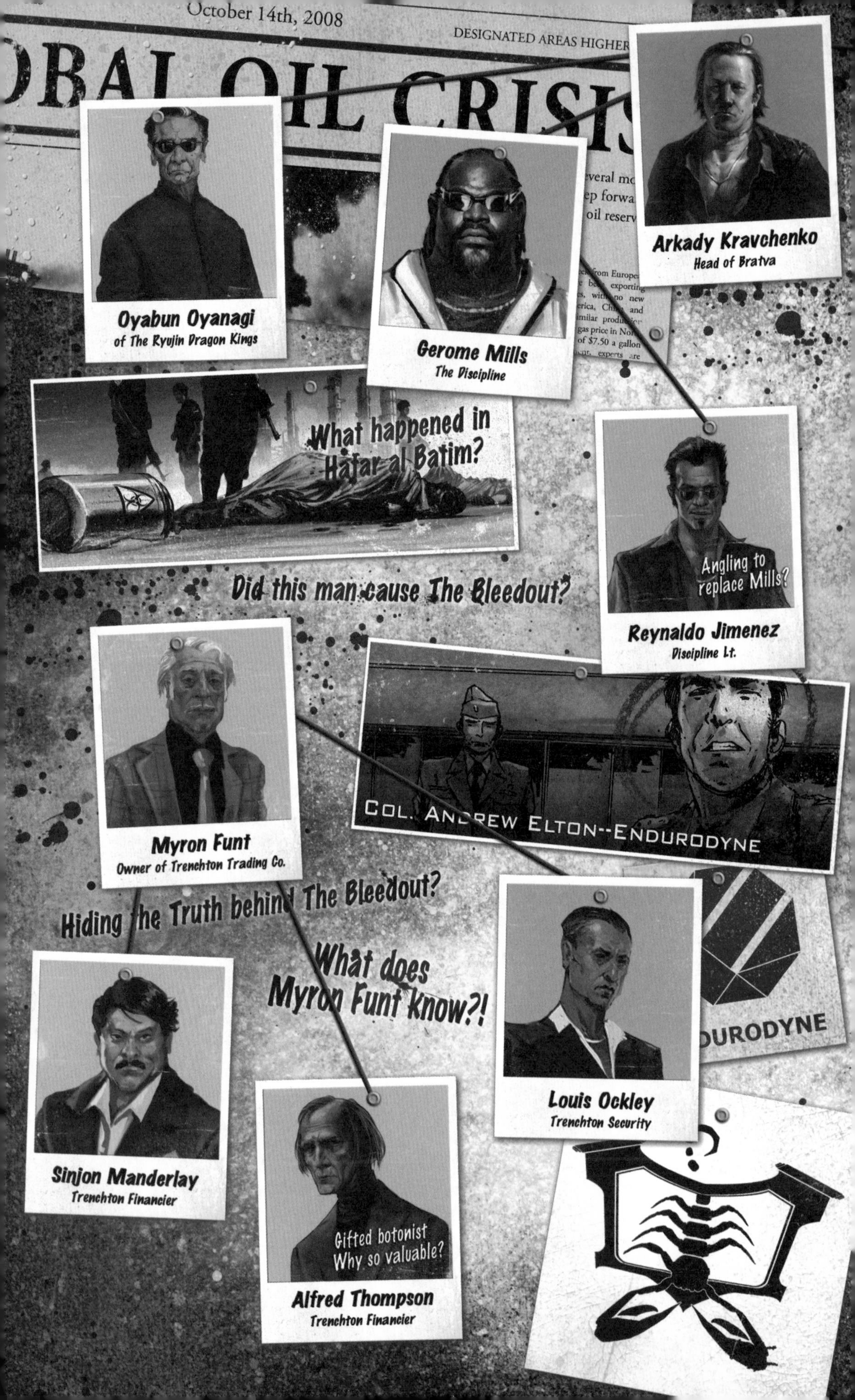
October 14th, 2008
DESIGNATED AREAS HIGHER
OBAL OIL CRISIS
Oyabun Oyanagi
of The Ryujin Dragon Kings
Gerome Mills
The Discipline
Arkady Kravchenko
Head of Bratva
What happened in Hafar al Batim?
Did this man cause The Bleedout?
Angling to replace Mills?
Reynaldo Jimenez
Discipline Lt.
Myron Funt
Owner of Trenchton Trading Co.
COL. ANDREW ELTON--ENDURODYNE
Hiding the Truth behind The Bleedout?
What does Myron Funt know?!
ENDURODYNE
Louis Ockley
Trenchton Security
Sinjon Manderlay
Trenchton Financier
Gifted botonist
Why so valuable?
Alfred Thompson
Trenchton Financier